P9-CEM-015

80E

WITHDRAWN

Rape,
Incest,
and
Sexual Harassment

Rape, Incest, and Sexual Harassment

A GUIDE FOR HELPING SURVIVORS

Kathryn Quina
and
Nancy L. Carlson

PRAEGER

New York
Westport, Connecticut
London

Library of Congress Cataloging-in-Publication Data

Quina, Kathryn.
    Rape, incest, and sexual harassment : a guide for helping
survivors / Kathryn Quina and Nancy L. Carlson.
        p.   cm.
    Bibliography: p.
    Includes index.
    ISBN 0-275-92533-1 (alk. paper)
    1. Rape victims—Mental health.   2. Incest victims—Mental health.
3. Sexual harassment—Psychological aspects.   4. Counseling.
I. Carlson, Nancy L.   II. Title.
RC560.R36Q56   1989
362.88'3—dc20   89-16160

Library of Congress Catalog Card Number: 89-16160
ISBN: 0-275-92533-1

First published in 1989

Praeger Publishers, One Madison Avenue, New York, NY 10010
An imprint of Greenwood Publishing Group, Inc.

Printed in the United States of America

The paper used in this book complies with the Permanent
Paper Standard issued by the National Information Standards
Organization (Z39.48-1984).

10 9 8 7 6 5 4 3 2

Contents

Tables and Figure   vii
Preface   ix
Acknowledgments   xi

Part I. The Issues Raised by Victimization

1. Introduction and Perspectives   3

2. Understanding Victimization   19

3. Helping Approaches   41

Part II. The Immediate Aftermath of Sexual Abuse

4. Posttraumatic Phases   63

5. Medical Intervention   83

6. Legal Intervention   101

Part III. Counseling Survivors of Sexual Abuse

7. Promoting Recovery   125

  8. Emotional Aftereffects   143

  9. Counseling Models   175

10. Individual Considerations   199

Epilogue: Empowerment   221
Appendix I: Types of Professional Counselors   229
Appendix II: The Victim Booklet   231
Bibliography   233
Name Index   253
Subject Index   259

Tables and Figure

TABLES

9.1 Steps for Crisis Counseling   176

9.2 Steps for Individual Resolution Counseling   183

9.3 Steps in Group Therapy   190

FIGURE

1.1 The Continuum of Sexual Exploitation   11

Preface

We became involved in caring about and caring for survivors of sexual abuse in different places and different roles. In the mid–1970s Kat Quina embarked on a project to educate herself about the issues of sexual abuse. In speaking with survivors, she was saddened by the lack of resources to help them recover and the harmful treatment some had encountered. In speaking with therapists, she recognized that many knew nothing about sexual abuse, or held blatantly harmful attitudes. She began applying her training as a research psychologist and educator to the issues of sexual abuse with a team of students at the University of Wisconsin–Milwaukee. In the process, she also found personal discovery and recovery.

Nancy Carlson was already confronting sexual abuse issues in her clinical work. In the very early 1970s several young college women described to her in individual therapy the devastating effects of being raped. Through their courage and willingness to ask for help in resolving their hurt and rage about such abuse, insult, and betrayal, she was quickly informed about the depth and breadth of the problem. Subsequently, she cofounded and supervised the first campus women's crisis center at the University of Maryland, then developed and supervised centers at the State University of New York at New Paltz and later at the University of Rhode Island. Through working with the training and crisis intervention efforts of those centers, and also through working with so many clients in psychotherapy who had been raped, incested or harassed, she had the privilege of being with women, and on occasion men, who shared this experience of deep and almost indefinable pain, so great it seems to be from the soul. Releasing the tears and rage was crucial, she recognized, to the recovery of a sense of control over one's self and a sense of empowerment and rights in the world. Understanding, support, and acceptance provide the environment and clear the way for healing of the soul and release of the painful memories locked into the body and psyche. The healing itself is through love in the best and most profound sense of that word.

In 1978 our paths merged at the University of Rhode Island, where Nancy became Director of Counseling and Career Services and Kat joined the faculty in Psychology. Our cooperative projects there were bolstered by our complementary interests and skills. When Nancy moved to Portland to pursue a private practice, the distance imposed a heavy toll on her car, but the mutually enriching process of coauthoring has continued undaunted. We are both grateful that we could find ways to produce a book in spite of our different schedules, styles, and situations, and that our friendship and mutual respect have emerged healthy.

Because so many humans—some say all women and most men—have experienced violations of their bodies and psyches by the woundings of abuse, the importance of creating a handbook for helpers became clear to us. Consider the huge numbers of people who now are relaying their stories of heartless misuse and neglect as small children—survivors of incest and sexual and physical abuse at the time when they were most vulnerable. Writing this book has been a continuing reminder that when one member of humanity suffers through abuse, humiliation, and disrespect, we all do.

The women and men who shared their stories with us so that they might help others deserve a special tribute. Without them, there would be no book. Their strengths and their wisdom have allowed us not only models for the book, but models for our own lives. They have shared with us their pain and their joy, and they have shown us the light at the end of the tunnel of victimization. We have also woven into these stories our own lives and those of our loved ones, and we thank them for their willingness to contribute so openly.

May this effort help in the healing of wounds and in recreating respect for all beings.

Acknowledgments

There are many who have helped in important ways. The University of Rhode Island Alumni Foundation funded a research assistant, Nancy Jackson, at a critical time, and her work was invaluable. MaryAnn Paxson, Pamela Gibson, and Susie Hamin suggested helpful revisions. Karen Bachus and Carolyn Brooks assisted with typing.

Joanne Herbst gets credit for launching my interests in this area, and the members of the Milwaukee Rape Action Team, notably Pamela Webber and Willa Lunsford, share credit for the direction my interests took. The staff and fellow volunteers at the Rhode Island Rape Crisis Center, especially Peg Lang-hammer, provided personal and professional role models, and it is to their important work that I will donate my share of any proceeds from this book. My colleagues in the URI Psychology Department, especially Janet Kulberg and Bernice Lott, and collaborator and friend Mary Zahm have been constant sources of support and praise, which kept me going when it seemed easier to quit. Throughout, the people who entrusted portions of their training to me made allowances for the time taken away from them. In this regard, Karen Bachus, Pat Gallagher, Nancy Jackson, Sharon Michael, MaryAnn Paxson, and many others deserve heartfelt thanks, for their support and for their friendship. To my parents, Charlotte and Herbert Quina, I repeat my gratitude for providing a loving, nonviolent home. To my nieces, Mariana and Jessica, and my nephews Marco, Andre, and Eric, I repeat my hope that they may grow up in a safer world. Last but not least, my husband David Miller has been my life support system through this whole process, encouraging me from the first hint to the final details, providing technical support, home management, and best of all, love.

K.K.Q.

I would like to express my profound appreciation to all those courageous beings who have wanted more than anything to find a way to heal their own lives and to create ways to help others. The long list includes clients, students, colleagues and friends, crisis center volunteers, teachers, and acquaintances. Support at many levels came from the generosity of my brother and sister-in-law, Bob and Karen Carlson, and my mother, Elizabeth, and for that I am deeply grateful.

N.L.C.

Part I

The Issues Raised by Victimization

1

Introduction and Perspectives

WHO ARE THE VICTIMS?

Ann lives on a quiet street in a large city, and works the three-to-eleven shift as a nurse. One night, as she was walking the block from the bus stop to her home after work, a man wearing a stocking mask jumped out from an alley, held a knife to her throat, and threatened to kill her. He dragged her into the alley and raped her, then stole her purse and ran away.[1]

Brenda was three months pregnant with her second son. After an argument with her husband, she went to a local restaurant for coffee. As she left the restaurant, two men grabbed her. She attempted to run away, but she fell and broke the heel of her shoe. She was taken to an apartment where she was tortured and raped for over eight hours.

Every ten minutes, a woman is forced to perform a sex act in the violent assault we call rape (U.S. Department of Justice, 1983). A representative survey in the San Francisco area found that one-fourth of the adult women respondents had been raped at least once, and nearly half had experienced either an attempted or a completed rape (Russell, 1984). While a gun or knife is used to terrify about a quarter of the victims into submission (U.S. Department of Justice, 1982), sheer physical strength or the surprise of a sudden attack overpower many others. Violent stranger rapes like Ann's and Brenda's capture our sympathy and our imagination, sometimes stirring up public anger over unsafe streets and a call for death to the offender.

Acquaintance and Date Rape

The most frequent assailants are not the strangers Ann and Brenda encountered. Their rapes represent extreme versions of the multitude of sexual assaults that take place daily in our society. Most abusers are family members, "friends," coworkers, acquaintances, dates, or even marriage partners.

Carol was seventeen, and a virgin. She had dated Andrew for two years when he was drafted into military service. The night before he left, she visited his home. Although she didn't normally drink, he persuaded her to share a "toast." Soon she felt dizzy and had to lie down. With his sister and mother in another part of the house, Andrew raped her.

Donna was visiting friends who were giving a party. She grew tired and went into the guest bedroom to sleep. She was awakened by another partygoer, a friend of her hosts, who raped her while warning her of the consequences of telling. He would say she was lying, and she would have no more friends.

Early studies based on figures from police records suggested that acquaintance rapes such as Carol's and Donna's accounted for only a small proportion of rapes. Surveys from the general population, however, have revealed that nearly three-fourths of adolescent and adult rape victims know their rapists (Katz & Mazur, 1979). The reason for the discrepancy is clear from the victims' own stories. Like most of the victims we have worked with, neither Carol nor Donna reported the assault to the police. Surveys show that perhaps as few as one in ten rapes or attempted rapes is likely to be reported to the police (Russell, 1984); even the most optimistic reports estimate that figure to be less than 40 percent (Law Enforcement Assistance Administration, 1985). The assaults that are reported are not likely to lead to a satisfactory resolution for the victim; of reported sexual assaults, only about 20 percent are prosecuted (Russell, 1984) and less than 10 percent result in convictions. That finding conforms to estimates that fewer than 1 percent of rapes result in punishment of the offender (Russell, 1984).

Marital Rape

A devastating type of sexual assault only recently recognized by legal and social authorities occurs when a woman is raped by her husband.

Elaine married a man she had dated for seven months. He had been rough physically on occasion before they were married, but now he seemed more aggressive. One night, he hid in the house when she came home from work and viciously attacked her. He held a gun while he raped her, saying he "performed better." The next day he was gentle and sweet. This assault was to be repeated every few months until Elaine left him.

Russell (1984) found that 12 percent of the married women in her sample had been forced to perform sexual intercourse against their will, usually with physical violence, by their husband or ex-husband; 5 percent had been raped by a lover or former lover. Acts of marital rape reported by wives include role-playing aggressive fantasies (e.g., acting out pornographic movies), sexual acts as a component of general brutality (Frieze, 1983; Gelles & Cornell, 1985), and forcing unwanted forms of sex, such as anal intercourse (Russell, 1984). Sexual abuse within intimate relationships tends to be more physically violent than other forms of rape (Finkelhor & Yllo, 1985). Yet many states still exclude sexual abuses committed by a spouse from legislation, because of traditional assumptions that marriage guarantees sexual access regardless of circumstances.

Adult Male Rape

For years, people believed that rape only happened to women, and most laws reflected that belief. In 1973 Robert A. Martin, a Quaker pacifist jailed for protesting the Vietnam war, was raped repeatedly in his jail cell. His description of his abuse brought the issue of male rape in prison to the public (Brownmiller, 1975), but most continued to believe that it was an exceptional situation and not likely outside of prison walls. Yet in a 1975 random survey of campus men and women, Quina and Tyre[2] identified one male victim of adult rape (by men) for every three female victims, and the men's stories were not very different from those of their female counterparts.

Bill and Carl were travelling across the country for a spring vacation from college. Their car broke down in a small town, and two men stopped to help. The men produced a tire iron, which they used to force Bill and Carl into submitting to rape. During the assault, Bill hit one of the attackers in the face. When Bill and Carl reported the rape to the police, they were told to get out of town immediately, or they would be charged with assault and battery on the two attackers, who apparently were "civic leaders."

Most rapes of adult males are carried out by men, although rapes by women do occur on rare occasion (Sarrell & Masters, 1982). In either case, the men's responses to the trauma and the sexual violation are very similar to those of women.

Child Rape and Sexual Abuse

Perhaps the greatest shame—yet one of the most common experiences—in our society is sexual abuse of children.

When Frances was seven, a man attacked her in a park and raped her. She didn't tell anybody. Then, when she was nine, Frances fell off her bicycle and broke her pelvis. In the examination, it was discovered that she had contracted gonorrhea from the assault.

While most sexually abusive childhood experiences may not appear to be as physically harmful as Frances's assault, most leave considerable psychological trauma.

Gail was six years old and about to receive her First Communion. The priest, a family friend, came from another city to officiate and stayed at her house. The night before the ceremony, he asked her to come into his room to say goodnight. When she did so, he pulled her into bed with him and fondled her. The next day, he served communion as if nothing had happened.

Harriet recalled, years later, the "strange man who sat in his car on a busy city street exposing himself to me. I can still vividly remember the feeling that overcame me when I encountered the middle-aged white male fondling his flacid penis as I passed his car."

In nearly one-third of all sex crimes reported to the police, the victims are under the age of fourteen (Burgess & Holmstrom, 1974; Rush, 1980). A report commissioned by the Canadian government found that up to 40 percent of women and 20 percent of men had suffered from at least one sexually traumatic experience during their childhood (Harvey, 1984). Kinsey et al. (1953) reported that 25 percent of his female respondents had been sexually abused as children; Finkelhor (1979) concurred, finding sexual abuse histories in nearly 20 percent of his female and 9 percent of his male respondents. About 15 percent of female children and up to 8 percent of male children suffer severe emotional and physical consequences from an experience of being molested, kidnapped, or raped (Finkelhor, 1979; Landis, 1956). One physician decried the fact that, in his experience, sexual abuse of children is "more common . . . than broken bones and tonsillectomies" (Dr. Frederick Green, quoted in Rush, 1980, p. 5).

Perhaps the most devastating aspect of these childhood assaults is that most of them—75 percent to 95 percent—are committed by someone the child knows and trusts, as in Gail's experience (Groth, 1979). The experience of sexual abuse is particularly confusing to the child when the abuser takes advantage of a loving familial relationship.

Ike adored his older brother Dan and tagged along with him everywhere. When Ike was eight, Dan informed him that in order to "be his brother," he had to do what Dan said. Dan's orders included various acts of sexual molestation, which continued until Ike left home ten years later.

Irene recalled, "While I was a little girl of nine, my mom went into the hospital, and it became up to me to run the household. My father drank for the two weeks Mom was away. During this time, my father first began to sexually abuse me. He told me that if I did Mom's work, I had to sleep in her place. This continued until I finally left the house at age eighteen. I tried several times to tell my mom but she never believed me.

At least 10 percent of females, and perhaps 5 percent of males, are sexually abused by a relative during their childhood, often by their own father or stepfather

(Finkelhor, 1979; Herman, 1981; Russell, 1984). Family offenders often assault the child repeatedly, over a period of years, increasing in frequency and intensity as the child matures. Children rarely feel safe or comfortable reporting an abuse, especially when they depend upon—and often love—their abuser. Among Russell's (1984) survey respondents who were assaulted as children, fewer than one in twenty cases had been reported to the police. Although reports of abuse have risen dramatically in recent years, sexual exploitation of children within families has remained our society's "dirty secret."

The long-term implications of intrafamilial sexual abuse are enormous. Professionals working with problem adolescent girls have estimated that 80 percent of juvenile offenders, 80 percent of drug abusers, and 70 to 95 percent of young prostitutes have been sexually assaulted, many by members of their own families (Bianco, 1984; Rush, 1980; Weisberg, 1984). Caldwell (1989) found that teen mothers were more than twice as likely to have been sexually victimized as children than successful contraceptors. Childhood sexual abuse, particularly incest, may lead to greater vulnerability to subsequent abuse as well (Russell, 1984).

Jane's favorite uncle always brought her gifts and showered her with attention, although sometimes he also scared her by touching her genitals. When she was eleven, he woke her up in the middle of the night and forced her to have oral sex with him. She didn't tell anyone, and thought she had overcome her ordeal. However, when she was 26, a trusted older friend demanded sex. She froze. She couldn't react soon enough to prevent his assault.

Sexual Harassment

Sexual harassment is the term applied to a variety of sexual abusive behaviors that generally do not involve physical violence. Sexual harassers often use economic or social power to dominate their victims. To distinguish sexual harassment from voluntary sexual relationships, the generally accepted definition is "unwanted sexual attention . . . ranging from leering, pointing, patting, verbal comments, and subtle pressure for sexual activity, to attempted rape and rape" (Alliance against Sexual Coercion, 1981, p. 9).

Karen, who had been sexually abused as a child, was attending her first office meeting at her new job. Arriving early, she found two male coworkers telling rape jokes. When she asked them to stop, one turned on her, saying, "Lighten up." After he told another joke she was in tears, as other men entered the room and looked on.

Linda was hired as a janitor on a night shift. Her male supervisor started commenting almost immediately on her attractiveness, stating that he "looked forward to working alone with her at night." Over the first few weeks, his verbal harassment increased. As she checked in one night, he reached out and pinched her side, quite roughly. He told her he would "be down to see her later." She was terrified of his approaches, but with three young children to support, needed her job.

Mary was a freshman science major at a large university. She took a student assistant position in a science department to support herself financially. One of her professors began stopping by her desk, leaning over her and touching her breasts "accidentally" while talking about her course work. Fearing for her grade and her job, she remained silent. At the end of the semester she filed a letter of complaint and quietly left school.

Nearly every woman has experienced catcalls or whistles on the street, and most can recall unpleasant subjection to sexually offensive jokes, as happened to Karen. Women who enter a "man's world," racial minority women, and gays and lesbians often report being singled out because they represent a group the harasser dislikes, as was the case for Linda, who was the only woman in a blue-collar job. Other vulnerable employees and students, like Mary, are subjected to repeated physical contact by a socially powerful assailant and are expected to act as if nothing has happened. In still other cases, a supervisor or professor demands sexual favors from employees or students, who may see no alternative but to submit. Even without physical violence or threats, acts of sexual harassment can usually be clearly distinguished from mutually desired behaviors by both the victim and the harasser (Stanko, 1985).

A study of federal employees found that 42 percent of the women and 15 percent of the men responding had experienced sexual harassment in the workplace (Merit Systems Protection Board, 1981). Over 90 percent of working women responding to surveys by organizations of working women and by magazines like *Redbook* considered sexual harassment to be a serious problem, and most described incidents of harassment affecting themselves and coworkers (Alliance Against Sexual Coercion, 1981). The stories told by victims confirmed their powerless state. Most of those who did not complain found that the harassment continued or increased, but a number of the women who had spoken up had been fired after filing a complaint.

Studies in universities show similar patterns of extensive sexual abuse. One-fourth of Harvard coeds reported experiences of sexual harassment by professors, and studies at Yale, the University of Rhode Island, and other schools echo those figures (Lott et al., 1984; Hall & Sandler, 1982). A survey of university professors revealed that a fourth of male faculty members had engaged in sexual relations with students (Fitzgerald et al., 1988). Although some relationships began as "voluntary," over 80 percent of the women students later reported negative consequences. Abusing professors are almost never reported, because the young victims fear their grades, graduate work, or future jobs may be jeopardized. That fear is often justified.

Nan was in her first year of graduate school when her professor invited her to have coffee after class. Thinking he wanted to discuss possible research projects, she readily accepted. Instead, he propositioned her. She thought she had turned him down tactfully, but still felt flattered because he had noticed her. The next day an exam was returned with a much lower grade than he had told her she had earned.

Olivia was just about to go to court for her divorce. Her lawyer, who until this time had been quite helpful, suddenly demanded an additional payment and refused to continue unless she "paid up." She was offered an alternative—have sex with him. When Olivia refused, he dropped her case and threatened to sue her for nonpayment. She had to go to court without a lawyer because she had spent all her savings on his retainer.

Professional Misconduct

The line between voluntary and nonvoluntary sexual relations may be blurred when there are large differentials in power or status between two people. Clients who seek help for emotional problems are particularly vulnerable to any kind of attention from their helpers (Pope & Bouhoutsos, 1986). Most professional codes of ethics, recognizing this special vulnerability of clients, prohibit any sexual contact with clients (e.g., American Psychological Association, 1981; 1988).

Pamela sought out an assistant pastor in her church to discuss a relationship that had recently broken up. A few sessions later, the minister asked her to lie on the floor nude. He told her this was to build trust, an important part of the healing process. Several months into the "therapy," he climbed on top of her and, without a word, entered her and climaxed. He began talking about his feelings for her, although he refused to see her outside her regular appointment or receive her calls. Even though the physical contact was distressing and physically unsatisfying, she felt she owed it to him because he said he loved her. Five months later, another woman in her church reported him for rape, and Pam realized he had been raping her, too.

Rhonda was taken to a physician by her sister because she was losing weight. Rhonda had been going to a counselor but seemed to be getting worse, not better. She finally admitted that she had been having sex with her counselor for about six months. He had diagnosed her as emotionally frigid, and the cure he insisted upon was "opening up" to him. She hated the sex, but believed she had to continue, or she would have no hope of "becoming sane."

A client like Pamela may not physically "resist" the sexual relationship, and in fact, like Nan with her professor, may welcome the attention at first. Some, like Pamela, submit to unwanted sex out of a need for approval or a desire for a "nice relationship." However, like Pamela, in nearly every case the client eventually experiences the relationship as abuse, along with other characteristic victim reactions (Pope & Bouhoutsos, 1986). Often these victims had believed the other person was motivated by the same caring, helping concern they felt, or the same emotional bond, and only later realized the negative effect of the sexual relationship. In other cases the offender uses a more direct, authoritarian attack to entrap the victim; for example, Rhonda's abusive therapist combined the promise of a cure if she complied with the terrifying threat that she would lose her sanity if she did not.

Estimates of the incidence of professional misconduct are hard to obtain. In various surveys, up to 14 percent of male therapists and up to 3 percent of female therapists reported that they had had sex with a client during their professional careers; insurance estimates place the figure even higher, at 20 percent (Pope & Bouhoutsos, 1986). There is evidence that these therapists' primary targets include the extremely vulnerable incest victim. In a survey of thirty incest victims who had sought professional help, seven reported sexual involvement with male therapists (Armsworth, 1987).

FRAMEWORKS FOR INTERVENTION

The victim profiles we have presented suggest the variety of situations comprising sexual victimization. The circumstances of their stories raise some of the problems facing a sexually abused individual: What decisions need to be made in a crisis situation? What legal resources are available to victims of sexual harassment? What kind of treatment should a distressed survivor expect? How can the negative long-term consequences of sexual victimization be prevented? The answers to these questions for any individual must be developed in the context of larger social and clinical perspectives on sexual victimization. We will begin by outlining two important frameworks for understanding sexual abuse and its consequences.

Social Framework: The Continuum of Sexual Exploitation

In this book rape and sexual assault, harassment, and incest are considered together as related forms of social exploitation. The common features among various kinds of sexual abuse, and the characteristics that distinguish sexual abuse from other kinds of victimization, are fundamental aspects of this framework:

Various forms of sexual abuse form a continuum, with underlying commonalities in cause and effect, varying primarily in the degree of violence or physical injury to the victim.[3]

Presented in Figure 1.1, the continuum includes physical and psychological attacks involving unwanted sexual behavior or the threat of a sex act. These attacks range from verbal offenses, which create fear, distress, and annoyance, to the most extreme form of violence, rape-murder. While the level of lasting physical and psychological injury generally increases across this spectrum, certain social features are present at all of these levels of assault. While individual circumstances vary dramatically, the perpetrators of these various acts, the targets they select, and the cultural and institutional reactions to both exhibit striking similarities across the continuum.

Figure 1.1

The Continuum of Sexual Exploitation

Increasing Physical Injury

Jokes	Verbal Harassment	Physical Harassment	Rape (Including Incest)	Rape-Murder

Commonalities among different acts of sexual exploitation have been noted by several scholars studying attitudes in our society (e.g., Beneke, 1982), the politics of rape and its presence in our culture (e.g., Brownmiller, 1975; Russell, 1984), and the socioeconomic and cultural predictors of sexual abuse (e.g., Schwendinger & Schwendinger, 1983). The social perspective provided by considering this range of assaults as part of one related continuum is vital to understanding and offering more effective services to the survivors of sexual abuses.

Four common links among the exploitative acts on this continuum are particularly relevant: their definition as aggressive rather than sexual acts, gender roles and relationships, cultural stereotyping, and survivors' reactions. In the discussion that follows, evidence for these commonalities is presented to support the theory that sexual abuses form a social continuum.

Abuse as Aggression, Sex as the Weapon. In spite of the fact that a sexual act is involved or implied in harassment, rape, and incest, these abuses are not sexually motivated. As we will elaborate in Chapter 2, eroticism and sexual satisfaction are rarely significant factors to the abuser. To sexual abusers, the assault or harassment represents a demonstration of power, a power defined in terms of aggressive domination, humiliation, and degradation, where sex is merely the weapon of choice.

Gender and Gender Roles. Statistically, the most striking commonality across our continuum is the gender of the assailants. Whether a soft-spoken neighbor molesting children or a drifter violently strangling a prostitute, the offender is almost always a male: an estimated 99 percent of rapes and 90 percent of incest and harassment offenses are committed by males (Groth, 1979). Most abusers start their sexually abusive behavior in their teens, with less serious offenses, and commit their most violent assaults in their twenties and thirties. They either believe they fit, or wish to fit, an extremely stereotyped gender role of masculinity, which for them is defined in terms of sexual dominance (Beneke, 1982; Groth, 1979). Although young males also carry out the majority of other violent activities in our culture, there is no other crime perpetrated so predominantly by offenders from one sex, who are imbued with such strong gender-role stereotyping.

The victims of sexual abuses across our continuum are also linked by a set of gender, age, and social characteristics. Unlike all other crimes, the victims of sexual abuse are overwhelmingly women and children. An estimated 95 percent of rape, 90 percent of incest, and 75 percent of harassment and child sexual abuse victims are female, and the majority of the abuses occur before the victim is eighteen (Finkelhor, 1979).

There are also clear links between sexual abuse and socialized gender roles of masculinity and femininity. Men in our society are supposed to be strong, dominant, powerful, and aggressive; women and children, including young boys, are stereotyped as passive, powerless, and weak. These gender stereotypes are the same roles acted out in sexual aggression. Abusers believe they are more masculine when they have dominated a woman, especially sexually. Studies of rape in prison indicate that even when men rape men, they objectify their targets as feminine, calling them "gal boys" or "women." Rather than raising issues of homosexuality, the prison rapist sees himself as a masculine "wolf" (Weiss & Friar, 1974).

While the aggressive acts of sex offenders may be extreme, the fact that these behaviors are only extensions of culturally sanctioned masculine aggression allows us to discount their severity (Russell, 1975). Abusive sexual aggression takes place in a culture where normal male-female interactions are expected to maintain differences in power and strength, where men and women are trained to act out sexual roles of aggressive pursuer and submissive pursued, and where men and women who deviate are punished.

Cultural Stereotyping of Sexual Abuse. Survivors of sexual abuse are cast into a cultural context of proscriptions and roles, from which they and their treatment are viewed. In no other crimes have the voices of society been so hostile to the victims, and so sympathetic to the perpetrators.

The defense lawyer bragged about a client recently acquitted with his help. The client had admitted beating up his victim, who had a broken arm and other injuries. But the lawyer bragged that "we were able to prove she had a bad reputation, so we got him off from all the charges. It was her fault. Women lie to cover up when they've been sluts."

When Carol told her therapist about how her boyfriend had so unexpectedly raped her, he seemed sympathetic. But when he learned that she was a virgin, even though she had dated Andrew for two years, he exclaimed: "No wonder he raped you. You were holding out! Poor guy, you can't blame him! You frustrated him into it!"

Interviews have documented the extraordinary extent to which the victim of sexual abuse is blamed for the assailant's actions and given negative characterizations such as lying or immorality (APA Task Force on Victims of Crime and Violence, 1984). Placing blame on the victim also attenuates anger toward the male abuser. Whether he has committed a violent assault, a date rape, or incest, the man who abuses is likely to be judged the "victim," either of his own socially acceptable masculine drives or of a female's "seductiveness."

The responses of institutions—police, hospitals, and courts—have too often reflected these blaming attitudes, causing postrape interventions to be described as the "second victimization." Reports of unsympathetic treatment by medical, legal, and other helping professionals demonstrate the extent to which our social systems have incorporated assumptions about sex offenders and victims into their treatment practices (Holmstrom & Burgess, 1978). Over the past decade, dramatic changes in cultural attitudes have been reflected in improvements in laws, policies of treatment facilities, and training of mental health professionals. However, some institutional reactions continue to reflect strong stereotypes, and the attitudes of individuals can negatively affect treatment of victims even in supportive institutions (President's Task Force on Victims of Crime, 1982).

The Personal Meaning of Sexual Abuse to Victims. Serious physical injury occurs in less than 5 percent of sexual assaults and in few incidents of harassment (Burgess & Holmstrom, 1974; MacKinnon, 1979). Yet all of the abuses described by our continuum have been known to cause severe psychological consequences long after the physical scars have healed. We can observe highly consistent emotional reaction patterns for victims across the abuses on our continuum. Certain responses are typical of any traumatic event, like cancer, an accident, a natural disaster—for example, fear, stress, and anxiety (Sales, Rich, & Reich, 1984). In addition, sexual abuse has personal meanings of violation not found in most other traumas, meanings that make survivor reactions different and often more difficult to resolve. Blaming and misunderstanding perpetrated by cultural and institutional responses to sexual abuse are internalized by the survivors themselves, leading to feelings of guilt, shame, and isolation.

In Chapter 2 we will discuss the issues raised by this social framework, including gender and power, cultural stereotyping, and the ways survivors describe their experience. Subsequent chapters will examine specific emotional sequelae of the social context of sexual abuse.

Clinical Framework: From Victim to Survivor

We use the terms "victim" and "survivor" to refer to clients within a clinical context. The term victim is used to emphasize the abusive dynamic, the experience of being targeted for sexual abuse; the term survivor is used to describe the person in recovery. Being a survivor is an ongoing process, but the successful survivor has self-esteem and self-respect, copes with the emotional aftermath of her victimization, and has taken back control over her life. Our primary goal for those who have experienced sexual abuse is to help them transcend feelings of being a victim, by achieving feelings of being a survivor.

The framework structuring our intervention guidelines contains three important assumptions about resolution: (1) it has a temporal course (the phases); (2) there are individual paths to resolution (the phenomenological approach); and (3) it should be a process of growth. We have labeled our framework the Phase Framework, because the term "phase" does not connote a universal time line or sequence. The four phases that structure our intervention framework and the organization of subsequent chapters are the *acute phase* and *avoidance phase* (Chapter 4) and the *transition to recovery* and *resolution phase* (Chapter 7).

Recovery Phases. The process that takes place after a sexual trauma has been described in terms of "stages of recovery" by several researchers. Temporal patterns in recovery have been observed in victims of any kind of violence, with impressive consistency in timing and order of appearance of reactions. In 1944 Lindemann identified two reaction patterns in survivors of the Cocoanut Grove fire in Boston, distinguished by time course and symptomology. The acute phase, lasting four to six weeks after the trauma, was characterized by physical and emotional distress and disruption of routine behavior. Over a much longer period, the survivors worked through an active process of reorganization. Subsequent researchers have applied Lindemann's framework to victims of all types of crises, including criminal assault, war, and natural disasters. Researchers working with rape victims have added an intermediate stage, a latency period during which the survivor attempts to overcome the acute stress symptoms by utilizing strategies of denial or repression of the event (Horowitz, 1976; Sutherland & Scherl, 1970). This avoidance reaction may continue for months or years, as long as the victim's need to control stress is greater than the need to resolve the experience, or as long as the social environment allows her or requires her to "forget" the incident.

Sharon, a 40-year-old woman, called a suicide prevention line, saying that she was unable to cope with life and that her behavior had caused her husband to threaten to leave. She was obsessed with worry because her daughter was going to her first prom. On probing, the woman suddenly remembered her own experience: she had been raped by her date after her first prom 23 years before. She had never told anyone and had repressed the incident, blaming herself for "leading him on." She was relieved to see a reason for her unexplained anxiety, but confused by the fact that she had forgotten such a traumatic incident.

As with so many others, during Sharon's teen years support and sympathetic counseling were not available. Like many others, she hid her assault from her husband, family, and friends and denied her own feelings about it. Keeping sexual abuse secret is so common that a survey of women assaulted before 1970 found that half had not told anyone about their experience for at least ten years (Tsai & Wagner, 1978). Male child victims are even less likely to disclose their experience (Finkelhor, 1979).

The Phenomenological Approach. Temporally structured descriptions of recovery can provide extremely useful tools for understanding a client's current reaction, for anticipating future reactions, and for helping a client move through transitional periods. Perspective on recovery as a process that changes with time allows the client to see a "light at the end of the tunnel," something to grow toward. As with all intervention approaches, however, there is danger in assuming that particular stages apply to every person recovering from trauma. No single, predictable time line applies to every individual, and some survivors never move through clearly defined stages. The tendency to label may result in an attempt to fit a victim into a category that is not accurate, leading to improper helping efforts. Worse yet is the tendency to try to force a client to behave in an "appropriate" manner for the stage she "should be in" or to try to push her on into the next stage. Misapplications of stage theories can harm an already vulnerable client, further taking away her control, and can delay or even reverse the recovery process.

To avoid such problems, intervention must honor the phenomenological approach. Described further in Chapter 3, this approach requires consideration of the individual's own style, experiences, and perceptions of her or his situation, as individualized guides to handling all phases of intervention, advocacy, and counseling.

Resolution as a Process of Growth. This phrase contains three key words on which any intervention should be founded. *Resolution* recognizes that the survivor will never be the same again and will not forget the experience. Effective intervention, however, can help a person find a new level of understanding and coping, even a new perspective on life. Resolution, in this sense, is potentially a better outcome than restoration of the previctimization level of functioning. But it is not a product; it is a *process* that is never complete. Even the most healthy survivors report occasional moments of grief, anxiety, guilt, and suffering. Intervention must empower survivors with skills for taking back control over those feelings. The process can lead to a continually increasing strength and flexibility.

Finally, the outcome goal for intervention should always be *personal growth*, not just recovery. The discovery of inner resources, the energizing effect of anger, the flexibility in dealing with life issues that sexual abuse recovery demands and the ego strength that emerges when self-esteem is rebuilt from within can all lead to a more mature survivor. It is the promise of a better future that keeps many survivors, and their helpers, moving forward.

PLAN OF THIS BOOK

We have written this book with three audiences in mind. To the professional in mental health, medical, or legal services, we offer guidelines for the treatment of survivors. To the layperson, the information will provide a better grasp of the options available and typical procedures to expect. For the survivor, we hope our approach will serve as a guide for taking control over her own recovery and a path for that process.

We have laid out this volume in a progression, starting with the issues raised by victimization in Part I. In this chapter, we have begun with a sense of the problems created by sexual abuse, and offered frameworks for understanding and intervention. Chapter 2 describes the various contexts in which individual reactions to sexual abuse must be approached. Chapter 3 provides general principles for helping clients.

Part II deals with the immediate aftermath of sexual abuse and focuses on crisis intervention and advocacy with respect to emotional (Chapter 4), medical (Chapter 5), and legal (Chapter 6) needs. In these chapters we have attempted to summarize the most effective approaches developed by rape crisis centers and other professionals. The specifics of medical procedures and legal systems differ from one locale to another and are constantly changing; therefore we speak in generalities. The helper should become familiar with current local resources, laws, and policies prior to client intervention.

Part III is written for counselors working with victimized clients, although the information will be helpful to other interveners and to survivors. Chapter 7 describes various approaches and stresses matching the intervention to the client's individual situation and needs. Common specific post-abuse symptoms and appropriate treatments are reviewed in Chapter 8. In Chapter 9, models are offered for putting these treatments into short-term counseling frameworks.

Chapter 10 addresses the special needs of clients who are male, minority, disabled, gay, lesbian, or older. Traditional therapy based on white, middle-class young women has often failed to note many issues that arise with other populations. We have tried to raise some of these issues without contributing further to stereotyping or exaggerating group differences.

Working with sexual abuse is difficult, not only because the crime is so devastating, but also because at this time in our culture we cannot report many positive outcomes. However, we can begin to empower individuals and perhaps help reduce vulnerability in the future through new approaches to self-defense and prevention. The epilogue deals with our hope for the future.

We have had to make tough choices along the way. One was to cover a wide range of issues and treatment approaches, rather than focusing on a single type of client or therapy. We have provided references to these more focused works and hope the reader will follow up on individual interests. Another decision was to focus on older adolescent and adult clients. The issues for child clients have been treated very well in other works, and thus we refer the reader to Biller and Solomon (1986), Finkelhor (1984), MacFarlane and Waterman (1986), Sgroi (1981; 1988), and Walker (1988).[4] Finally we decided to use the pronoun "she" in most references to victims and clients, and in some references to the helper, and "he" to refer to most abusers. We recognize the importance and prevalence of victimization in men's lives, however, and have written this book to cover the needs of both men and women. Sexual abuse is an important *people's* issue, and our pronouns should not suggest that we think otherwise.

NOTES

1. The names and some personal data of the women and men who shared their stories with us have been changed to protect their identity.

2. This survey was funded by the University of Wisconsin–Milwaukee, whose assistance is appreciated.

3. The continuum framework was suggested by Hazel Temple of the University of Rhode Island.

4. Other resources are the National Committee for the Prevention of Child Abuse (332 S. Michigan Avenue, Suite 950, Chicago, IL 60604) and the Clearinghouse on Child Abuse and Neglect Information (P.O. Box 1182, Washington, DC 20013).

RECOMMENDED READINGS

Alliance Against Sexual Coercion. *Fighting Sexual Harassment: An Advocacy Handbook.* Boston: Alyson, 1981.

Finkelhor, D. *Child Sexual Abuse: New Theory and Research.* New York: Free Press, 1984.

Russell, D.E.H. *Sexual Exploitation.* Beverly Hills, Calif.: Sage, 1984.

2

Understanding Victimization

In this chapter we will describe the various dynamics shaping the unique experience of sexual abuse victims. For this analysis, it is helpful to look first at the people who commit sexual abuse, in order to give helpers and clients a better understanding of the personal characteristics of their victimizers and the control strategies they employ. We will then examine the personal meaning of sexual abuse to its victims, viewing it respectively as a trauma, a crime, and a sexual attack. These personal meanings will be enlarged with discussions of the social relationships and the cultural context, which are critical to understanding the individual's difficulties in the process of seeking resolution.

SEXUAL ABUSERS

Only a small minority of abusers are ever publicly identified, and even fewer become the subjects of research projects. The most extensive research has been conducted on convicted rapists, estimated to be less than 1 percent of all rapists (Abel, Blanchard, & Becker, 1976; Koss & Leonard, 1984; Russell, 1984), or from stories of daughters of incestuous fathers (e.g., Herman, 1981). Little research has been done on sexual harassers (Fitzgerald et al., 1988). Nevertheless, some important information about sexual abusers has emerged from the research. We will consider two aspects of sexual abusers, their characteristics and the control strategies they employ, and the implications of these aspects for victim reactions.

Characteristics of Sexual Abusers

The data that exist on men who commit various sexually abusive acts suggest that sexual abusers share some features in common, confirming our continuum framework. Among abuser characteristics are four of particular importance: they appear to be normal; they abuse repeatedly, using a modus operandi; they are motivated by anger and a need for power, not sex; and they believe rape myths, particularly that it is okay to rape.

Apparent Normalcy. Our culture tends to imagine that sexual abusers are insane sex maniacs, much like the deviants described by Krafft-Ebing (1965) in his famous *Psychopathia Sexualis*. Rapists are seen as bizarre, distorted creatures; poor, ignorant, rural men commit incest; and sexual harassers are harmless older men with sexy secretaries. Exceptions to these stereotypes are difficult for some people to comprehend: a "normal" man doesn't rape, especially not his own children.

In the past ten years, research has revealed a very different portrait of sexual abusers. There is no single abusive "type"; the stereotypes are rarely applicable. In fact, male sexual abusers cover the full range of age, race, culture, and intelligence; very few are "psychotic" (Gebhard et al., 1965; Henn, 1978). Perhaps the best summary statement of the profiles that emerge from this research was made by Beneke (1982) upon his first meeting with convicted sexual offenders, including some who had murdered their victims. "The first experience I had was blinding: a feeling of *identification*. . . . They were not different from the men I knew. They could've been my brother, . . . my father, . . . my friends, . . . me" (p. 41). This conclusion is even more astounding in light of the fact that these convicted assailants are highly unrepresentative of all sexual abusers. Those abusers who are convicted and incarcerated have committed the most frequent and most violent crimes, and because of prejudices in the justice system, they are far more likely to come from a lower socioeconomic level, a minority or culturally disadvantaged group, be poorly educated, or suffer from a mental disorder (Brownmiller, 1975). The vast majority of sexual abusers, who never come to the attention of authorities or become subjects of research studies, are even more likely to seem "normal" (Kanin, 1985; Koss & Leonard, 1984). Most rapists, child abusers, and sexual harassers behave in socially acceptable ways most of the time.

More recent studies reveal just how widespread the potential is for sexual abuse by "average" young American men. In surveys across the country, 10–20 percent of male college students admitted to already having coerced a woman into sexual acts that they knew were against her will, although few of them defined their actions as rape (Rapaport & Burkhart, 1984; Koss & Leonard, 1984). Surveys suggest that up to 14 percent of male counselors and 20–25 percent of male professors have engaged in sex with their clients and students (Glasser & Thorpe, 1985; Pope & Bouhoutsos, 1986; Fitzgerald et al., 1988). Other men have not committed forced sex, but would under the right circumstances. When asked whether they would be likely to imitate a man who raped a woman in a parking lot at knifepoint, about 35 percent of the college males surveyed responded affirmatively, if they could be assured they would not be caught (Malamuth, 1981). Obviously, these men are aware of the legal implications of their actions, but the personal feelings of their victims are of no concern.

The fact that an abuser seems normal is extremely distressing to his victims. Their faith in judgment about other people is shattered, and often survivors say they "don't know who to trust anymore." The abuser's seeming normality may also lead the survivor to question her own perceptions of the abuse—did it really happen, or did she imagine this nice guy was so violent? In cases of incest, sexual harassment, and acquaintance rape, there may be further contact with the abuser, who acts as if nothing has happened. Victims of some family members or friends may experience a split reality, as others tell her she is lucky to have such a wonderful brother or father. Distortions in fundamental issues of "what is normal," "who is good," and "who can be trusted" affect other relationships long after the abuse.

Repeated Abuse with a Modus Operandi. For any sexual abuser, the likelihood that he has performed a similar abuse in the past—and that he will repeat it in the future—is extremely high. Most sexual abusers act out with alarming regularity; on the average, convicted sexual offenders have performed hundreds of sexual abuses over 15 or more years before their first arrest (Freeman-Longo & Wall, 1986; Rosenfeld, 1985). The low likelihood of being caught and the virtual nonexistence of punishment for those who are caught only reinforce repeat offending.[1] Furthermore, each abuser tends to show consistencies in the cycle of frequency, the planning, the approach to the victim, and the behaviors during the assault. Case workers frequently document abusers who have assaulted younger sisters and brothers, then daughters and sons, then grandaughters and grandsons, in turn as they reach the age the abuser has designated for starting his assaults. Harassment follows the same pattern: abusive professors often target one student in each class; abusive bosses approach each new secretary hired in the office; and abusive counselors often have sex with several clients at a time (Holroyd & Brodsky, 1977).

Recognition that sexual abusers typically repeat their offenses using a modus operandi, or pattern, is important for helping survivors of sexual abuse. Repetitive abusive patterns are often not well understood by victims or authorities, who tend to look at the individual's story as an isolated incident. The problem is compounded by many victims' unwillingness to report sexual abuses, which, although understandable in light of their embarrassment and shame, makes it difficult to compile an abuser's profile and seek justice. We have worked with cases in which several women working within an office or restaurant were harassed by the same individual or several children in the same neighborhood were abused by a neighbor, without each other's knowledge. Information about other victims of the same type of abuse reduces self-blaming and isolation, as the survivor realizes that her assailant had planned his assault according to his own timing and style, without reference to her appearance or behavior.

Two general modus operandi of sexual abusers deserve special description. Some aggressors rely on a surprise attack against an unknown victim, called the "blitz attack." Others use deception to manipulate their targets into vulnerability, called a "confidence" or "con" assault (Burgess & Holmstrom, 1974). Each style has implications for the victim and for others' reactions to her (Koss et al., 1988).

In the blitz attack, a stranger appears suddenly, as if "out of nowhere." The victim's responses resemble reactions to any other sudden, unexpected, dangerous event: (1) the shock often interferes with defensive action; (2) the shock precludes seeing or remembering much of the incident, so that subsequent identification may be difficult; (3) the event is perceived and experienced as an assault, and the survivors more readily identify themselves as survivors. Because the assailants are unfamiliar, victims of blitz assaults often experience hopelessness of avenging the abuse, along with self-directed expressions of anger for not defending themselves or acquiring better information during the assault.

Confidence assaults, on the other hand, involve a scheme set up by the abuser, which requires that he gain his target's confidence. The term "con artist" is apt, since he works through his script like an artist. The victim's trust is used to manipulate her into physical and psychological vulnerability. Victims are usually completely shocked by the abuser's change in behavior from a "nice guy" to an aggressor. By the time the victim realizes she is going to be assaulted, the confidence aggressor has already assessed her potential for escape or defense and has usually eliminated many of her options. For example, one seemingly kind gentleman used the excuse of a dangerous neighborhood to key-lock his door after letting in women visitors, thus preventing his victims' only means of escape from his home—an action that seemed protective and reasonable at the time. A con-harasser first convinced his young assistants that it was to their benefit that he work late with them at the office.

A confidence victim experiences the shock of the blitz attack, but her other reactions are more confused. Seeking an explanation for the sudden change in behavior, she may blame her own actions in the prior relationship (Katz & Burt, 1988). Confidence victims often have difficulty convincing themselves and others that a "nice, normal person" could be abusive. Trust is devastated after a confidence attack.

Motivated by Anger and Power. When caught, sexual offenders almost universally protest that their victims "liked it" or "wanted it." Yet serious confessions by mentally competent sexual abusers reveal consistently that most know they have exploited another human being for entirely personal reasons (Beneke, 1982; Groth, 1979). Furthermore, research clearly shows that very few sexual abusers, from street harassers to rapists, are motivated primarily by sexual needs. In fact, sexual satisfaction is often absent, or only occurs with the humiliation of the victim, and is inseparable from psychological needs (Groth, 1979). The primary goals are the expression of anger and a feeling of power, a special kind of power often defined in terms of dominance and humiliation. The patterns of motivation that emerge in research suggest that sex offenders

- show little concern, trust, or empathy for others, especially their victims (Groth, 1979);
- cannot express anger in normal ways, but take their anger out on women, weaker men, or children because they are less likely to confront their power;
- have exaggerated gender-role ideals that could be called "macho" and view sexual dominance as an element of masculinity (Beneke, 1982; Russell, 1975; Scully & Marolla, 1983);
- blame women for a wide range of problems, rather than taking on responsibility themselves or blaming the appropriate target (Groth, 1979; Scully & Marolla, 1983);
- may have been sexually abused themselves (Freeman-Longo & Wall, 1986; Groth, 1979), although this relationship may not be causal; and
- are likely to repeat their offense, because the underlying psychological problems are not resolved by the assault.

The profile of men who physically abuse their wives is strikingly similar (Cantrell, 1986), suggesting that our continuum might be expanded into some types of physical violence.

Belief in Rape Myths. Kanin (1985), Koss and Leonard (1984), and Malamuth (1981) have examined college men with a propensity to rape, evaluated by the men's questionnaire responses. A strong relationship emerges between likelihood to rape and beliefs in "rape myths," cultural attitudes described later in this chapter. A particularly important belief among these men is that rape does not have serious consequences for its victims; some men contend that women secretly like it, particularly since they themselves are such "good lovers." This assumption is mirrored in some abusers' beliefs that sex with a child is merely a form of education, good for the child (O'Brien, 1983). MacFarlane (1978) quotes an incest father who felt he was a moral man because he didn't have sex outside of his family—only with his wife and children.

More thorough descriptions of specific types of rapists (Gebhard et al., 1965; Groth, 1979; Koss & Leonard, 1984; Rada, 1978), of incest and other child abusers (Abel et al., 1976; Starzecpyzel, 1987), of sexual harassers (Dzeich & Warner, 1984; Paludi, in press), and of abusive therapists (Pope & Bouhoutsos, 1986) are useful resources. Clients frequently can recognize their abusers in these profiles, which helps them to place the motivation, and thus the blame, for the abuse with the offender, and not with themselves.

Control Strategies

We tend to define coercion as physical force or use of a weapon. Data collected from rapists and their victims show an average advantage of three inches and twenty-four pounds for the rapist, even when both assailant and victim are male (Brownmiller, 1975, p. 360). In about 25 percent of reported rapes, further superiority is obtained by the use of a weapon (U.S. Department of Justice, 1982). While these weapons are rarely used to inflict physical harm, their presence is sufficiently intimidating to most victims to prevent self-defense.

The majority of sexual abuses on our continuum, however, do not involve physical violence (Finkelhor & Yllo, 1985). A wide variety of resources are employed by abusers to force victims to submit. This range of coercive tactics underscores the fact that abusers look to their own experience, individual advantages, and level of acceptable violence for the most effective means of controlling their victims. In most cases their selection of a control mechanism is part of the planning that occurs prior to and during a sexually abusive act. Some of the physically nonviolent but tactically effective methods of control commonly used by sexual abusers are described here.

Fear of Harm. The recognition of a physical strength advantage often frightens victims into submission. For women this fear is nearly automatic, as we have been taught from early childhood that men are stronger and that fighting them is futile. Fear of harm coming to another person is also an effective controlling tactic. Mothers assaulted in their homes, or older children assaulted incestuously, have often submitted in order to protect their children or younger siblings. One day care center worker got preschool children to submit to abuse by threatening to kill their parents.

Economic Advantage. Jobs, grades, letters of recommendation, promotions, and legal and medical services are all critical to economic stability. They are also key areas of vulnerability to abuse by those holding the economic power. Abuse of economic power is particularly evident in sexual harassment cases. The Working Women United Institute found that physical harassment was negatively correlated with income; that is, the lowest-paid women were the most frequently harassed (Alliance Against Sexual Coercion, 1981). Only 1 percent of abusers in a survey by the Working Women United Institute were less powerful subordinates (MacKinnon, 1979). The victims of economic abuse we have seen are emotionally devastated and experience a lack of options, like a victim of physical force. Their specific fears are different, but they leave no less devastating emotional effects.

Vested Authority. Some roles in our society give the individuals who occupy them a special power base, in the form of real or perceived authority. The most obvious example is family authority, usually that of the father or stepfather. Children are instructed to respond to his authority without question because of his role: many incest victims cannot imagine defying such a powerful person as their father. Nor can their mothers; studies suggest that mothers of incest victims have often been victims of incest or physical violence themselves (MacFarlane, 1978). In many states, sex within marriage is legally sanctioned, and abused wives report submitting to marital sexual abuses from the multiple burdens of social pressure to "obey" their husbands, their emotional desire to please, and the reality that no one can or will help.

Certain professionals are vested with social authority and entrusted to act in the best interests of their constituents. We have worked with victims of sexual abuse by men who relied on their social authority: physicians, ministers, priests, policemen, teachers, and political power brokers. Social authority makes recourse nearly impossible; no one will believe the victim because the abuser has a role-defined presumption of exceptional behavior and/or has the power to make the victim's life worse if the abuse is reported.

Psychological Manipulation. Some abusers weave a psychological trap to make their victims believe they must cooperate with sexual abuse. The key to the success of psychological manipulation is convincing the target that she wants or needs the sex, that she is a participant. This psychological force is utilized by many child molesters, as revealed in an interview obtained by a reporter under the pretext of "learning the ropes" from a more experienced molester. The man, who bragged of abusing dozens of young children, advised him not to do it just once, because in time they might tell, to do it several times right away, because then they will start to believe they they have participated and that they carry some of the responsibility. That "guarantees they won't tell." (CBS, 1984; see also O'Brien, 1983). In similar fashion, abusive therapists take advantage of their clients' need for a supportive, loving partner and abusive mentors manipulate the admiration of younger protegees.

Helpless Victims. People who are mentally or physically handicapped or rendered helpless by alcohol or drugs are extremely vulnerable to abuse. In addition to their inability to prevent the abuse physically, these victims are often unable to report it or are not believed. Abuse of the institutionalized mentally ill, as chronicled painfully in the Frances Farmer story (Farmer, 1972), may be compounded with implicit or explicit threats related to the length of stay: "If you report this, you'll never get out." Elderly and physically disabled people are vulnerable targets because of their physical limitations; in addition, because of stereotyping, they may be treated as if they have a mental handicap as well.

Abusers also render their victims temporarily helpless. "Plying her with drink" is one of the oldest means known for obtaining sex and still perhaps the most used. Alcohol or drug use is a factor in about half of sexual assaults (Koss et al., 1988), a serious problem since these abuses are not likely to be reported, not clearly enough remembered, or perhaps not defined by the victim as rape. From society's perspective, staying sober and in control is viewed as an individual's responsibility, so the drunk victim is allowed little sympathy. Yet this control technique is not very different from those of the dentist who assaults his clients when they are under the influence of laughing gas, of the father who gives his teenager addictive drugs that become his "payment" for sex, or of the man who slips a sleeping pill into his date's drink. Each abuser wants his target physically and mentally incapable of fighting off his assault, and wants no one to believe her if she does report his actions.

Additional Control Issues

This range of control strategies points out the need to understand the many meanings of coercion in sexual abuse. We have tended to define force in terms of observable physical violence, not in economic or social terms. Sometimes it is hard to understand just how incredibly trapped by these other factors a victim can feel. Furthermore, there is a tendency to assume that the survivor of economic or social coercion was not severely harmed. The survivor may not identify herself as a victim ("It wasn't rape, because he didn't have a weapon"); authorities may not act on her case because the assault doesn't fit legal or social conceptions ("Why didn't you just quit the job?"); and the survivor may deny her own feelings ("Other people are hurt so much more, mine was just a minor thing"). The helper must be vigilant to prevent these perceptions. With the perspective offered by an inclusive definition of coercion, such attitudes can be counteracted while the client comes to appreciate the reality that, for a short time in her life, control was taken away from her.

PERSONAL MEANINGS OF SEXUAL ABUSE TO VICTIMS

The word "trauma" can be applied to nearly everyone at some point in life. We may experience trauma when we are caught in a violent storm, when our home is vandalized, or when we have a car accident (Dlugokinski, 1985; Siegel, 1983). We are faced with others' traumatic experiences every day in the news, in pictures and the words of survivors of events ranging from earthquakes to terrorist bombings. Few of us can see those pictures without a perceptible chill, and we often express relief that the problems are someone else's. We often have nightmares of an imagined trauma, waking up in a realistic state of terror that takes a few minutes to shake.

Victims of criminal harm experience a special kind of trauma created by the intentionality of the criminal act (Bard & Sangrey, 1986). Sexual abuse has additional meanings for its victims, caused by the fact that it is such a personal violation. Fear of rape is one of the strongest fears reported by women, and the level of fear women report is extremely high (Riger & Gordon, 1981). Rape is perceived by women (but not by men) as worse than murder (Quina-Holland et al., 1977). In this section we will review the experiences of trauma, criminal harm, and sexual victimization as the first step in providing a structure for understanding emotional responses to sexual abuse.

The Experience of Trauma

Studies of victims across a wide range of events reveal two consistent features in personal descriptions of traumatic experiences: *fear of harm* and *loss of control*. These represent actual or potential threats to the individuals' physical and psychological integrity and to their sense of safety and security.

Fear of Harm. In life-threatening situations, most people describe a gripping sense of terror and speak of "seeing their life passing before their eyes" or making emotional preparations for death. Physically, the victim may be "frozen with fright," speechless, or unable to control voluntary activities. To believe that death is imminent, or to fear mutilation or major life disruption, can change one's whole life. Lifton (1982) describes the psychological impact on victims of the atomic bombings at Hiroshima as follows:

The most striking psychological feature of this experience was the sense of a sudden and absolute shift from normal existence to an overwhelming encounter with death, an emotional theme that remains with the victim indefinitely (p. 50).

Most sexual abuse victims experience these terrors. Nearly all victims of physically violent assaults report that their primary concern—indeed, their only thought—during the assault was that their assailant planned to kill or mutilate them. These fears are frequently reported even without physical violence, as in many incest and harassment cases, where the size, power, and unpredictability of the assailant form implicit threats. While such terror is common to many traumatic events (Harris Poll, cited in Stark & Goldstein, 1985, p. 2), the feelings created by sexual trauma translate into a particularly wide range of negative aftereffects, including anxiety about personal safety, generalized avoidance of large segments of life (outdoors, men, school), phobias attached to specific places or stimuli, or panic attacks. The survivor of an assault or abuse taking place in her own home may never feel safe, even in personal quarters.

Victims of less violent assaults often focus their terror less on the actual abuse and more on a "worst-case" scenario, which includes fears about personal and economic-support systems, potentially affecting the victim's whole future. Ongoing sexual abuse such as incest is a special kind of trauma, which shares some features with the person waiting out a long-term illness or unemployment. For example, Irene knew she might someday become pregnant from her father's incestuous assaults; her terror came to be focused on a fear of pregnancy rather than on the abuse itself. Nan fixed her terror on receiving a bad grade and losing five years of professional training, rather than on the individual incident of sexual harassment.

Loss of Control. The unpredictability of events and the resulting loss of self-determination are another fairly universal trauma-victim experience. Whether the power is in the hands of nature or of an assailant, helplessness to prevent or stop an event is a profound blow to psychological integrity (Bard & Sangrey, 1986). This blow stems in part from a strong need for predictability in our lives. We expect a high degree of personal control over our own destiny. We rarely plan for minor inconveniences like flat tires, much less major disruptions in our life patterns like accidents or floods.

A common psychological response to loss of control over events, observed in survivors of various traumas, is a generalized paralysis from action. Although for most this inability to respond is temporary, the experience of helplessness may affect emotional and relational realms of life: "If I ultimately have no control, why bother?" For victims of multiple traumas, especially childhood incest, who never have an opportunity for consistent self-determination, learned helplessness increases vulnerability to subsequent abuse.

The opposite response is also observed. A trauma survivor may compensate for prior helplessness by increasing control over future experiences. One option is to avoid the location of the trauma altogether—a hurricane victim moves away from the coast. Others may gain control through new knowledge and skills related to the event—a man nearly killed by a shark becomes an expert on their behavior (National Geographic Society, 1982); after an auto accident, a driver takes up professional racing. Among sexual abuse survivors, the effort to regain psychological predictability may include changing residence or jobs, strict regimens of behavior ("I'll take karate. I'll kill anyone who tries to mess with me again"), or highly controlled emotions ("I won't trust anyone").

Increasing control is important, but controlling reactions can also become problematic if the control dominates normal activity or relationships. In extreme cases, more likely among males, an angry victim may attempt to regain a feeling of control by victimizing others.

Crime Victim Experiences

Disasters, terrorist acts, and accidents are usually perceived as having a random nature. In contrast, victims of crime know there is a responsible perpetrator, who has carried out the crime knowing that their victim will be harmed in some way. Threats to physical and psychological integrity are individualized, even if the identity of the victim is not known to the criminal. This *intentionality* affects victims of crimes ranging from property theft or vandalism to sexual or physical assault and the family survivors of murder victims (Bard & Sangrey, 1986). However, the reactions are far more intense after sexual abuse. Janoff-Bulman and Frieze (1983) have pointed out a particularly important effect of intentional harm, the disruption of *personal belief systems*, three of which will be described here.

The Goodness of Humanity. The notion that someone could intentionally harm another person is difficult to contemplate. Most victims react with disbelief: "How could anyone do this?" To explain the action, some develop theories that the offender was crazy or desperate ("He needed money" or "He was drunk"). The interpretation of sexual abuse is usually more complex, particularly in situations where violations of trust have occurred. The more intimate or trusting the prior relationship, the more disturbing the experience of intentional harm is, and the greater the loss of faith in human goodness.

The Just World. We have a well-documented belief, called the "just world hypothesis," that if we behave according to social rules, we will be accorded respect and not be hurt (Lerner, 1980). Many of us were raised by the "golden rule" that if we treat others nicely, they will do the same for us. In spite of the fact that crime violates personal justice theories by failing to distinguish between "good" and "bad" people as targets, we still try to apply these old views to explain misfortune. Many victims and their friends and families develop incorrect theories about particular incidents, or about abuse in general: "I was a bad daughter; my father was punishing me." "It must have been the way I sat in class." or "That's what you get when you hitchhike." Searching for a personal reason for one's selection as a target is an active part of the resolution process for victims of all crimes. For sexual abuse victims, this search is complicated by social and cultural factors, as we shall see in the next sections.

Personal Invulnerability. We tend to underestimate our own chances of being a victim of a crime, contracting a serious illness, or undergoing other forms of trauma (Perloff, 1983). This illusion is a protective mechanism, shielding us in normal times from a range of fears. When a crime such as sexual abuse occurs, we are forced to recognize not only that we are not specially protected from harm, but also that the same crime may happen again. The silence surrounding sexual abuse in our culture enhances the illusion of invulnerability for nonvictims and the intensity of its loss for victims.

The loss of protective belief systems, such as the goodness of humanity, the just world, and personal invulnerability, are accompanied by grief for a world that "used to be." Rarely is a person ever as naive or trusting in others after a crime, especially after sexual abuse.

SEXUAL VICTIMIZATION

The personal meaning of sexual abuse differs in important ways from those of other traumas or crimes. Of course, individuals react differently to life experiences. Such factors as the circumstances, the length and severity of the abuse, the victim's relationship to the abuser, coping strategies, and support from others are crucial. Even so, the various forms of sexual abuse constitute unique personal violations that must be taken into account if we are to understand the individual experience of sexual victimization.

Violation of the Intimate Self. Sexual abuse is deeply invasive. Our sexual body parts, and our sense of our own sexuality, are highly protected personal possessions, even among sexually active individuals. When sexual penetration occurs through force, the victim is violated in a way very different from other physical assaults. The sexual offender violates the intimate self, a far more devastating experience than an assault on an external possession or an outer physical region (Bard & Sangrey, 1986; Wilson et al., 1985). Incest and rape victims speak of their abusers as "taking something very special away from me," of feeling "invaded." When sexual body areas have been threatened but not penetrated, as in attempted assaults and some forms of harassment and child molesting, the reactions are strikingly similar. Descriptions and nonverbal expres-

sions of internal violation are present for most sexual abuse victims, whether or
not penetration has occurred.

Violation of Trust. The majority of sexual abuses are committed by a person
the victim trusted. The violation of the victim's trust is one of the most devastating
aspects of the abuse ("How could he say he loved me and still do this to me?").
However, some loss of trust can be observed in most sexual abuse victims, who
may come to mistrust "all men" or "all relationships" even when the abuser
was a stranger. Violations of trust create a range of emotional aftereffects,
including distancing, isolation, and difficulty with future relationships and will
be discussed in later chapters on recovery.

Violation of Identity. A victim feels *objectified* and *depersonalized* by sexual
abuse, becoming the property of the offender during the assault. Victims report
losing their identity as they are being treated like the offender's "wastebasket,"
as one victim described the experience. As the property of the offender, to be
used for his needs and then discarded, the victim is stripped of personal dignity.
Looking back at his gang rape by Turkish authorities, T. E. Lawrence (Lawrence
of Arabia) said, "to earn five minutes' respite from a pain which drove me mad,
I gave away the only possession we are born into the world with—our bodily
integrity" (letter to C. Shaw, 1924, quoted in Knightley & Simpson, 1970, p.
245).

Some incestuous fathers express their "right" to their daughters' virginity,
as if virginity were an object separate from the child's body. Employers remind
their targets of the ease with which they can be fired or otherwise disposed of.
In addition, many victims experience specific efforts by the assailant to deny
their human qualities, by making them be quiet or covering their faces. Other
abusers impose different identities on their victims, treating them like players
in a fantasy, as when Irene was treated like her father's wife during incestuous
assaults.

Violation of Dignity. Sexual abuse is also degrading and humiliating. These
elements are most obvious when foreign objects are inserted in the victim's anus
or vagina during a rape, or when the abuser soils his victim. Even without such
acts, however, feelings of humiliation are common to victims of all the abuses
on our continuum. Women often react to whistles on the street with a physical
withdrawal, accompanied by discomfort and disgust (Sanford & Donovan, 1984).
A child may interpret a male abuser's ejaculation as "peeing on me," an act
most children view as "dirty."

The effects of a degrading experience are different from other traumas. Victims
develop a self-image of being soiled, ruined, dirty, or evil. Self-hate and disgust
at one's own body are often expressed. Personal shame may interfere with seeking
help, as the embarrassed survivor fears that others will react with the same
disgust.

SOCIAL DYNAMICS OF SEXUAL ABUSE

After any trauma, survivors need a great deal of social support from individuals
and institutions. They need to be with people who can offer support and caring,

a feeling of security, and a situation clearly separable from the traumatic incident. From institutions, assistance is needed on medical, legal, and economic problems. These kinds of assistance are usually made available to trauma victims.

For sexual abuse victims, however, the social response is often very different. Many experience disbelief, rejection, and blaming by others. At a time when their greatest need is for stability in the rest of their lives while coping with the trauma, there may be major changes in relationships. All of these are appropriately perceived as betrayals and contribute to the victim's isolation and silence. Already suffering from the trauma and its personal meanings, the sexual abuse survivor enters a social dynamic unlike that of any other experience.

Loss of Safety Net

Social support is a major factor in recovery for victims of sexual abuse (Burgess & Holmstrom, 1974). Instead of active, supportive responses, however, the people and institutions who should be providing support are often uncaring or hurtful. The loss of this safety net, the support structure that should form the base for recovery, thus becomes an additional source of distress. Many survivors report that harmful actions by other individuals and institutions have been the worst part of the post-traumatic experience. A single woman who pursued a sexual harassment complaint against her boss told us, "Nobody ever warned me about what would happen if I reported this. My coworkers testified against me; my company falsified documents to make me look bad. I was alone, personally and professionally."

Repression, Isolation, and Blame

After most traumas, others urge the survivor to tell them about it, and respond with concern and responses like "I'm so sorry this happened to you." In contrast, sexual abuse survivors are often unable to discuss their experience openly, even with good friends or family. A few may refuse to believe her story and treat her as "crazy"; others may attempt to prevent her from thinking or talking about the experience, thinking that "forgetting the whole thing" is helpful. When survivors do describe their trauma, their listeners' obvious distress may cause them to feel different or strange. Silence becomes a normal response, because attempts to talk about the experience are unsuccessful or painful. Some victims begin to isolate themselves even from caring relationships, feeling that no one can understand. The everyday experience of keeping a dreaded secret has emotional consequences of its own, as documented for other "secrets" such as abortion (Lemkau, in Quina, Lott, & Lemkau, 1987).

"It was really awful in high school," Irene recalled. "My girlfriends would giggle about boys and wonder what sex was, and I had to pretend I was like them. And every night my father was having sex with me. It made me hate the other girls, partly because they seemed so naive and silly, but mostly because they were having a normal adolescence."

Other social responses are more vicious. A number of studies have asked college students to evaluate the respectability of a female rape victim in a hypothetical situation and the extent to which she is seen as causing her own fate (e.g., Jones & Aronson, 1973). The findings are probably good indices of the way the families and friends of most sexual abuse victims respond; between 10 and 50 percent of the responsibility for a rape—by a stranger at knifepoint in a parking lot—was attributed to the victim, depending on the way she was described. More recent studies find a generally lower level of victim blame in violent rape assaults (Kanarian & Quina, 1981), but evidence persists for victim blame in acquaintance rape, incest, and sexual harassment (Burt, 1980; Muehlenhard et al., 1985; Quina, in press). A survey of over 4,000 sixth-to ninth-grade students found that 16 percent of young women and 24 percent of young men felt that "a male on a date" has "the right to sexual intercourse against the woman's consent" if he had "spent a lot of money on her" (Kikuchi & Marceau, 1989). These proportions increased to over 50 percent when the hypothetical couple had been dating a long time, were planning to get married, or had previously had sex. Although this most likely is the other person's way of denying the personal threat of random abuse (Shaver, 1970), the effects are painful to the victim. Every survivor of sexual abuse we have worked with has experienced some blaming by lovers, family, friends, or institutions dealing with the assault.

The mother admitted, with some embarrassment, "My daughter was assaulted by a male student while taking a shower in her coed dorm. I was very upset for her. But you know, I would never have said it, but I wanted to know what she was doing taking a shower at seven o'clock at night!"

Blaming reactions have their roots in cultural myths, as we shall discuss in the next section, and affect self-attributions as well as social relationships.

Changes in Relationships

After abuse, survivors often find that close relationships change, sometimes dramatically. Well-meaning family members and partners may respond with overprotectiveness, creating a new, dependent status that can interfere with subsequent social relationships. In other cases, they respond with rejection. Some avoid a victim because they don't know how to treat the "different" person who has been identified; others simply want to avoid the emotional drain of reality the victim creates for them.

If sexual contact has been a part of the abuse, subsequent voluntary physical relationships are likely to be affected. In addition to sexual difficulties, partners may express disgust or anger at her, as if the sex had been a willing breach of faithfulness.

Brenda, whose story was told in Chapter 1, finally made her way home after a night of brutal rape and torture. She showed her husband her wounds, which included cigarette burns on her thighs and multiple bruises. He remained quiet, but obviously angry, for about an hour. Then he approached her and gruffly announced, "I've decided to forgive you." They never had sex again, and within a few months she filed for divorce. She became a single parent with two children, one of whom she was carrying during the rape.

Most partners want to help, but simply don't know how to act. Men who have been raised to be protective often feel like failures and want to fight back against the abuser—which directly conflicts with the survivor's need for a gentle, supportive partner's presence. These conflicts are enhanced when the male partner feels that his spouse or child is his possession and that the damage to his property must be avenged. The survivors' rapidly changing moods and conflicting messages about their own needs add to the helplessness and frustration of their partners.

After twenty years of marriage, Vera finally told her husband about her father's incestuous abuse. He became furious and announced he was going to kill her father. His rage so frightened her that Vera told him she had made the story up, rather than face the consequences of his violence. Her marriage continued, but he thought of her as a hysterical liar.

CULTURAL DYNAMICS OF SEXUAL ABUSE

Sexual victimization must always be interpreted in the context of the culture in which the abuse takes place. Only in this context are victim reactions fully comprehensible. Culture is always relevant to trauma. For example, we tend to express greater indignation at murders of beautiful young college coeds than at murders of prostitutes. For sexual abuse, however, there are unique cultural standards and attitudes that shape the victim's experience and act to maintain the existence of sexual abuse in the society. Two important cultural contexts are the offender's cultural *power base* and the culture's *mythology* of women and sexual victimization.

Cultural Power Base

Individual sexual abusers are allowed to get away with their offenses by our forgiving culture, as attested by short prison sentences, low prosecution and high acquittal rates, and a general sympathy for abusers. This is made possible by the fact that individual abusers also have a larger cultural power base. Power in our culture is based on the same factors as power in a sexual abuse: physical strength, money, and ascribed roles of authority. Since men predominate on each of these dimensions, they hold a wide general power base in the culture. Non-minority men, particularly, dominate in power bases of money and authority roles. Women and children hold less power than men, and minority women and children, including social minorities such as the elderly and the disabled, have the least cultural power.

This relationship of gender and race to power is not coincidental to abuse. In fact, Baron and Straus (1986) found a negative correlation between economic and social gender equality and sexual abuse: The less powerful women were, the higher the rates of rape. Women and children are far more vulnerable to sexual abuse than men, and minority women and children are the most vulnerable.

These gender differences are promoted by cultural gender roles and expectations. Definitions of power are virtually synonymous with our culture's definition of masculinity: physical dominance, economic superiority, and authority. Without at least one of these, a male is perceived as not masculine, or worse, as "feminine," as derogatory terms like "sissy" and "wimp" imply. Gaining masculinity, by whatever tactics necessary, is socially approved, and men who fail to "act manly," even if people are harmed by their actions, are social outcasts (Beneke, 1982; Kahn, 1984). The net result of this power-gender role mix is that sexual abusers can readily justify their actions as expressions of masculine needs or drives. This justification fits well enough with cultural expectations for males that others may not strongly censure an abuser for his actions, however reprehensible, thus providing cultural supports for continuing abuse (Burt, 1980). The response to a rape or harassment story is dulled by social acceptance of every male's need to "prove" his masculine power.

These cultural values for men and masculinity are complemented by values for women and femininity. Our culture's definitions of femininity include traits that are synonymous with vulnerability: sociability, submission, dependence, and weakness (Lott, 1987). Girls are taught to be nice, not to confront, to try to please men, and always to obey their elders. Girls grow up knowing how to be afraid and how to seek protection through dependent relationships, but not how to react in the face of danger. Regardless of their actual capability, many women believe they are weaker than men and that escape from a male abuser is impossible (Kidder et al., 1983). This belief denies women a range of options when faced with a threat of assault.

The power dynamics of sexual abuse extend into the institutions that respond to the individuals. Victim powerlessness is reinforced by medical, legal, and social service systems that are based on the same assumptions about masculinity. These systems are usually led by men trying themselves to achieve personal masculinity, and these men believe the same myths about sexual abuse. For example, Field (1978) found that the attitudes of police officers toward rape were closer to those of convicted rapists than to those of the general public. Minority women abused by nonminority men and gay male victims experience this reality the most harshly. A survey carried out by women living in the inner city of Milwaukee found nearly half of the 32 sexual abuses against Black women were committed by White men, but only one of those had been reported to police, much to that victim's subsequent regret. In contrast, about one-fifth of intraracial assaults had been reported.[2] These women recognized that their cultural powerlessness as minority women assaulted by White men would only reinforce their individual powerlessness as victims. Gay men experience the same reality: since homosexuality is a violation of the social norm, pursuing justice is often futile (Krueger, 1985). Unquestionably, their assailants recognize the same fact.

Analyses of the ways sexual abuse has functioned to maintain social control reinforce this conclusion. Brownmiller (1975) presents a brilliant and devastating historical review of tactical uses of rape to destroy troop morale in war, by degrading the women associated with the men who are fighting. Her work is backed up by statements from Vietnam veterans who used these tactics (Beneke, 1982). Farley (1978) and Stanko (1985) demonstrate tactical uses of sexual harassment to prevent women from moving into male-dominated fields and gaining economic strength. Even without specific experience, women college students report limiting their activities—not taking evening classes, going to the library or computer center at night, or working late in the laboratory—out of fear of sexual assault (Hall & Sandler, 1982). In prison, stronger inmates achieve and maintain control through systematic sexual abuse (Brownmiller, 1975; Weiss & Friar, 1974; Wooden & Parker, 1982; see also Morokoff, 1983).

Cultural Mythology

Stereotypes and myths about sexuality and sexual abuse have persisted throughout the recorded history of humanity, from biblical writings to cocktail party jokes, as the excellent review by Brownmiller (1975) and research by Burt (1980) attest. Contemporary professionals have too often believed and perpetuated these myths, creating the backdrop for what some have called the "second injury" (Symonds, 1980). These myths, well ingrained in our culture, directly affect the experience of sexual abuse victims, creating levels of shame, guilt, and confusion rarely arising from other traumas. We will review some major myths and stereotypes and provide examples of their impact on treatment and reactions of victims.

Myth No. 1: There Is a Fine Line between Coercion and Seduction. Ever since Adam took his first bite from the apple, women have been accused of causing otherwise normal men to lose control. From Homer's sirens, to the European and early American witches burned for driving men crazy, to Nabakov's pre-adolescent "nymphet" Lolita, history has held females from age one to ninety-five responsible for man's animal instincts. This notion still forms the basis for today's "double standard" for sexual behavior. It also has permeated sexual abuse work. Until the mid–1970s, the "handbook" for legal professionals on sexual assault listed 27 ways in which a victim could precipitate a rape (MacDonald, 1971). Although MacDonald's statistics were subsequently demonstrated to be false (Hursch, 1977), his erroneous claims are still cited.

This myth of seductive female sexuality has been extended into images of sexually abused children. Freud's notion of childhood seductivity was used to "explain" incest (Westerlund, 1986). The most often cited study on child victimization prior to 1974 examined 16 preadolescents who had "had sex relations" with adults (Bender & Blau, 1937). They concluded that these unusually charming and outgoing children could be labeled seductive personality types and that they bore at least some of the responsibility for initiating and maintaining the sexual contact, even though they "rationalized" their own behavior with "excuses" of fear.

In cases of harassment, the seduction myth maintains a firm grip as well. Although the notion conflicted with their own data on the extent and nature of harassment of vulnerable office workers, Meyer et al. (1981) warned readers about the complexities of sexual harassment because "women send out a variety of signals that are not always easy to interpret. The manner in which they dress, use makeup, and walk across a room can indicate that banter and even serious sexual come-ons would be welcome" (p. 40).

Myth No. 2: Women Want to/Need to/Love to Be Forced. Each year a joke circulates on college campuses in which a girl screams "Rape!" and the other girls run out screaming "Where?" Portrayals of passion in film and in popular "romance novels" promote the fantasy of a strong, handsome lover (usually on a white horse or in a new Porsche) sweeping a protesting maiden off her feet. In fiction she winds up loving it every time. Unfortunately, this fantasy, in which the "victim" knows (or creates) and loves her attacker, who himself is consumed by passion, has been labeled "rape fantasy" and is assumed to be a desire for real sexual abuse.

Sexual aggression has been offered as a "cure" for many types of women, from assertive to frigid. Gloria Steinem (1984) related an early opponent's proposal that she should have met up with Richard Speck, the convicted rape-murderer of eight student nurses. Her opponent believed she deserved such a fate for stepping off the narrow feminine path with her writings. Another woman related being forced into excruciatingly painful sex by her husband on the advice of her gynecologist, who called her husband after examining her and told him to ignore her protests because the pain was "in her head." (Years later, a physical problem was identified.)

Helene Deutsch (1944–45) contributed greatly to professional acceptance of this myth by her psychoanalytic theory of feminine development. In her view, adult females must learn to submit to the pain of sexual intercourse and childbirth for the joy of having (male) children. Therefore she reasoned that pleasure through pain, or masochism, is essential to a normal mature feminine personality, as well as to survival of the species. Pornographic portrayals of feminine masochism are common, as in two of the most popular X-rated films of the 1970s, *Story of O* and *Emmanuelle*, in which women find complete sexual fulfillment and "true womanhood" through being raped, degraded, and physically defiled.

Children do not escape this myth, either. In a widely referenced book, Abrahamsen (1952) stated:

Unconsciously, a woman would like to be taken by force. In literature, such a theft as that of the bride in Peer Gynt for instance is quite a common phenomenon, and is undoubtedly instigated by the unconscious wish of the woman to be raped. Frequently we find this seductive inclination in small girls, in their being flirtatious, seeking out rather dangerous or unusual spots where they can be picked up, or exposing themselves more or less deliberately to sexual attacks (p. 181).

The concept of masochism also leads to a common misconception in our culture that women "like it rough." In studies across the United States and Canada, a large percentage of college men reported their belief that women like to be forced into sex (Malamuth, 1981). Although Caplan (1984) has debunked the myth of women's masochism effectively, some psychiatrists have continued to insist that it is an inherent aspect of women's personality (see "Self-Defeating Personality Disorder," in American Psychiatric Association, 1987).

Myth No. 3: The Truth of Claims by Women and Children Must Be Evaluated Carefully, Especially concerning Sex. Another of Freud's legacies affecting victims of sexual abuse is his concept of hysteria. Freud attributed neurotic symptoms in his young female patients to unresolved psychosexual seduction fantasies about their fathers from early childhood. Ironically, as Masson (1984) has now documented, Freud originally believed his patients had been incestuously abused, but he bowed to pressure from other professionals who could not accept the horrible implications for human nature. Despite restricted clinical definitions, even for modern therapists the label "hysterical" conjures up images of a seductive woman unable to discern truth from fantasy. "Hysterical" is also used to mean "out of control," placing victims in a double bind: If a victim is emotionally controlled, her plight is not deemed serious; yet if she is distraught, she is labeled hysterical and her words will not be trusted.

Children and elderly victims are further stigmatized by their age. Developmental psychologists and parents are well aware of the rich imagination of the normal child. Although most experts concur that young children simply do not make up the kind of detailed story told by a child who has been abused (MacFarlane & Waterman, 1986), defense attorneys and others will counter that any story from a child under eight is most likely fantasy, and some states automatically consider testimony from a child under five to be suspect. (See Chapter 6.) The elderly suffer a different stigma; the "failing memory" image. Defense attorneys have been known to purposely confuse elderly victims on the witness stand in order to render their testimony about the identity of an abuser "unreliable."

Sexual harassment victims are treated with suspicion because of cultural images of women seeking revenge against an innocent professor or boss. As with rape victims, in case after case we have seen the victim's life scrutinized for "reasons for wanting to get even" before authorities take any formal steps to halt or redress her harassment. Recently a university lawyer told a group of administrators that when a person charged with harassment is not found guilty, universities should consider charges against the claimant for making false and malicious accusations. Given the already wretched record of success in obtaining guilty judgments in harassment cases, the effects of this practice could be chilling.

Myth No. 4: A Truly Virtuous Woman Would Not Have Been Abused. Shakespeare's Lucrece took a knife to her breast because she had been unsuccessful at avoiding rape.[3] Today our literary refinement may be lacking, but the sentiment remains: "Nice women don't get sexually harassed/raped." An astonishing number of men, and a few women, that we have talked to believe it is impossible to complete a rape without some cooperation on the part of the victim and that an "innocent" victim would not provide that cooperation. This myth shows up in a variety of judgments about the victim; her prior sexual behavior and dress are considered relevant to the abuse, if not in causing the abusive act, then in the extent to which the abuse has caused her harm. In some states, until the mid–1970s, if one could prove a rape victim was of "immoral" character (e.g., a prostitute), the rape was not a crime.

The common threads of this myth are woven into attitudes about other victims of sexual exploitation. Colleagues of sexual harassment victims may say, "I don't understand. Nothing like that ever happens to *me*" —often following with descriptions of the moral prudence of their own behavior. Parents often believe their child's abusive experience will reflect badly on them, and punish the victim for her "misbehavior."

The Effects of Myths on the Victim

Perhaps the most dangerous outcome of these cultural ideas is the survivor's own acceptance of blame (Quina-Holland, 1979; Quina, in press; Symonds, 1980). Self-blame is one of the most prevalent survivor reactions, and will be treated extensively in in subsequent chapters.

Karen's meeting wasn't her last experience of harassment. She recalled, "After four coworkers approached me during my first year, I became convinced I must be doing something to entice them. It never occurred to me that I had been hired by a group of sexual harassers. This wasn't my experience of normal male behavior—I had had lots of male friends in college—but since so many colleagues were involved, I figured it must be my fault. For a few years I couldn't relate to any men, because those first professional interactions had led to such disastrous results. Later, one of them was brought up on charges of sexual harassment by two other women.

Wendy was hitchhiking, as she had often done for short distances around the city. But this driver pulled out a gun, drove her to an isolated area and raped her, keeping the gun in his hand throughout her entire ordeal. She called a crisis line about a month later, in tears. She had come to believe that she could have avoided being raped and that by missing the chance to get away from her attacker, she must have wanted the rape to happen. When queried about her opportunities to escape, she replied, "We were on the interstate, and the car slowed down to about 40 because of the traffic. I put my hand on the door handle to try to jump out, but he put the gun up against my head and said,

'Don't try that or I'll kill you. I should have gone ahead and jumped.'' While she agreed that such a move would have been foolish and perhaps fatal, she still felt that if she had been "innocent" she would have jumped anyway.

NOTES

1. The average prison sentence for convicted child sex abusers is less than one year (Stark, 1985); various reports place the mean stay in prison for convicted rapists at less than five years.

2. This survey was organized by Judith Jasper and Willa Lumsford and coordinated by Kathryn Quina.

3. Pamela Webber deserves credit for her excellent literature review.

RECOMMENDED READINGS

Brownmiller, S. *Against Our Will: Men, Women and Rape*. New York: Simon & Schuster, 1975.

Figley, C. R., ed. *Trauma and Its Wake*. New York: Brunner/Mazel, 1985.

Groth, A. N. *Men Who Rape: The Psychology of the Offender*. New York: Plenum, 1979.

Stanko, E. A. *Intimate Intrusions: Women's Experience of Male Violence*. Boston: Routledge & Kegan Paul, 1985.

3 _____

Helping Approaches

WHO IS THE HELPER?

Teachers, counselors, lawyers, law enforcement officers, nurses, physicians, social workers, and crisis agency staff members and volunteers are likely to serve clients who have been abused. Helping is not limited to professional roles, however. A parent, child, partner, or friend who has been victimized may ask for help. This chapter will explore the formal and informal roles assumed in working with victims and offer general guidelines for helpful intervention.

A question often heard from the general public, even from volunteers for sexual abuse centers, is "How can I help? I'm not a professional." Professional training is not a requirement for being helpful to others. Most survivors are able to resume a normal level of life functioning after a brief recovery period. The majority of crisis needs can be met effectively by a supportive, informed helper (Carrow, 1980). Professional counselors can add their in-depth training and experience, and the special expertise of medical and legal professionals is vital, but there are plenty of other helping roles to be filled by people without these specializations. A healthy, concerned ally is often the most helpful person of all.

Requesting assistance after sexual abuse can be very difficult. While most families and friends provide strong support after a trauma, in some cases they are unwilling or unable to respond. Some survivors don't want to cause pain to their families and friends, or they fear a negative reaction, and thus choose not to tell them about the experience. In these situations a new person, often a crisis worker, becomes a primary source of help and support. When a family member or friend is the offender, a teacher or social worker may be the initial contact for help. As the survivor moves through the medical and legal systems, people in a variety of roles may affect her emotional process and resolution.

Because of the negative attitudes surrounding sexual abuse, most survivors have a heightened sensitivity to the kind of treatment received and to the attitudes of the provider. Effective helping must include comforting, supporting, defending, and educating the client and others, along with specialized victim assistance.

The helper is someone who lends the survivor physical and moral support, provides information, advises about options, clarifies and explains, and makes the survivor comfortable. The helper also keeps track of incoming information, reduces external stress, and takes care of details. The helper validates the client's experience as a victim, helps others understand it, and may also serve as a liaison between the client and institutions or agencies, provide referrals and a source of contact with resources, or if qualified, enter a longer-term relationship with the survivor as her counselor.

The helper is *not* someone who makes decisions for, forces assistance on, or reacts for the client. The helper does not cajole, push, insist, or interrupt a client nor diminish or deny the client's feelings or reactions. The helper is not there to take over for the victim, except in emergencies. Above all, the helper is not authoritarian or defensive with a client or with others. The helper role is one of intervention, not interference.

THREE HELPING FUNCTIONS

There are three functions a helper may serve, depending on the client's needs and on the helper's training and experience. These are the functions of *crisis intervention, advocacy*, and *counseling*. While one person may be qualified to serve all three functions, such as a social worker who is also a crisis worker, other helpers serve only one, during a time-limited interaction, as may a nurse in an emergency room who serves as an advocate for a patient who has been abused or a crisis line volunteer who talks to victim clients over the phone. The three functions address different, but often overlapping, client needs.

Crisis Intervention

Intervention during a crisis is the most intense and in some ways the most important helping function, because effective early help can reduce the severity of long-term problems. The definition of "crisis" depends on two factors: the recency of the abuse and the urgency of the client's needs. Crisis-level needs are greatest during the hours and days following an incident of sexual abuse, but crises may also arise at any time, even months or years after the abusive treatment ends. A crisis intervention function should always be assumed during the first contact with a client, unless a referral has indicated otherwise.

Crisis intervention is specific to an incident and short–term in nature. It results from a specific trauma and in no way implies any general psychological dysfunction of the client. The short-term, issue-oriented model of crisis intervention focuses on the traumatic incident and gives that incident a clear priority over other issues in the client's life (Burgess & Holmstrom, 1974). The goal of crisis intervention is to help the victim cope with her ordeal. The crisis intervener should help the client to (1) develop and maintain realistic perceptions of the event, (2) manage the affective responses to the event, and (3) develop coping strategies appropriate to the client's post- victimization knowledge and experience (Golan, 1978). Longer-term efforts, such as integrating the meaning of the abuse into the survivor's life, are best left to later phases of resolution.

Advocacy

The advocacy function involves intervention with the institutions that work with victims, such as social welfare agencies, hospitals, police departments, and court systems. As mentioned earlier, these places and their procedures are often unfamiliar, confusing, and frightening. An advocate accompanies a client through the procedures, serving her in any way that reduces the fear and confusion and helps to meet both institutional and client needs. The needs of institutions are very different from those of their clients. An institution can often be impersonal and bureaucratic, and rigid in procedure, while the client needs personal contact that adapts to her special situation. The institutions are task-oriented and time-limited, while she needs gentleness and patience. Few institutions have specialists in sexual assaults, so her case is treated like any other, yet she has unique needs. Finally, most institutions are public, noisy, and open, while she needs privacy and quiet.

In interactions with institutions, the advocate can explain and prepare the client for procedures, keep track of information, and maintain personal contact. Most victims need and appreciate someone who functions as an advocate. These functions are especially important with the elderly and with child victims (Warner, 1980). At the same time, most institutions also appreciate an advocate who can supply accurate information and provide the personal support they cannot offer. Many referrals to rape crisis centers come from hospitals and police stations with personnel who have come to rely on volunteers for those functions. Some larger institutions have even hired their own advocates for their victim clients (Chapter Appendix 3A). Staff members of an institution, such as a hospital, may incorporate an advocacy function into other roles for serving individual victims. Gilmore and Evans (1980) describe an advocacy model for emergency unit nurses using a primary nursing approach.

Another important function of advocacy is the protection of victims' rights. Occasionally problems arise with institutional responses to a sexually abused client, when standard or acceptable procedures are not followed or when personal treatment of the client becomes cruel or offensive. Effective advocates try to turn such problem situations into an education for institutional personnel by gently but firmly explaining the problem and offering a more appropriate treatment or procedure. If the mistreatment continues, the client should be fully informed of the problem and of her rights to receive appropriate treatment and allowed the choice of continuing or terminating the procedure. If an institutional employee questions the presence or role of an advocate, the advocate should ask the client clearly, "Do you want me to remain with you?" An affirmative response from the client justifies the advocate's continuing presence. Few institutions have rules that prevent a friend or advocate from staying with a client, except during emergency procedures such as surgery. If an advocate or a client is mistreated in any way, the advocate should send a detailed letter of complaint to administrators and public officials as soon as possible, with a copy to the local rape crisis center if it is not already involved.

Counseling

Counseling involves a more complex relationship between a client and a trained and qualified counselor. While some counseling may occur immediately after an assault, or for only one or two sessions, most sexual abuse counseling starts after the crisis needs are met and takes place over a few weeks or months. The counseling process may be specific to the abusive incident or may span a range of issues in addition to the assault.

The goals of counseling are to help the client to (1) clarify perceptions of the abuse and reactions to it, while increasing understanding and self-acceptance, (2) relieve the emotional discomfort and pain caused by the trauma and by others' reactions, and (3) establish new ego patterns that integrate the abusive experience and allow for growth.

Counseling is more intense interpersonally than other helping roles because it requires a deeper relationship with the client and a broader range of listening and facilitating skills. The client shares her victimization experience, reliving her trauma, and works through it with the counselor, who helps her move toward resolution. Effective counseling also often requires the ability to recognize, and to help clients with, problems that are unrelated, or only peripherally related, to the abuse.

To be a qualified counselor, one needs to have knowledge of psychological theory and research, training in therapeutic skills and techniques, supervised experience, and the ability to recognize and treat a range of problems. Most qualified counselors have a minimum of a master's degree. Special expertise in working with abuse survivors is also very important. The more complicated the client's problems, the more essential the counselor's training and experience become.

RESPONSIBILITIES OF THE HELPER

The helper has the responsibility to the client to establish a healthy relationship, to promote positive attitudes, and to provide accurate information. Each helper also has a responsibility to herself or himself not to exceed personal limitations. These responsibilities can best be met in a comfortable and mutually agreed upon relationship, where helper and client form an alliance, facing tasks as if they are "in this together." Trust is essential if such an alliance is to work, so it is crucial for the helper to be open, honest, and clear about values and commitments.

Informed Consent

Upon meeting a client, the first responsibility is to establish the nature of the helper's relationship and services. These issues can be covered in as little as a few sentences, but it is important that the client enter a relationship of informed consent. Every potential client must have the option to refuse or to discontinue intervention at any time. Many victims are reluctant to talk to a stranger, especially someone they perceive as a "shrink," at a time when they are feeling disorganized and vulnerable. Some refuse to talk to anyone, even a close friend. If a potential client refuses intervention, a card should be offered with a phone number for future contact, along with gentle words like, "Sometimes people want to talk about this kind of thing later on, when they're feeling a little better. If you feel this way, please call me; my name is _____." A hospital social worker who used this technique with considerable effectiveness pointed out that the calls she received months later in the middle of the night were proof that seemingly "uncooperative" victims just needed more time.[1] Staff members at police stations and hospitals have found it important to repeat offers of help to victims who initially reject it, since they often become ready to accept help after some time.

Informed consent must include the *capacity* in which someone is serving the client, and the amount of *time and energy* that person can be expected to spend. "Blank check" promises like "I'll stay with you as long as you need me" should not be offered, and promises of cure must never be made. Time limits must be clearly stated; for example, a volunteer on a crisis line with a one-hour limit on phone time or a hospital staff member who will go off shift in two hours should let her client know well before the time is up. An opportunity for additional contact or referrals to other appropriate resources should be provided before the meeting terminates. If an agency has specific rules against such practices as transporting a client or going to her home, its representatives must make sure that the potential client understands these rules. If a client has requests that cannot be met, the limitations should be explained in such a way that she is not rebuffed. The agency's rules, and its trust, must never be violated.

Volunteers or staff members from an agency or institution should give each of their clients their card or write down their name and position. If there are any charges or requirements associated with the intervention, such as a report of an incident to the police, the potential client must be informed immediately. If she cannot afford services or meet requirements, she must be offered options.

All services must be *confidential*, and the client should be assured of that confidentiality. If for some reason strict protection of information about her is not possible (as in a case where the helper is a nurse who may be asked to reveal the content of discussions in courtroom proceedings), the client must be apprised of the limits on confidentiality, preferably in writing.

An effective working alliance requires *honesty*. Difficult personal questions often arise. A helper who has herself been sexually exploited may feel awkward about revealing her own experience, yet this is one of the first questions many victims ask. A helper who has been sexually abused and who is comfortable talking about her own experience may help the client realize that she is not alone, and provide a role model of healthy resolution. However, those who are not comfortable revealing personal information, or who have not been a victim of sexual abuse, should never lie. A direct answer may be avoided by mentioning a close friend or relative who was abused, or another type of severe personal trauma, so the client can feel the helper can understand what her experience is like. In either case, it is important to keep the focus on the client's experience. Sometimes both helper and client will be tempted to talk about the past in an effort to avoid the present reality. The client only needs to know that she is not unique or alone; she does not need the added burden of responding to another's trauma.

Nonjudgmental Treatment

For men counseling women victims, Silverman (1977) titled an article "First Do No More Harm." This message should be foremost in the training of all counselors and advocates, male and female. In the role of expert, the helper has the power to be either a positive or a negative influence. Some of the potentially negative influences, which must be eliminated, arise from harmful attitudes: personal prejudice against the client, false assumptions based on first impressions, stereotypic attitudes about sexuality and sexual abuse, and projections of blame and politically based anger onto the client.

Personal Prejudice. Most of the volunteers with rape crisis centers around the country are white, middle-class, and often young (Carrow, 1980). Many people seeking the services of these centers are from lower socioeconomic and less educated backgrounds, partly because of the greater violence in poor neighborhoods and partly because women with higher incomes are more likely to seek private treatment. Because of their economic vulnerability, minority and poor women are frequent targets of sexual harassment and assault. Unfortunately, with the exception of neighborhood centers, most organizations and crisis centers have not been able to bridge the gap between cultures as effectively as they would like. Utilization of services by minority women has often been embarrassingly low, and efforts to reach out to minority populations have too often been unsuccessful (Carrow, 1980). Thus it is especially important for counselors to avoid being influenced by racial or ethnic prejudice.

Other personal prejudices are difficult to identify in oneself in an honest way, but they must be eliminated from helping behavior. For example, it has been well documented that there is discrimination against women who weigh more than average (Brown, 1987) or who speak with a different regional or class accent. Every client should be appreciated for her individuality and must be approached with a "blank slate": nothing can be known about this person's ability or personality until she shares it. The client is the only expert about herself.

Impression Formation. People tend to judge other people by their behavior and appearance on the first meeting (S. Asch, 1945; Briscoe et al., 1967). A client who is disheveled or exhibiting symptoms of emotional stress may create a negative first impression. It is easy to slip into assumptions of instability or low competence in such a case. It may be especially tempting for professional counselors who have been trained to look for problems to try to "diagnose" the client right away. It is more appropriate to insist that each client is a psychologically healthy person who has undergone an externally inflicted stress and should be assessed and helped as one would any other victim of trauma.

Sexual Stereotypes. In spite of generally high awareness, the stereotypes and myths discussed in Chapter 2 influence the attitudes of even well educated helpers. Their impact on a helper's effectiveness can be seen in the example of Jean and Mary (Chapter Appendix 3B). Faced with a client who was open about her prostitution, Jean found that her attitudes were more judgmental than she had believed. Even for a strong political activist working with rape victims it is not uncommon to criticize someone who could "get themselves into" a long-term harassment situation or attribute some responsibility to adolescent incest victims.

Helpers must be prepared to deal with different lifestyles and sexual situations, including some quite unlike their own experience. The focus must be on the client's trauma, not on her lifestyle. If an unbiased relationship cannot be established, the client should be referred to a more appropriate source of assistance.

Projections of Blame. Some judgmental attitudes arise from the helper's own needs, especially the need to feel safe. Notman and Nadelson (1980) have used a psychodynamic approach to explain the threat presented to the counselor's own feelings of security when confronted with a client's experience of victimization. To avoid this conflict, a helper may try to distance herself from the client, either by making her different ("she isn't like me, she is poor, not educated, dresses badly") or by making her behavior different ("she did a dumb thing, she could have fought harder"). This blame may not be expressed directly, but may emerge in subtle comments or treatment choices. Even skilled professional counselors may resort to victim blame as self-protection. As someone whom the client has entrusted the evaluation of her actions, a helper must be especially wary of blaming tendencies. From the victim's perspective, if an "expert" blames her, then she may feel even more guilty.

Some blaming reactions are more harsh and dangerous. As an adult, Irene went to a psychiatrist for help resolving her incest. With justifiable bitterness she related,

I paid this man $60 per hour to have him tell me that it was *my* fault that my father molested me, something he called the 'provocative child syndrome.'' He also blamed Dad's alcoholism on me, saying that Dad became an alcoholic because he felt guilty for molesting me!

Fortunately, Irene had enough self-esteem to leave this therapist, but many are so vulnerable they are unable to break away. Armsworth (1987) has documented similar cases of therapist blame for incest victims seeking help.

Political Anger. A serious dilemma often arises for experienced helpers. Most clients see their victimization as a deeply personal trauma, especially when it is inflicted by someone in their own intimate circle. On the other hand, the helper may recognize in the client's experience the common characteristics of sex offenses, the gender imbalance in these crimes, and the perpetuation of sexual abuse by social institutions. This awareness that a client's individual assault is part of a cultural pattern creates a tendency to minimize her individual reaction, seeing abuse as a problem out of her reach or control and resulting for many in an intense anger. To be helpful, however, the helper's political anger must be subdued. Balancing personal and political views is not easy for most helpers, but it is essential. Over time, the client may develop the same understanding of the way social norms have helped to create and maintain victimizations like hers. Such understanding is a long-term process, however, and not an immediate goal.

Accurate Information

Clients may base life decisions on the information provided during sexual abuse intervention, so each helper has a special responsibility to be informed and accurate. Incorrect information leading to a bad choice will lessen the client's confidence in herself and her trust in others. Agencies doing victim advocacy often depend on the good will of the institutions with which they work, and errors reflect back on them.

If the answer to a question is not known and no written materials are available, the closest authority should be consulted before the client is given a response. However, there are situations in which the local authority may give incorrect information. Police officers in one city, who were required by law to offer rape victims the option of a female officer, had done so in only about half of the cases studied (McCahill et al., 1979). We have worked with victims who were given seriously misleading information and even blatant lies. One harassment victim was told by a supervisor to avoid a counseling center because "they couldn't help her," probably because the supervisor feared that the center would tell the victim about the option to sue her institution. When in doubt about the advice or information a client has received from an authority, the local rape crisis center is probably the best resource. Most centers maintain information banks and know which "insiders" to consult on specific questions.

Reasonable Intervention

A helper's level of involvement must be based on personal limits as well as on strengths of experience and training. Individuals have the responsibility to appreciate and respect their own limitations in training, experience, ability, and tolerance for personal stress. Helper and client may suffer emotional consequences from inappropriate intervention; in some cases, overstepping bounds may have legal consequences for the helper. Professional counselors, physicians, and attorneys are accountable for their work, and most have liability insurance and training, so they should be utilized when appropriate. A nonprofessional volunteer or the agency she or he represents may be sued if a client is dissatisfied with inappropriate therapy attempts, medical treatment, or legal advice.

Most agencies specializing in sexual abuse intervention give their representatives extensive training, including skills for crisis intervention and advocacy. However, emotional problems other than sexual abuse issues may arise, placing most volunteers outside their range of experience. Even highly trained therapists experience uncomfortable counseling situations. At the first sign of an unfamiliar problem, a qualified specialist should be consulted or the client should be referred.

Helpers also need to protect themselves from excess personal stress. Experience can help determine how much pain, fear, and conflict one can listen to without losing too much personally or interpersonally. If the intensity and trauma of crisis intervention work are creating too much stress, the helper should seek relief, such as a transfer to another kind of work. For volunteers who wish to continue to contribute to an agency there are usually other roles, such as public education or fund-raising, or the option of a leave of absence. Employees such as nurses or social workers may try to shift into a role with a different focus or a new position. Personal stress also varies with time and other life stressors, and the need to move away from direct victim contact may be only temporary. However, any stress should be taken seriously, as evidenced by the high rate of counselor and volunteer *burnout*.

Freudenberger (1980) has listed symptoms of burnout: chronic fatigue, irritability, cynicism, guilt, inability to joke and laugh, physical complaints, and reduced sex drive. Most also experience denial—of feelings, of problems, and of their own needs.

Sarah, a rape crisis hotline volunteer for two years, described her feelings: "I sit by the phone and hope it doesn't ring, so I won't have to hear about another victim. But if it doesn't ring, I feel guilty because rape is still going on, and someone isn't getting my help. My husband keeps bugging me to stop working with such depressing people and to spend more time with him. He makes fun of my friends' "feminist martyrdom." I want to be happy, too, but too many people need me.

These reactions are not a sign of incompetence or lack of commitment; rather, they are caused by overdedication and lack of support. They are particularly problematic for sexual abuse helpers because there are so many victims, their problems are serious, and positive outcomes are slow. Recognizing, responding to, and preventing burnout are discussed in Chapter Appendix 3C.

HELPING TECHNIQUES

The intervention techniques offered in this section are adapted from standard counseling approaches to address the special needs of survivors of sexual abuse. These general techniques form the background for more specific recommendations in subsequent chapters.

Leaving Choices to the Client

By definition, in sexual exploitation the victim is made powerless. From the beginning, the victimized client should be given back as much control over her life and her environment as possible. Most clients appreciate help in defining their needs, giving them priority, and meeting them. The helper, however, must not push the client toward any action and must try to prevent others from doing so, too.

There are specific tactics that are useful in helping a distressed client make decisions. The impact of tasks can be lessened by helping her focus on only those decisions that need to be made right away, such as immediate shelter and safety needs or whether or not to tell someone. Large decisions can be broken into smaller problems to be solved, with a maximum of two or three options each. If a client appears to have reached a point, through fatigue or stress, where she cannot make reasoned choices, the helper can suggest a break to rest, possibly overnight. Except for safety, there are rarely any decisions that can't wait a few hours if necessary.

Most people undergoing trauma are overwhelmed in part because they see no alternative to their present situation. Identifying real options gives back some sense of control, which in turn can reactivate the desire to get on with the rebuilding process. It is helpful to keep a list of the options and the choices a client has made, both for her information and as a concrete record of progress. Written material is frequently easier to handle than verbal and can be reviewed whenever needed.

Interventions for each client must also be evaluated in the larger framework of the victim-to-survivor model, promoting recovery and even the personal growth that comes with a successful coping process. While the immediate comfort and needs of the client are primary, the long-term consequences of actions and decisions should always be considered. A person under stress may not be able to recognize when a quick solution may be detrimental to her later interests. For example, a sexually harassed employee may want to quit an otherwise good job, a desire that is understandable and probably meets an immediate need for a reduction in stress. On the other hand, if there is a chance that the harassment can be ended and if she might not be able to obtain an equally good job right away, quitting may create even greater stress for her in the future. When short-term and long-term interests conflict, a client should be asked to weigh both sets of interests and consider the larger framework of options for the long run. A delay of even a few hours may allow her to see the impact of her decision more clearly. As always, the final choice belongs to the client and must be respected.

Validating the Victimization Experience

Believing the client is essential to a helping relationship. Victims need to vent feelings and review their experience, often repeatedly (Mills, 1977). However, venting is not helpful without validation. Validation is a process in which the client is encouraged to express all the feelings, thoughts, or emotions that surface, with minimal interference and maximal acceptance. Validation requires complete acceptance of the client's pain and support while the painful memories are being described.

The quality most essential to validation is *empathy*. Empathy means putting oneself in the other person's place, feeling that person's emotions but not taking them on, anticipating her reactions as if they were one's own but not acting them out. Empathic treatment places the client's needs first at the time; everything is done in her best interest. Empathy also requires objectivity and a nonjudgmental approach. Sympathy, or feeling sorry for a client, is not helpful because it diminishes the client's belief in her strength to get through the process. Bullmer (1975) and Mills (1977) provide thoughtful exercises to enhance empathy.

Feelings of helplessness after a traumatic experience do not mean that a client is inept. The natural desire is to protect a victim from further pain, but taking over for a client at this time may be harmful in the long run. An overprotective helper may "infantilize" the client, reinforcing a helpless self-image. Survivors need gentle support to rebuild their own power, with some protection from unnecessary additional stress, while building independence in making their own life choices.

Devoting Individualized Attention

An effective helper does not demand that a client meet her expectations, but appreciates her as an individual. In this phenomenological approach, the client determines the level of intervention, and the helper adapts. Individuals must not be pushed to conform to a helper's predictions, and symptoms should not be diminished or dismissed because they do not match expectations. For example, a rape victim who does not experience disruption of normal functioning in the days following a traumatic assault should not be questioned because her coping style seems atypical; nor should a harassment victim who continues to grieve months after losing a cherished job be told to "forget it and get on with your life."

Intervention should be gauged to the client's age and life stage. For example, with younger victims, especially children, information should be concrete (Kempe & Kempe, 1984). Questions should be matter-of-fact, short, and to the point, free of confusing grammatical tricks like double negatives. Dolls and puppets are often helpful tools in eliciting information from children. However, anyone talking to a young child must be especially careful not to suggest acts or experiences that might or might not have happened, because of legal implications (Eberle & Eberle, 1986). With elderly clients, special care should be taken to speak clearly and more slowly than usual, and anything an older client may need to remember later should be written down. Life-stage issues may impact the recovery process for individual clients as well (Notman & Nadelson, 1983). After sexual abuse, secondary or compounding problems often arise from transitional issues, like the struggle for independence in adolescent clients.

The client's language-level and terminology should be used wherever possible, and highly professionalized or medical terminology should be avoided. When more formal terms are used, they should be explained if the client does not appear to understand them.

Listening Effectively

Reflective listening is the best way to gather information from a client. This process directs the helper's full attention into the listening process (Rogers, 1951). The client is allowed to talk freely; during meaningful pauses, the helper restates the client's ideas, with the meanings extended and filled in. The helper continuously moves to a level deeper than what the client has said, by suggesting an implication or interpretation. If feedback from the client indicates that the helper is wrong, the client is asked to repeat her ideas, perhaps in a different way. This reflective process lends itself to greater validation of the client's experience, as she realizes someone has heard her and understands.

Reflective listening requires that work proceed at the client's pace. No conclusions should be drawn before the client is ready. Putting words into her mouth, or second-guessing her, may invalidate her experience instead of helping her. Rather, the helper must adjust to the client's level of responsiveness. This is perhaps most difficult when the client is silent and the helper is nervous. At such times, expressing anxiety is not helpful. With these clients, a helper should always be ready to shift gears; a client who has been silently mulling over options may decide to move and want action rapidly!

Asking questions may be a help in gaining insight into a client's experience and needs. The questions should only be requests for information that will help in the intervention process, always asked in the context of reflecting, clarifying, and understanding.

A good listener does more than analyze the words spoken by a client; she listens with something that has been referred to as the "third ear" (Reik, 1948). The "third ear" hears the meanings the person has attached to her words, as if reading between the lines. Cues are obtained from inflection, gestures, body language, emotional expressions, contradictions, and silences. If a client says, "I don't really need anything," with a sigh, but seems to be looking for something, perhaps she is temporarily overwhelmed and can't decide what she wants. Her need may be as simple as a cup of coffee, or she may be worried about a family member. Concrete offers like getting a snack or making a phone call may help her focus her attention on what she wants. The "third ear" picks up on things that frighten a client, that seem to inspire anger, withdrawal, or tears. Meaning may also be found in seemingly unimportant comments. For example, a passing reference to a friend's rape by Ann (from Chapter 1) was accompanied by unusually strong nervous expressions. Followup on the unspoken message revealed that Ann's friend had suffered serious emotional problems following her rape, and Ann feared a similar fate for herself. Attention to nonverbal reactions may also help to identify sexual abuses that have not been revealed.

Silence may indicate that a client is thinking through the experience and that the time is being used productively. On the other hand, silence accompanied by stress behaviors may mean that the client is overwhelmed. If the latter seems to be the case, several tactics can help: calling attention back to easy, concrete matters; redirecting thoughts to a subject less difficult to handle; focusing attention on more specific thoughts, such as a single aspect of the assault, or how the client is feeling now, or the reaction of one family member; or a physical action, like going into another room to get a drink of water.

Regardless of a client's apparent stamina, no one can stay with intense, painful work for too long a period of time. Occasionally the helper should change the subject and try to get the client's mind off the most intense aspects of her experience. This is self-protective and may lead to greater progress in the long run. The analogy to breaks for rest during exercise should be sufficient.

Viewing Recovery as a Process

One of the most frightening victim experiences is a fear that one will "always feel this way." For clients experiencing extreme stress, this fear is especially disturbing. The victim-to-survivor approach emphasizes that recovery is a process that takes time. The general orientation of "past-present-future," as Mills (1977) describes it, is helpful. Victims need to be reassured that what they are feeling is very real and should not be diminished, but that they won't feel this way forever. Survivors go through mood swings, from sadness to rage to feeling glad to be alive, from feeling better to feeling worse and back to better again. With this perspective on the healing process and the normalcy of their feelings, clients typically report less fear and find the ratio of good days to bad days increasing over the weeks and months following a trauma.

Some clients also need emotional protection. Someone who breaks a leg is allowed time to mend without demands to move around as that person normally would. A cast physically protects the limb from outside intrusion and prevents further stress to the person in general. But when people are injured emotionally, no one can see the wound or its cast. Thus it is harder to allow the time or the protection for mending psychologically. The client and her significant others may need help in developing a respect for her wounded internal state and her need to heal.

Clients may also need explicit permission and time to grieve. Sexual abuse always involves losses, yet many survivors don't recognize their grief responses and try to prevent or fight their depression. Emotional "downs," unless they are suicidal in nature, are a normal part of the process of grieving for the past, and the freedom to grieve can be liberating for the future. Appreciating present grief is self-validating; once grief is expressed, most survivors experience feelings of relief.

TERMINATING AN INTERVENTION

The end of any relationship is difficult, but for the client who has been traumatized and perhaps betrayed by sexual victimization, ending a helpful relationship can be particularly frightening. Yet it is important for both helper and client that a clear closure be given to the relationship, even when the intervention has been short.

Termination should take place with the achievement of the client's goals or the fulfillment of the helper's role. If the intervention is time- or task-limited, as in phone work or advocacy roles, the end of the relationship is often more predictable. However, when helping roles are more extensive, as in ongoing crisis cases or in counseling, it may be more difficult to determine when and how to end the complex relationship that has developed over time. Nevertheless, counseling is not an endless process, and its end must be addressed as soon as the goals are met. In either case, both helper and client need to have an awareness, prior to the last meeting, that the relationship will be ending.

Many therapists believe that the termination process can determine the outcome of the whole therapeutic intervention. Chodorow (1978) and Gilligan (1982) have described the importance of relationships to women and the difficulty women experience in severing or separating from important relationships. In the helping relationship, this problem is compounded by the fact that clients may experience the strength and comfort they so badly need when they are with their helper. The result is a fear of losing that strength and comfort, even when the client is fully recovered. However, when the client's goals are achieved, there are clear benefits of termination: the client can view herself as having completed her tasks successfully, or as being "recovered," and the normal tendency to become dependent on another can be avoided or relieved. In other cases, the client may still have needs that have not been fulfilled by the helper's function in that intervention. Many clients benefit from referrals to support groups, medical or legal assistance, or counseling. These referrals should be in place before termination where possible. Guidelines for the referral process are offered in Chapter Appendix 3D.

Terminating the helping relationship does not mean that the client and helper will never work together again. But if the client recontacts the helper, or if they see each other in some other context, their initial relationship will be history, and a new relationship must be renegotiated.

As the end of the relationship nears, the helper may try to ask the client the following questions:

- What have you accomplished? The client can review her achievements and good feelings about the relationship.
- Do you need anything else? If there is need for further intervention, an extended relationship can be renegotiated or appropriate referrals offered.
- What will you do (in the future)? The client needs to acquire a future-oriented outlook and to recognize positive options that can be achieved by herself.
- How do you feel about the termination of this relationship? Clients may experience mixed feelings about a helper who is ending a relationship. Anger and grief are not unusual after extended counseling. In complex relationships, the helper may find that her own reactions include sadness or guilt. Airing those feelings openly can reduce many of them and the confusion they cause.

The process of closure should be positive and honest, but the fact of termination must be clear. Even a brief interaction deserves a "best wishes" ending. If sincerely felt, a statement like "I'll miss working with you" is fine.

NOTE

1. This and other information was provided by Kate Greenquist of Milwaukee, Wisc.

RECOMMENDED READINGS

Carrow, D. M. *Rape: Guidelines for a Community Response*. Washington, D.C.: Department of Justice, 1980.
Egan, G. *The Skilled Helper: Model Skills and Methods for Effective Helping* (3rd ed.). Monterey, Calif.: Brooks-Cole, 1985.
Mills, P., *Rape Intervention Resource Manual*. Springfield, Ill.: Charles C. Thomas, 1977.

CHAPTER APPENDIX 3A: INSTITUTIONAL ADVOCACY

In the 1970s, some institutions recognized that their existing treatment was not adequate for sexual abuse victims. Specialized clinics were established at a few large hospitals, and some court systems set up rape prosecution teams. One exemplary hospital-based program was established at Family Hospital in Milwaukee, Wisc. Prior to the establishment of this center, rape victims had to go to the large county hospital and wait several hours in the general emergency waiting room. The staff there was not particularly sympathetic or trained to work with rape issues.

The Sexual Assault Treatment Center was designed to offer a quiet atmosphere and individualized care by specially trained nurses, physicians, and social workers working as a team. The following characterizes the program: The normal emergency room is bypassed, and a room is provided for family members or friends to wait with the client or for police interviews. Choices of medical treatment and whether to report the rape are left up to the client, but the center can collect evidence for prosecution if the client wishes. The initial contact includes treatment for injuries and psychological counseling; followup counseling and tests for pregnancy and venereal disease are available to any client. Other exemplary programs at Beth Israel Hospital of Boston and Santa Monica Hospital are described by Gilmore and Evans (1980) and Abarbanel (1980), respectively; these programs offer community education and professional training and consultation as well as direct victim services.

The district attorney's office of Milwaukee County developed another model victim advocacy program with funding from the Law Enforcement Assistance Administration. Specially trained prosecutors were assigned to rape cases, from start to finish, so the client only had to tell her story to one person. Adjunct services located in the same suite included a social worker who performed advocacy work with external agencies (such as social services), as well as individual counseling with clients. The staff also identified flaws in the existing rape statutes and worked to reform sexual assault legislation. Unfortunately, this was a pilot program for a few years in the 1970s and ended after its funding expired. However, other districts have followed some of the more general principles of minimizing turnover among prosecutors and increasing understanding through inservice staff training. Furthermore, more generalized victim services, such as hot lines for information on the status of a case, funding for restitution of damages or pay lost as a result of the case, and education about courtroom procedures, have evolved in many areas. Justice Assistance, a national organization, also provides general court advocates for victims of all types of crimes (633 Indiana Avenue, NW, Washington, DC 20531).

CHAPTER APPENDIX 3B: DEALING WITH CLIENT DIFFERENCES

Jean is a college student from a middle-class family who has volunteered with a rape crisis center. She is asked to work with Mary, a client living at a women's shelter. The first thing Mary says is that she "gets tired of johns beating me up," and she relates a story of "beating the shit out of this pimp who tried to rip me off." She is wearing clothes that are very tight. She speaks sharply to her children, who have come in from playing outside. After a few minutes of awkward silence, Mary eyes Jean and laughs, "I suppose you are shocked by me."

A good helper-client relationship can almost always transcend differences in gender, race, class, sexual preference, and life circumstances. However, some helper-client differences may be large enough to interfere with helpful intervention. The mismatch of Jean and Mary was evident in more than dress or language. Jean found Mary's history of giving and receiving violence and the way she treated her children shocking and repugnant.

Recognizing her feelings, Jean steered discussions away from Mary's life experiences. They spent this initial meeting helping Mary list her needs and offering resources for each, and Jean referred her to the center's professional counselor. Jean contacted the counselor herself with her concerns about the welfare of Mary's children.

Below are some general reminders for dealing with such differences, particularly with clients who differ dramatically from the helpers in their lifestyles or beliefs.

1. Recognize and admit feelings of discomfort. Denying or covering them may turn the intervention into a harmful experience, in that the client may sense the unspoken discomfort. Once feelings are recognized, they can be set aside more readily. If it is appropriate to disclose them to your client, do so gently and assure her that you will not judge her life, indicating that you will not deviate from your normal role.

2. Your responsibility is to determine the client's needs and attend to them. Focus on the task at hand rather than on your reaction to words or stories that upset you. However, if you suspect any child abuse has been committed by the client, inform her of your responsibility to report it and follow up. If you are not protected by confidentiality laws, you should let her know of your legal position with respect to confessions of any crimes she may make to you.

3. As with any other client, this client needs to tell her story, even if it is longer than most others. Listen, within the time frame allowed by your role, with the same nonjudgmental attitude any client deserves. Avoid comments or expressions of amazement—they reinforce the client's sense of being unusual and may even encourage her to tell irrelevant but shocking stories.

4. Be careful to decide which, if any, psychological needs you can meet. A client with a drug addiction, a financial crisis, or deep emotional problems may need more help than any one person can provide, even if the helper is a professional. Know your limits and make referrals, and help the client follow up on them (Appendix 3D).

5. Don't be offended if the client rejects offers to help or denies emotions. Look for small signals about needs, and respond with reassurance and sensitivity to her position. Individuals who have strong "tough" exteriors have developed these as barriers against enormous amounts of suffering. Don't take on a crusading effort to "break the ice" in a short-term intervention.

6. Remember that your goal is to help the individual cope with sexual abuse, not to reform your client or others around her. Never confuse your goals for her with her own. If she requests help in changing her life, provide resources and assistance, but remember that her growth is not your responsibility. You can help, particularly by your understanding and solid support, but she must carry the responsibility for setting her own goals and maintaining her growth process.

CHAPTER APPENDIX 3C: BURNOUT

Do you feel tired all the time, especially when you have to go to work (or volunteer)? Do you often feel overwhelmed by the number of victims and the intensity of their experience? Are you giving every spare minute of your time to victim advocacy or counseling, and no time to yourself? Do you feel guilty about friends or family because you don't spend as much time with them as you used to? Do you see no joy, no end to the pain, no change of pattern in your future? If you have answered yes to several of these questions, you may be suffering from what some have labeled *burnout*.

What to Do about Burnout

1. Recognize the symptoms of burnout, and admit your feelings to yourself and others. Do not attack others who express concern or try to help; listen, and let them help.

2. Take time off to rest—as much time as you need. If you feel guilty about not helping, recruit a friend to volunteer or apply for your job. Remember, healthy professionals take vacations, and you can too.

3. Evaluate the sources of your feelings. Have a complete physical examination; you may have an illness, like mononucleosis. Look at yourself and your relationships. Freudenberger (1980) used his rest time to talk into a tape recorder daily, replaying each tape the next day and writing about his insights. Your feelings may be precipitated by the behavior of others, as was the case with Sarah, whose husband was doing things that she responded to with guilt, like his attempt to cut her off from the feminist friends he feared would change her. Distinguish between personal and structural or organizational sources of burnout—some agencies do not provide adequate resources to maintain the intense commitment required of helpers. An unsupportive or hostile supervisor, or client, can create the same feelings. Work to change or to end unhealthy relationships.

4. Regenerate positive feelings about the rest of your life. Reacquaint yourself with your lover, family, friends, pets. Spend time with fun people making joy—singing, laughing, playing—*and* time alone enjoying yourself—reading, hiking, watching funny movies, or just sitting.

5. Adopt a schedule that is reasonable for you, a schedule that balances work and play.

How to Prevent Burnout

1. Develop a support structure, one that will encourage you and allow you an ongoing expression of your own feelings. Many rape crisis centers have regular volunteer meetings and infrastructures that allow such communication. The cocounseling model is an exciting way for professional counselors to achieve mutual help (Jackins, 1987).

2. Set more realistic goals for victim work. See value in even small positive outcomes; a little help is better than none. Don't obsess about problems or "lost cases," but use them to help consider ways to change the intervention process to reduce their likelihood in the future.

3. Commit only to those things you feel good about doing. Some prefer one-on-one client contact; others would rather it be public speaking, legal advising, or support work like answering phones or typing. Some volunteers go back to school to change careers, to have an impact from within the system. There are always alternative ways to help.

4. Expect clients to be responsible for their own lives. Don't allow excessive dependency to develop or continue. Utilize other resources when appropriate. Realize you are not omnipotent; you cannot solve everyone's problems.

5. When you need help, ask for it. You may be amazed at how many people would be happy to help out, especially if you are enthusiastic with them. Keep your organization or service viable by encouraging others to become involved.

6. Spend time in positive life experiences, and maintain a sense of humor. Playing with children can help you develop thoughts like "the world will be a better place for them because of my nonviolent role modeling." During playtime, clear your head of negative or anxiety-provoking thoughts like "these children may be scarred for life by rape."

7. Nurture yourself first. Appreciate what you do for others, as an "extra" special quality of life, not as a way to avoid guilt or to fill time. After a client intervention, pamper yourself to refresh your own spirit. Do something you enjoy doing, and remember to define that for yourself!

For more information, see Cherniss (1980), Freudenberger (1980), and Pines et al., (1981).

CHAPTER APPENDIX 3D: REFERRALS

If a client needs more than you can offer, such as long-term counseling when you are intervening as an advocate, you must be firm in refusing. Explain why you are not the right person, and offer to help find someone who can do what they ask. If possible, offer to remain as a support person while they work with the new helper.

The need for referral may raise delicate questions. If you have been successful in building an alliance with a client, she may feel betrayed by your refusal to work with her. Stress that your action is not a rejection, but an effort to find the best help for her. Indicate that the need for a referral is not based on her level of "sickness," but only on your own level of expertise or experience. Discuss her fears about referral. One client suffered debilitating anxiety for two years after she was referred to an incest specialist, because her only available analogy was a medical specialist to whom one is sent when they are "very sick."

In making a referral, (1) consider the client's physical location and financial resources; (2) make sure the referrals are competent, empathic, and appropriate to the client's needs; (3) contact the referrals in advance to make sure they are currently accepting clients; (4) give the client options of more than one person, where possible; and (5) follow up on all referrals. While some dropout is inevitable, a more informed and more structured transition can avoid many delays or client losses.

Many rape crisis centers have a staff therapist for short-term rape or harassment counseling and special groups for incest and rape victims, often free of charge. Private therapists and institutions may wish to refer clients in for specialized work on the sexual abuse as part of the overall therapeutic process. For longer-term work, most rape crisis centers maintain a list of therapists who are effective with sexual abuse issues.

The more personal the referral, the better. It is tough enough to make a new contact, and having a name and a brief description of the person will take away some of the client's fear of the unknown. If you cannot locate an individual for referral, help the client contact the local mental health center and state her needs and preferences clearly. For any referral, it is helpful to prepare the person or agency to accept her as a client. Go with the client as a support on the initial visit if appropriate, or ask her to report back to you about how the initial contact went. If any problems are suspected, review them carefully and recommend a different referral if necessary.

If the referral is to a counselor, the client needs to appreciate her role as a consumer of services and her rights in obtaining those services. Consumer handbooks on women and counseling (Aftel & Lakoff, 1985; Bruckner-Gordon et al., 1988; and Liss-Levinson et al., 1983) are excellent resources. Appendix I, at the end of this book, provides a summary of the training and special characteristics of various types of professionals and paraprofessionals who might be called upon to help a sexual abuse victim. Develop your own list of the qualified individuals available in your area, and do not hesitate to call them when a client will benefit from their intervention.

Part II _____

The Immediate Aftermath of Sexual Abuse

4

Posttraumatic Phases

Immediately following an abusive incident, many victims need assistance in obtaining safety and medical assistance. Other needs arise during the next days or weeks, particularly for security and for legal assistance. During this time the survivor is likely to experience intense stress reactions and disruption of normal physical and psychological states. The most severe symptoms are felt during the first few days; however, the *acute crisis phase* generally lasts up to six weeks, depending on the severity of the experience and the support received.

Psychological trauma is the response to a sudden and unexpected event in which the person believes her or his life or physical health is in danger. In the immediate aftermath of a traumatic victimization experience, a number of emotional reactions are common. From moment to moment these reactions may vary from helplessness to rage, from composure to terror. The stress of trauma also causes somatic problems, including nausea, gastrointestinal distress, shaking, and sleep disturbance (Lindemann, 1944).

An acute crisis reaction is frequently followed by a period of relative calm. During this *avoidance phase*, the victim may claim to be all right and request a termination of all intervention. The same person who insisted on bringing the assailant to justice last week may now refuse to press charges or to appear in court; the counseling she had found so helpful may be rejected. This combination of apparent composure and refusal to deal with the trauma are, for many, a normal phase of posttraumatic recovery.

In this chapter we will review interventions appropriate to the immediate postabuse phases, emphasizing crisis intervention approaches. We will then identify five areas of decision making, which we call *choice points*, and take a crisis intervener or advocate through the issues a client should consider in each area. Finally, we will examine the common emotional reactions during the acute phases and suggest ways to assist a client who is experiencing these reactions.

ACUTE CRISIS INTERVENTION

Crisis intervention techniques are designed to help a client manage emotional trauma and make effective decisions under difficult circumstances and can prevent more serious problems later. In most instances the initial contact can be assumed to be a crisis even if the trauma occurred years ago. Subsequent contacts during the acute phase may also warrant crisis intervention, depending on the individual and the situation.

The goals for the helper during the acute phase should be (1) to help the client secure physical safety; (2) to reduce the client's stress; (3) to inform and support the client's choices and (4) to reduce the long-term effects of the trauma. The most difficult, but also the most important, choices arise at the same time the survivor is feeling intense stress.

Crisis intervention must begin with physical safety. The first issues to be determined are whether the client is safe from further harm and whether medical attention is required. If she is not safe or has serious injuries, the police and/or an ambulance should be summoned immediately. Active intervention is also warranted if a client indicates suicidal behaviors (See Chapter Appendix 4A.)

Once the client is clearly safe, a private place to talk should be secured. Advocacy for arranging such a place may be needed in institutional settings such as hospitals, where clients may be left in the large, public waiting area of the emergency room. Most buildings have a private area, such as a conference room, that can be made available.

To start the conversation and establish rapport, the helper-client relationship should be negotiated, using the guidelines in Chapter 3. If the client does not want additional help, her wishes must be respected, even if she appears to need assistance. However, she should be offered information about options and a way to reach a helper. If possible, a followup contact should be made in a few hours, because the client may not yet recognize her need for help or comfort.

If the client can tell her story in depth, she can begin to sort out the details of the incident and clarify some of the confusion that frequently follows a trauma. If she has an opportunity to express the intense emotions raised by the trauma, she may then feel less overwhelmed by them before she begins making decisions. Three critical issues to be alert to are whether the assault is likely to recur, how the client is responding to the stress, and how much support she is likely to receive from others. Above all, an empathic, nonjudgmental response from an understanding helper will reduce her fears about her situation and increase her sense of self-worth.

Based on her story, the five choice points described in this chapter should be addressed. The helper guides the client through an assessment of her wants and needs in order to help her make initial decisions. These choice points generally represent decreasing orders of immediacy, but individual clients may express different priorities. Some will reject any emotional thoughts and will initially focus on medical or police attention. Others may feel that their most important decision is whether or not to tell a family member or friend about the assault. Thus the choice points are provided only as a guide and must not become demands placed on a client.

There are wide individual differences in response to crises, regardless of the type of abuse suffered. One of the first rules of crisis intervention is that the way an individual client will react to a trauma is not predictable. Some will cry uncontrollably, some will be quiet and seem to lack emotion; others will display nervous reactions such as laughter. Some will be expressive, freely demonstrating emotions; others will be reserved and unexpressive. Some react immediately to their trauma, while others seem calm at first, but react after the immediate tasks are completed. These individual differences, very noticeable during the acute phase, must be recognized and respected for any client.

AVOIDANCE PHASE INTERVENTION

The avoidance phase represents a "time-out" from the intensity and disorganization of the initial posttraumatic period. The victim attempts to defend her psyche from further pain and grief by withdrawing from the stress-causing situation, a response that can be viewed as self-protective. Extending the analogy of the broken leg from Chapter 3, the avoidance phase is like the leg encased in its cast. After the initial pain and shock of recognition and treatment of the fracture, the vulnerable limb is placed into a protective casing while the the rest of the body resumes normal activity. The cast reduces pain because external pressure can't come near. No progress may be apparent, because the casing prevents anyone, including the victim, from viewing the wound. However, considerable healing activity is going on inside, with tissues regrouping and reconnecting and surface wounds losing their ragged edges. In the same way, the defenses of the avoidance phase act as a psychological cast for the trauma victim. Thus its functions, and for some, its importance, become understandable, even though the client's behavior may seem puzzling. For highly traumatized, sensitive individuals who find the stress of the acute phase extremely disorganizing, this phase may be essential to halt the intensity and destruction wrought during the acute crisis phase. In rare cases, where anxiety reactions and sleep disturbances are excessive, avoidance may be a way of preventing psychosis.

As with the broken leg, however, it is false to assume that the client has closed off options permanently. As we shall be discussing in Chapter 7, the issues will probably reemerge, but with a more stable base from which to seek resolution.

As a period of defensiveness, the avoidance phase is a difficult time for intervention of any sort. Efforts to keep clients interested in pursuing actions related to the abuse frequently fail during this period. Looking forward to enormous tasks, such as two years of litigation, may simply be too overwhelming. Denial and rejection also characterize responses to emotional support. Clients say that they are fine, that they have gotten over the abuse, and that they do not want to talk about it. Attempts to convince them otherwise are met with anger or silence. Clients may forget appointments, refuse to return for medical checkups, or not return phone calls. Many survivors move away, some to another city, and drop contact with the helper.

Faced with these reactions, it is important to keep in mind the phase perspective of recovery and if possible to convey it to the client. This temporary process framework allows a frustrated helper to understand changes in a client's responses, particularly rejection or hostility. The feelings make sense and may be viewed as best at this time. The phase framework reminds us, however, that while the client feels better than she did during the acute crisis phase, her avoidance gives only temporary relief and is usually not a satisfactory long-term resolution. The helper and the client can be better prepared for future reactions with this phase perspective in mind.

Given the meaning of this phase to overall recovery, intervention should address three goals: meeting the client's pragmatic and emotional needs, increasing her self-esteem, and helping her return to a normal life. The client should never be forced to talk about the abuse or to undergo unwanted counseling. If she does not want intervention, it may be helpful to provide a contact or counseling referral in case she feels the need for them at a later time. If she wishes to continue the relationship but not to talk about the abuse, a supporting and stabilizing role can be negotiated in which her work, relationships, or interests are the focus of discussions.

If a client is considering dropping out of ongoing legal or medical proceedings, she should be encouraged to think through her decisions, perhaps aloud with another person. Regardless of the outcome, it is better when choices are made, based on an articulation of the potential outcomes. First the client should determine what needs to be done, and when (e.g., appear in court tomorrow, have a check-up next week). If tasks can be delayed, she may wish to request rescheduling, leaving her options open for the future. If an upcoming task cannot be postponed, such as facing her assailant at a hearing, it may be helpful to have her draw up two lists: why she would want to do the task, and why she would not. The first list should include the reasons she wanted to press charges in the first place. Gentleness during this process is important, but she should fully understand the implications of her decisions. If she sticks with the task, she will do so with preparation for its requirements; if she withdraws, she will know the options that are foreclosed as well as those that remain available. As always, it is the client's decision, and the helper's role is to offer nonjudgmental support.

Professional counselors may want to utilize this phase to work on other issues, especially any problems that can interfere with the resolution of abuse issues when they arise. Problems with parents, current relationships, or concerns such as whether or not to have children or to change jobs are often aspects of resolution work but may not seem so threatening to the client. Some clients need assistance getting through immediate tasks, such as an upcoming exam or business deal, with a stress on practical strategies. In most cases, the client will indicate when she is ready to move forward to the resolution phases.

CHOICE POINTS FOR INTERVENTION

At a time when the victim needs most to feel comforted and secure, she is faced with a number of choices to be made, problems to be solved, and demands from outside systems. In this section we provide a systematic approach to helping clients work through acute-phase tasks so as to make choices in an orderly and informed fashion. Our approach, originally described by Carlson and Courtois (1972), targets the five *choice points* that must be considered in immediate post-abuse intervention. The choice points are structured to allow the client the empowerment inherent in making her own decisions and to define helpful roles for others.

Each choice involves consideration of at least one other institutional or personal support system. Formal charges may involve a complex set of negotiations with personal relationships and institutional systems. For example, a sexual harass-ment grievance within a corporation may be addressed by a union, the company, private physicians and psychological examiners, and two sets of lawyers. Thus helpful intervention would incorporate the advocacy function, with several help-ers if necessary. A client who chooses not to take formal action may still request information regarding medical, legal, and personal issues in order to make de-cisions. Because of the variety of options, the helper can be a key resource during these choice points, not only to the victim but also to her friends and family and the institutions that serve her.

The five choice points are briefly described here, with greater detail given in subsequent chapters. At each choice point, the client should be made aware of the issues and concerns, the systems that may become involved, and the decision options and potential outcomes of those decisions. Then the client must be supported as she makes her own choices regarding each.

Choice Point One: Medical

Medical services may include one or more of the following: treatment of physical problems, collection of physical and emotional evidence to corroborate legal charges, and prevention of future problems such as sexually transmitted disease or pregnancy. The client's choices include whether and when to seek medical attention, where to go for medical services, which services or treatments to request, and the role(s) she wishes the helper(s) to assume.

Immediate medical attention should be urged if the abusive sexual contact occurred within the past 72 hours, if penetration or ejaculation took place, or if there is pain or physical injury. However, not all medical attention must be treated as an emergency. For example, if a victim of sexual harassment was not physically injured but is experiencing emotional distress, she can set up an appointment at her convenience with a competent physician willing to testify in court. A parent calling late at night about an incest case should not rush a sleeping child out for medical intervention unless there is physical injury, since waking a child up and taking her to an emergency room will only frighten the child more. In such cases the services of her private pediatrician or a clinic or hospital with specialized team intervention for child victims are more appropriate. A rape victim assaulted several days or months previously may wish only to be tested anonymously for sexually transmitted diseases at a clinic or to be examined for other problems in the context of a physical examination by a private physician.

An immediate physical examination will be required for anyone who chooses to pursue legal actions, and it should be a priority. However, a medical examination does not commit the client to report the assault or to cooperate in prosecution, although some hospitals routinely share information with the police.

The two major helping roles at this choice point are information and support. The helper should also provide four special kinds of information with respect to medical intervention.

First, because medical institutions vary widely in their services for sexual abuse victims, the advocate should be prepared with referrals appropriate to victim clients and should call to confirm that such treatment can be provided.

Second, it is important to collect medical evidence to support legal claims during the initial day or so after the assault, optimally within the first few hours, with as much evidence as possible intact. The advocate should encourage any recent victim who may decide to report the assault to police, even at a later time, to seek a medical examination immediately, before she changes, bathes, or douches. (She should be reminded to bring a change of clothing with her, as the clothes she was wearing during the assault will probably be retained as evidence). If she has changed clothes, she should wrap the clothes worn during the assault together carefully and bring them with her to the examination.

Third, the financial arrangements with the hospital or medical facilities should be considered with the client, and if she will be paying for the treatment, she should be reminded to bring her insurance information or checkbook with her.

Finally, during the medical intervention the advocate should keep a written record with information the client may later need, such as the physician's name, the medications prescribed, and the forms signed. Medical intervention will be discussed in greater detail in Chapter 5.

Choice Point Two: Justice

Choosing whether or not to report an incident of sexual abuse is often the most difficult decision a victim must make. The routes to formal justice cover a range of options: police and criminal court systems, civil courts, institutional grievance procedures, and public agencies.

It is best to report an incident of forced sexual contact or penetration to the police within the first 24 hours, although victims who delay reporting may still be encouraged to pursue justice. The police station is only the first step in a long legal process that may take up to two years. In the criminal justice system, the legal process is taken out of the victim's hands, and her role becomes that of a witness. If the case is pursued, she is asked to provide information and evidence, to identify the assailant, and to testify as a witness in legal proceedings. She may drop out of the process at any time, but she cannot force an unwilling police department or prosecutor to act on her case. Her choices, then, are whether or not to report the incident, whether to request a female police officer (available in most districts), whether to cooperate in the investigation and prosecution, and how she wishes others to assist her.

Most large corporations and institutions such as schools or hospitals have internal procedures for handling complaints of sexual harassment. In addition, federal, state, and local equal rights and equal opportunity commissions are provided for the protection of students and many employees. Guidelines for each should be consulted so that no technical errors prevent a successful complaint.

A victim has the additional option of utilizing civil court proceedings to seek financial redress directly from the alleged assailant. In this latter option she has more power, and treatment is more personalized, but the process is expensive in terms of time and money, and the chances for success are difficult to judge.

For the advocate, familiarity with the legal process is essential in helping the client to select from these options and then to adjust to the lengthy, stressful process. Supportive resources, such as preparation for court testimony, should be made available as needed. Special attention must be paid to the personal stress from delays, facing the assailant, and negative decisions. The legal system will be explained more thoroughly in Chapter 6.

Choice Point Three: Personal Support Systems

Victims often hesitate to tell others about their assault experience, for reasons including shame, a desire to protect others from the trauma, and fear of negative responses. On the other hand, opening up and sharing is helpful, and support from a spouse or lover, family, and friends is beneficial to short- and long-term recovery. Keeping a secret from an intimate friend or family member may be a greater burden than telling the person, especially since those close to the victim may already sense that something is wrong.

The client needs to choose whom to tell and how to tell them. An advocate can be particularly helpful in guiding the client through her reasons for and against telling others, sorting out sound choices—for example, not telling classmates whom she does not trust—from choices based solely on bad feelings about herself. She should consider the benefits as well as the risks of self-disclosure,

including the risk of losing a lover or friend. It is often helpful to see the problem
from the perspectives of the people she might tell. The advocate can probe these
perspectives with questions like, "If you were your mother, how would you
respond if you knew?" If the client forsees negative reactions, role playing of
possible outcomes can be extremely helpful. The advocate may offer to be present
when she discusses the incident with others, both to support her and also to
answer their questions and educate them about her experience. As a third party,
the helper can deflect accusations and anger inappropriately directed at the victim.
Additional issues with clients' relationships are discussed in Chapter 8.

Choice Point Four: Counseling

Many victims in the acute crisis phases do not feel they need or want to see
a therapist. Most were functioning well prior to an assault, and will again after
the intense stress decreases. Crisis assistance, personal support, and the healing
of time are often sufficient for helping a survivor recover normal functioning.
However, a skilled therapist can provide special help and emotional comforting,
and a referral for counseling may be extremely important for some clients.

The suggestion of therapy may lead the client to fear that others think she is
"crazy" or out of control. The helper should be careful to identify the positive
reasons for seeking counseling, viewing it as a resource for a more beneficial
resolution, not a requirement for normal functioning. As discussed in Chapter
3, extreme care must be taken in making referrals and recommending resources,
because poor or inappropriate therapy may be worse than none at all. Incest
survivors are at a particular risk for further sexual abuse by some therapists.
(See Chapter 10.)

If the client already has a working relationship with a counselor, she will
probably find it helpful to discuss the incident as part of her ongoing therapy.
If it happens that the helper is also a trained therapist, the client may prefer to
develop that relationship as a therapeutic one. However, therapy for sexual abuse
issues must be carefully negotiated and should proceed only with her informed
consent. Furthermore, in any counseling process, the client must retain clear
control.

At this choice point, the advocate has a responsibility to serve as an educator,
helping the client to recognize and assert her power as a consumer of mental
health services. Even after a referral has taken place, ongoing support may be
important.

Choice Point Five: Agencies, Institutions, and Employers

Agencies such as child protective or employment benefit offices, services such
as child care or overnight shelters, institutions such as universities or juvenile
detention centers, and the companies that employ the offender and the victim
may become involved in a complaint. In most cases the victim must define the

services she needs and then select the agency that can best meet those needs. Some agencies may be unable to accommodate a particular victim, while others, such as universities, may work hard to handle complaints efficiently and can save the victim from the difficult procedures required in formal legal proceedings.

The advocate may need to do extra work in locating the appropriate services from such agencies and institutions. In many cases it is necessary to confirm that services are available to the client, and the advocate may have to help the client negotiate with institutions on financial or other arrangements. An advocate is frequently important as a buffer between the client and the service providers, as she pursues help through each.

In cases involving children, the welfare of the child must be the highest priority. This priority is not a choice; it has been legislated. Under current laws, every state in the United States stipulates that any professional (teacher, physician, counselor, social worker, child care worker) who *suspects* that a child has been abused, physically or sexually, must report the incident to the responsible child protective agency. In some states anyone who fails to report child abuse may be criminally charged. Helpers and service providers should learn about their personal responsibility and know the legal requirements and the particular agency to be contacted in their area. If there is reason to believe that a client will reveal an abusive incident involving a child, the helper may choose to inform the client that the incident will be reported. In many cases, self-revelation of sexual abuse within a help-seeking relationship is viewed favorably by the legal system, and the abuser is likely to receive more lenient treatment, often continuing therapy.

ACUTE EMOTIONAL REACTIONS

Some of the acute reactions to sexual abuse are typical responses following any traumatic incident: fear, including heightened reactivity to frightening stimuli; disruption of normal routines and thought patterns, including psychic numbness; and reliving the experience through flashbacks, nightmares, and obsessive thoughts. These reactions have been observed in victims of a wide range of traumas, and the American Psychiatric Association (1987) has labeled this group of symptoms the Post-Traumatic Stress Disorder. (See Chapter Appendix 4B.) To be labeled a Post-Traumatic Stress Disorder, the reactions must deviate from the client's normal behaviors and must be preceded by an extraordinary event or trauma. Posttraumatic stress reactions may also appear months or years after the incident, and frequently reappear during victim recovery.

Other posttraumatic reactions are either created by, or heightened by, the meaning of sexual abuse to the victim and to our society. Unlike most other traumas, sexual abuse violates the most personal body areas. It is also likely to involve a violation of trust or love. After the abuse, others may be unsympathetic or blame the victim. In addition, as Warner (1980) points out, in sexual abuse (1) there is no apparent purpose other than overpowering and humiliating the victim; (2) many assailants force their victim to "participate" in the abuse; and (3) normal relationship strategies cannot stop the act. As a result, victims of sexual abuse usually experience feelings of being dirty or soiled. Humiliation, shame, and self-blame are almost universal. Feelings of violation of the most personal body boundaries occur even in victims who are not penetrated.

This section reviews common acute reactions and ways to help a client cope with them. It is important to be sensitive to the emotional needs of the sexually abused client during the acute phase, especially since some of the reactions are not readily apparent to the uninformed observer. Responding in a helpful manner at this time can prevent subsequent problems and reduce the long-term devastation of the experience.

Terror

Burgess and Holmstrom (1974) interviewed rape victims about their experiences and found that the overwhelming response during the assault was a fear of death—more aptly described as sheer terror. Even victims with abusers who did not use physical force or a weapon, such as the typical incestuous father, often reported a fear that this person would become violent and kill them. Harassment victims may not experience fear for their lives, but they report being extremely frightened by the potential consequences for their school, careers, jobs, or future plans. After an abuse, the most immediate fear for most victims is that the assailant(s) will return, that the abuse may become more violent the next time, or that implied abuse (as in harassment) will be carried out physically.

During the acute phase, the survivor's fear level is heightened in general, especially in situations reminding her of the experience. Rado (1942) described a similar "traumatophobia" in war victims. Specific fear responses also occur when someone resembling the assailant (in some cases, any male) approaches, or from loud noises. The survivor may react strongly to events that others don't even notice.

During the immediate crisis period, the helper can reduce fears with repeated verbal reassurance and a calm and consistent presence. The client needs to locate other people who will help to meet the same safety needs; one person cannot always be available, and excessive dependence on one person is not helpful. She may turn to friends or family whom she can visit, or who can sleep at her house or check in with her frequently, especially during the first few days. She should also be encouraged to recognize and describe her fears openly. Often a victim feels foolish admitting fears that seem unreasonable or excessive. Rather than challenging or ignoring a fear, the helper should work with her to understand its source. Realizing why she is afraid and accepting her fears as normal can provide the bases for gaining control over them. As soon as she is able, the client needs to begin to distinguish between her actual assailant or abusive situation and other people and situations, shaping general fears (for example, of all men or of ever being alone) into more specific reactions to the experience itself. Stern and Stern (1985) discuss intervention with the terrorized client along these lines.

Heightened fear responses give the advocate special responsibility during the acute crisis phase. The client may be confronted by situations or people who frighten her, such as an authoritarian male physician or a policeman carrying a gun. She needs to be prepared for this eventuality by the tactics described above, but she also may need an advocate to act as a buffer during potentially difficult interactions. If necessary, people approaching the terrified client should be cautioned against sudden or unexpected moves, physical gestures or contact that might be perceived as threatening, and loud or forceful speaking. If she does become frightened, the advocate should intervene, first asking the person causing the reaction to withdraw temporarily, and then comforting the client and allowing her the time and safety to recover.

Disruption of Behavior and Thoughts

A few survivors react with clear awareness and move through the choice points in well-organized fashion, but this is the exception. The more common reactions of disorganized mental and physical behaviors can be frustrating for everyone, including the victim herself. For law enforcement agents, whose tasks require attention to detail, as in identifying a suspect, disrupted thought processes may prevent effective intervention. Some survivors are too dazed to answer questions; others are willing but too confused or frightened to provide useful responses. Still others may appear to be calm and coherent but in reality are not listening or processing incoming information effectively. These reactions are often called *psychic numbness*, an analogy to the numbing of a limb after severe injury. Communication may be superficial, and memory is likely to be reduced. However, no one should assume that the client is not reacting to the trauma; she may in fact be reacting very strongly but be unable to express herself.

There are several ways to assist the disrupted client. Her level of organization and comprehension should be assessed before she is faced with demands from others. If she is genuinely unable to cope with complex tasks at that moment, a request to delay the task is in order. Since questions may not be clearly understood, they should be repeated or clarified before the client answers. All essential information should be kept in writing for later reference. Some rape crisis centers have advocates fill out a booklet for the client, with information such as forms signed, medications received, and names of professionals such as doctors and police who have worked on her case. (See Appendix II.)

Unusual behaviors also appear with extreme stress; these may include nervous activity, such as fidgeting, playing with the hair, or biting a lip, and repetitive activity, such as walking up and down halls, moving furniture, or compulsive housework. These represent the survivor's attempts to regain some sense of control over her environment and her own behavior, at a time when more complex tasks with longer-term goals seem overwhelming. Carol described her home life during this period as "full of unexplainable bizarre behaviors. . . . I would take all my clothes out of my closet, one by one, take them off their hangers and fold them. Then I would rehang them, one by one. It seemed to be the only thing I could do right." These behaviors, which seemed bizarre to her and her family because they deviated from her normal routine, made sense to her when the protective and control functions of stress reactions were explained. Labeling her behaviors as normal under the circumstances further relieved her, after years of believing she was "crazy." A warning, however, is in order about compulsive behaviors that interfere with safety or health, such as an eating disorder: Professional help should be obtained as soon as possible, as early intervention is the most effective.

The survivor's entire life-style may also be disrupted. Many rape victims change residences or phone numbers (Binder, 1981; Burgess and Holmstrom, 1974). Incest victims who report their abuse to the authorities are likely to be moved to another home and a new family or to have the abuser removed from their family, causing great disruption for any child. Sexually harassed students and workers frequently leave their schools or jobs, whether or not the harassment continues. Such concurrent traumas are important to consider; while some stress may be alleviated by distance from the abuser or the site of the abuse, new stresses associated with new situations may arise. Feelings may appear of isolation in new circumstances, exhaustion from energy-consuming tasks like moving, and guilt over disruption of others' lives. Clients experiencing these feelings may need to develop specific coping strategies, such as writing a resume to find a new job. Taking time out to rest physically and emotionally is essential, and clients should be encouraged to allow themselves that time.

Reliving the Incident

After any trauma, preoccupation with the experience is common. Specific moments dominate thoughts and images and may seem to be "the only thing she thinks about." Most survivors experience flashbacks and nightmares, especially during the first few days following the trauma (Kilpatrick et al., 1981). These further frighten the survivor, who may never before have experienced such intrusive and uncontrollable thoughts or dreams.

Flashbacks occur during waking hours and may precipitate the feeling that the traumatic event is reoccurring. They may appear suddenly, even without conscious thoughts of the experience, and are often accompanied by physical symptoms such as withdrawal, rocking, covering the face, or shaking. A flashback is an opportunity for expression of intense fear, often unexpressed during the height of the actual assault, and should be allowed and encouraged for a few days. The client should be given comfort and a safe environment for the expression of her terror, free from intrusion by anyone who might heighten her anxiety.

Nightmares take away the comfort and reassurance of sleep. Nightmares following a trauma are unusually severe, and often reenact the event in realistic detail. Victims may begin to fear sleep, because the nightmares are so terrifying. Disruption of sleep patterns produces an additional set of problems that complicate the recovery process. Behavioral disturbances ranging from an inability to think clearly, to physical illness, to hallucinations, to psychotic episodes can appear when an individual does not fulfill normal sleep requirements over a period of time (e.g., Cappon & Banks, 1960; Morris & Singer, 1961). Some simple techniques for regaining control over nightmares are described in Chapter Appendix 4C. A client who lives alone will need to develop a network of people she can contact if she is frightened during the night, including a crisis line.

If preoccupations, intrusive thoughts, flashbacks, or nightmares continue with frequency and intensity after the first few days, they may become hazardous to overall functioning. In these cases the client should be encouraged to seek more intensive intervention. A professional may consider prescribing a mild temporary medication to reduce anxiety or sleep disturbance, in order to allow her the rest needed to regain self-control.

Humiliation and Shame

One of the most striking reactions of sexual abuse survivors is a deep feeling of humiliation and shame. These feelings may be verbally expressed as being "dirty" and physically experienced as a desire to bathe or scrub oneself clean. Survivors frequently report that their first response after returning to a safe environment was to take a shower, often lasting an hour or more. Shame and humiliation are further heightened by degrading acts committed or suggested during the sexual abuse. Sexual body parts are our most personal areas, rarely exposed and, except in abuse, never without consent. Even the threat of sexual exposure, as in harassment, is sufficient to create a feeling of deeply personal violation. Victims of vandalism and burglary frequently report a similar feeling of violation, albeit of less intensity, because their personal life space has been invaded and degraded.

If others focus on the sexuality of the act rather than the degradation, the initial embarrassment can be compounded by the intervention process. Sexuality in our culture is replete with taboos, which may be transferred onto the victim of sexual abuse as if she has participated in a sexual act by choice. In turn, these feelings may become self-perceptions of being "bad" or "evil." From the myths discussed in Chapter 2, these responses of shame and humiliation are understandable, but they are all the more devastating because they are culturally imposed and often reinforced by the victim's friends and family.

Another negative outcome of humiliation and shame may be silence. Too ashamed to relate her experience even to her closest friends and family, the silent victim cannot receive help from those who could form the base for her recovery. A good listener can help break that silence, demonstrating through nonjudgmental, positive regard that others care and understand. The goal is to help the client share her experience without shame herself, free of such self-limiting emotions.

Guilt

The guilt reaction is perhaps the most irrational of victim responses, yet it is also one of the most common. Guilt has been described in survivors of the Nazi concentration camp horrors (Frankl, 1963), in cancer patients (Abrams & Finesinger, 1953), and in victims of natural disasters such as the Buffalo Creek dam burst (Titchener, Kapp, & Wingett, 1976) and the Mount Saint Helens volcano (Adams & Adams, 1984) and technological disasters such as Three Mile Island (Baum, Fleming, & Singer, 1983). It has also been observed in victims of automobile accidents, in battered women, and in surviving members of the families of murder victims. It is not surprising, then, that victims of all kinds of sexual abuse often express self-blame for their fate (Katz & Burt, 1988; Lundberg-Love, 1987; Quina-Holland, 1979; Quina, in press).

D. T. Miller and C. A. Porter (1983) discuss the types of self-blame observed in victims of violence and the possible meanings of these types of self-blame. Above all, survivor guilt represents an attempt to make sense out of the tragedy that has befallen the victim: Why did this happen, and why did it happen to me? Kegan (1982) describes humans as "meaning-making organisms," and others have discussed our need to have a rational world. The complete irrationality of a victim's fate is difficult to accept at face value. Instead, many survivors, like Wendy in Chapter 2, try to figure out why they in particular "deserved" or "allowed" this tragedy.

A special kind of self-blame occurs when a victim has reacted to the abuser with "frozen fright," a response of pure terror that disables the victim temporarily (Symonds, 1975). After the danger has passed, the victim and those who know her may say she "failed" to react. In these cases the first reaction of anger at oneself for not reacting effectively turns into a self-imposed guilt, often reinforced by social reactions such as "Why didn't you do something?" or "I can't understand why you let him do this to you!"

In addition to "justifying" the selection of oneself as a target, survivor guilt also offers hope, albeit false, for a safer future: "This wasn't pure fate; it happened because I did something wrong; so if I never do it again, I won't be abused again." This self-protective mechanism is one of the few ways some survivors can find reassurance and control, however unrealistic or tenuous, that the trauma will not be repeated.

The guilt following sexual abuse is distinguished from the survivor guilt felt after most other tragedies by the level of social support for blaming the victim. Institutions and individuals alike demand that the victim accept at least partial responsibility for her plight, as described in Chapter 2. A few years ago one of the authors had a minor car accident while at a full stop in a parking lot, with witnesses to the other driver's full responsibility. Even so, a few days later a guilt reaction occurred: "There must have been something I could have done. I could have moved the car rapidly; I could have stopped somewhere else; I must have done something wrong." Others responded to such worries, however, with reminders that the other driver caused the accident, and guilt quickly changed to anger. In contrast, victims of sexual aggression rarely receive this level of support or intervention to counteract feelings of guilt; instead, other individuals as well as the media actively promote victim blame.

The helper has a critical role in intercepting normal guilt responses, diverting responsibility from the client to the abuser each time the self-blame arises. When the client reviews her own actions, or lack of action, she should be reminded of the terror and uncertainty that influenced her actions at the time. Advice like "don't blame yourself" is probably not a sufficient response for the intense reaction the client is experiencing. Rather, a consistent message must be conveyed that the offender is the one to blame. Responses designed to develop anger and direct blame to the appropriate target may also help the client respond to others who may attempt to blame her.

At the same time, the protective function of self-blame cannot be ignored or stripped away when the client needs it most. Instead, expressions of "it happened to me because" need to be put into more useful discussions of prevention tactics, especially specific changes she can implement in her environment and her lifestyle.

Anger

When appropriately directed at the assailant and at insensitive others, anger is the most useful emotion during the acute phase. It can be energizing, allowing the victim to cope with crisis tasks. Anger can supersede guilt and provide motivation for enduring in the fight for justice.

Unfortunately, focused anger toward an aggressor is difficult to develop or maintain, especially for women. Victims frequently do not express any anger at their assailants, even with urging from others. In light of the social proscriptions against anger for women and their terror of further victimization, this lack of anger is not surprising. These obstructions to anger need to be overcome, since externally directed anger is essential to the long-term resolution of an assault. Furthermore, in the absence of a clear recognition of the assailant's responsibility, strong feelings may become self-directed, and the victim may become angry at herself, not at others. Self-blame and self-hatred are especially destructive.

The expression of appropriate anger can be encouraged by supporting the client's own anger response, letting her know anger is normal and right for the circumstances; adopting a modeling role, actively demonstrating anger at the abuser; and stressing his responsibility for the harm he has done to her. Statements such as "I'm furious that he has hurt you like this" or "I would like to make him sorry he did this to you" are often helpful. Reactions may also be elicited through calling the abuser names or describing visual images of retaliation against him. In general, anything is useful that helps the client recognize her right to be angry and enables her to get in touch with her own anger, always with some assurance that it is understood that she won't be taking such actions, just exploring her feelings.

Another anger problem is a diffuse rage response, often directed at everybody except the assailant. The client may be enraged at the world, at God, at the police, or even at her helpers. This unfocused anger is not productive because it creates energy without organization, overwhelming normal functions. Expressions of diffuse rage directed at the wrong people may further isolate the client from those who would help her. Others need to understand that a client reacting with generalized rage is not angry at them, but is expressing a deep sense of pain in the only way she can. While the client's right to be angry should be supported and encouraged, she needs to learn to distinguish between the people who are trying to help her and those who have hurt her. The helper should be very specific about who is, and who is not, responsible for her plight and point out inappropriate expressions of anger.

Once developed, even focused anger can pose problems if not exposed and released. The energy created by anger needs to be captured and utilized in a positive, productive way. One route is to seek justice through the legal system. Another is personal change, such as karate training or an exercise program, both of which also increase the sense of control and strength. A third is to take on tasks that require energy, focus, and physical effort, such as house painting. The angry client should write up a short list of options and be encouraged to pursue them. Above all, she needs to understand that she can use her anger in a productive way, as distinguished from the destructive way in which her abuser has used his anger.

FOLLOWUP ON ACUTE INTERVENTIONS

During the acute phase, most stress reactions are temporary. If any of these symptoms seems unresponsive to intervention, or if a client is distressed by their persistence, counseling should be recommended. Any client who displays additional problems, such as distortions of reality or self-abusive tendencies, should be encouraged to seek counseling immediately. In most cases, six weeks following the crisis is a good time to check with the client about a termination of the crisis intervention and suggestions for further intervention.

Termination at the six-week point should include a list of referrals for longer-term counseling and a mechanism by which the client can reach a responsible helper at any time. The client should be reassured that these referrals are provided in case negative symptoms persist or when resolution is needed. However, at six weeks posttrauma the client may have changed dramatically from the willing client of a few weeks earlier. She may be in the denial phase and unwilling to return calls or speak to anyone. If the crisis intervention has been successful and she is interested, she may return for more help when she is again ready.

RECOMMENDED READINGS

Burgess, W.A. and Holmstrom, L.L. *Rape: Victims of Crisis*. Bowie, Md.: RJ. Brady, 1974.

McCombie, S.L., ed. *The Rape Crisis Intervention Handbook: A Guide for Victim Care*. New York: Plenum, 1980.

CHAPTER APPENDIX 4A: INTERVENTION WITH SUICIDAL CLIENTS

If a client appears suicidal, or acts on a suicide threat with an attempt, the helper must respond immediately and responsibly. Even lighthearted comments about "doing myself in" should be taken very seriously. Suicidal individuals often leave hints with many people, which in retrospect seem obvious but at the time aren't understood. The helper is in a particularly good position to listen for and intervene if such hints are dropped. Furthermore, if the client is not serious, the actions that mark suicide interventions will cause her to think before she makes such comments in the future.

A particularly important symptom to watch for is an unexplained elation or sudden apparent resolution of problems, especially following a period of confusion or depression. The client may be saying, "My solution is set. I will end suffering by this act."

Some self-destructive acts are difficult to recognize as suicide because the individual masks them with cover stories. For example, an anorexic who starved herself to death had fooled her friends and her counselor into believing she was dying of cancer. The opposite may also occur; some disturbed clients will "practice" suicide many times, exhausting various friends and professionals with faked or minor attempts. Thus it is important that no one try to help a suicidal individual alone.

It is also important to realize that some suicides are successful, if not initially then later, regardless of how well intentioned or well executed the intervention. Guilt often haunts friends, families, and professionals after suicide. Such self-blame is normal but must be overcome by awareness that the suicide could not have been prevented and was intended to be that way.

If a suicidal intention is suspected, the helper should adopt the following procedure:

1. Assess the immediacy of the intent, that is, whether the person has a specific plan, date, or place in mind.

2. Act firmly and calmly to reduce potential resources for suicide, removing all pills (including aspirin and other nonprescription drugs), belts or ropes, and weapons (including kitchen knives or sharp instruments), closing windows on upper floors, parking automobiles away from enclosed garages, and taking whatever other precautions may be needed.

3. Try to make sure the suicidal client is not left alone; hospitalize her or ask friends to stay with her in shifts, if necessary. No one person should take on this responsibility alone for long periods of time because it is too exhausting.

Emergency Procedures

1. If possible, police and/or emergency rescue personnel should always be called to respond to suicide threats or attempts. It is not legal, ethical, or pragmatic to try to handle such dangerous situations alone.

2. If the client is calling on the telephone, it is important for the helper to try to engage her long enough to summon emergency help to that location. If another phone line is unavailable and she must be disconnected for the emergency call, arrange with her for a return call in a few minutes. Then talk with her until the emergency personnel arrive. Another option available is to ask her to call a local suicide crisis line, or get her number and permission for them to call her.

3. If the helper is with the client, emergency medical procedures can be applied as help is summoned. It is important to stay with her, comforting her and encouraging her to hold out for the help that will be arriving.

4. Do not confront a person at this time with questions like "why did you do this," but rather talk about specific reasons to live that will be meaningful to her—not "You're such a pretty girl, there will be lots of nice guys," but "You could see your niece growing up and be a positive influence in her life."

CHAPTER APPENDIX 4B: POST-TRAUMATIC STRESS DISORDER

In its *Diagnostic and Statistical Manual*, the American Psychiatric Association (1987) defines Post-traumatic Stress Disorder in terms of characteristic symptoms of "reexperiencing the traumatic event; numbing of responsiveness to, or reduced involvement with, the external world; and a variety of autonomic, dysphoric, or cognitive symptoms" (p. 146). Anxiety, depression, irritability, and impulsive behavior may also occur. These symptoms must follow a psychologically traumatic event outside normal experience. In delayed or chronic Post-traumatic Stress Disorder, these symptoms are likely to be intensified or reactivated by situations that remind the person of the original traumatic event.

Professionals making diagnostic decisions about clients where prior sexual abuse may be suspected should consider the possibility of Post-traumatic Stress Disorder. The specific criteria include:

1. A recognizable distressing stressor;

2. Reexperiencing of the trauma through recurrent and intrusive memories or dreams or "sudden acting or feeling as if the traumatic event were reoccurring" (American Psychiatric Association, 1987; p. 147); and

3. Reduced responsiveness to the external world, which begins after the trauma has occurred, shown by "markedly diminished interest, . . . feelings of detachment or estrangement from others, or constricted affect" (p. 147).

In addition, at least two of the following specific symptoms must be observed that were not present before the trauma: hyperalertness or exaggerated startle response, sleep disturbance, guilt, memory or concentration difficulties, active avoidance of activities that remind the client of trauma, and intensification of symptoms in the presence of reminders of the trauma (p. 148). Consult the American Psychiatric Association manual (1987) for complete details.

CHAPTER APPENDIX 4C: DEALING WITH NIGHTMARES

The very thought of nightmares frightens many of us, as we recall times we have awakened gripped with terror and gasping for breath. Yet we normally find ways to recover and return to sleep fairly readily. When the nightmare replays a real experience, however, it induces fear that can last long after awakening and interfere with further sleep. Therefore it is helpful to give a client tips for dealing with nightmares at the first indication either that she is susceptible to nightmares in general or that she has experienced one. These tips include the following:

1. Reassure yourself immediately, by turning the lights on and orienting yourself (time, place, where other people are or where the rooms are). It may be helpful to sleep with a dim blue night light. If you are alone, invite a friend to stay with you for a few nights. It may also be helpful to sleep at another place, but be sure to orient yourself to the new location before going to sleep, to avoid the additional confusion of waking up in a strange place.

2. Discharge the energy from the terror by getting up and moving around, reading, or carrying out routine chores like light housekeeping. It is helpful to exercise during the day, as it discharges energy and reduces depression. However, exercise just before bedtime or during the night is physiologically arousing and may interfere with sleep.

3. Remind yourself repeatedly that this nightmare is only a dream, that the real event is over, and that you are now safe. If there is no feeling of safety, it is important to seek additional protective measures.

4. Because this is a dream, one can exert some control over it. Return to the middle of the dream and create a new ending—a new way of getting away, getting revenge on the abuser, finding a helpful intervener. Thinking of these alternative endings, especially ones in which power is regained over the abuser, is often relaxing.

5. Sometimes insights can emerge in dreams, where thoughts are not censored by our waking defense mechanisms. Review the dream content carefully for new information about feelings, fears, and wishes for the future. Another person may be able to help sort it out, so telling a trusted friend about a dream may provide important information. In looking for hidden meanings, however, self-blame must be avoided.

6. Relaxation exercises just before going to sleep and upon waking during the night can reduce considerable stress. Avoid related topic areas; for example, a workplace harassment victim may refuse to think about any job-related issue. Replace frightening thoughts with other content— watch television (especially comedy), read, think about less frightening things. One client successfully overcame obsessive thinking by deciding, each night before she went to bed, on a task to work on, such as planning a trip or writing a paper for school. She kept a pad of paper handy (with the task written at the top) to take notes on her progress. If she woke up, she would focus on that task. Often she went back to sleep before the task was done, but if not, she would at least feel she had accomplished something with productive nighttime thinking.

7. Develop pleasant images on which to focus energy—make a list of strengths, of places that would be nice to visit, of people who are liked and trusted. Review the list just before going to sleep and try to keep those images and the feelings they elicit in mind.

8. Avoid alcohol. Although alcohol may help you fall asleep faster, it disrupts overall sleep patterns and allows more nightmares. Alcohol is a depressant; it dehydrates the physical body; and it may also precipitate a hangover lasting through the next day (Parker et al., 1987). Withdrawal from alcohol may also cause sleep disruption (Willoughby, 1979).

9. Avoid spicy foods, and don't eat a heavy meal late in the day. Many report that a small glass of warm milk before going to bed causes them to feel cozy and sleepy, although a few people have milk allergies that have the reverse effect.

10. Losing sleep one or two nights will not hurt anyone, so there is no need to worry immediately. The resulting tiredness will produce longer sleep the next night. If sleep disruption continues for several days, however, professional help should be consulted. The symptoms of sleep deprivation are similar to those of psychosis, so it is important to make sure that the professional consulted knows that the problem is caused by loss of sleep!

5

Medical Intervention

Medical intervention with sexual abuse victims has three primary goals: (1) examination for and treatment of injuries from the abuse, (2) collection of evidence in the event of prosecution, and (3) prevention of subsequent problems. Every victim has the right to receive as well as the right to reject any of these services. However, any client who is experiencing physical symptoms, who has been penetrated, or who may have been injured should be urged to seek medical attention.

Fundamental though these three goals are to the care of all patients, survivors of sexual abuse have experienced considerable difficulty obtaining the medical help they need. Refusal to treat victims, insensitivity on the part of personnel, and other problems have been reported, largely stemming from negative attitudes, outdated policies, and inadequate staff training (Holmstrom & Burgess, 1987; Gager & Schurr, 1976). Some physicians have avoided treating sexual abuse victims because of the possibility of having to testify in court. In response to these criticisms and to pressure from crisis advocates, many facilities across the United States have developed special intervention programs and techniques for abuse victims or have instituted more effective treatment policies. The guidelines in this chapter have been drawn from some of those intervention programs, described by Braen (1980), Burgess and Holmstrom (1974), Gager and Schurr (1976), Kempe and Kempe (1984), Kerns (1981), Klapholz (1980), Mills (1977), and Sproles (1985). The contributions to these resources by rape crisis centers are enormous.

SELECTING AND NEGOTIATING MEDICAL INTERVENTION

The extent to which a client's needs can be met by a medical facility depends on the the services provided and the cost; the location, privacy, and regulations of the facility regarding victims; and the client's personal preference. A private physician offers personal choice and private service and may be preferable for nonemergency care, such as a general examination, or for minor problems, such as vaginal infection. However, private treatment is costly and may not be available when the client needs treatment. Many private physicians do not have access to proper evidence collection techniques, and some are not willing to testify in court. Specialized clinics such as Planned Parenthood offer gynecologic exams, pregnancy counseling, and testing and treatment of sexually transmitted diseases (STDs) at low or no cost, and may be the option of choice when those services are all that are needed. In such clinics, however, other kinds of medical intervention, including treatment of injuries, are probably not available, and evidentiary requirements may not be met.

In most cases, clients who need immediate medical attention or who may seek legal intervention are advised to go to the emergency unit of a hospital, where a wider range of services is available. Hospitals vary widely in the treatment they provide. Small local hospitals, while convenient and less crowded, may not have a gynecologist on call, may not follow standard procedures, or may refuse to treat sexual assault victims. Clinics and hospitals specializing in the treatment of women and children may offer better specialized care for gynecologic problems but may not treat serious injuries. Large city or county hospitals often have greater expertise with sexual abuse treatment and evidence collection and frequently have a gynecologist on duty even during night hours, although their size and number of employees may not afford a client privacy and uniform treatment. In the best situations a single location, often a large hospital, has been designated as a center for sexual abuse treatment, and all victims in the region are referred to that center by police, crisis lines, and other hospitals. The best of these centers have staff members who specialize in crisis intervention and a team of helping professionals who can be called together for a sexually abused client.

The first major negotiation should establish the facility's range of services and policies regarding victim treatment. The client should be helped to choose one that best fits her individual circumstances. If possible, an advocate should check in advance with the facility and notify them to expect the client. The advocate should determine whether the victim can have privacy; whether the facility's personnel are prepared and willing to collect evidence for prosecution and to testify in court; and whether there are any special policies regarding sexual abuse victims. Some hospitals report all sexual assaults to the police regardless of the wishes of the victims. A few hospitals will only treat a victim who has been transported by, or is there by arrangements with, law enforcement authorities

(Mills, 1977). The facility's staff should inform potential clients of these policies before any other negotiations commence, but some institutions neglect this responsibility.

Even when an institution has no explicit policies regarding sexual abuse victims, its staff members may discourage victims from seeking their services, or they may not try to make the client's wait or examination comfortable. Some hospitals refuse to give the victim privacy; some of their staff members may treat her rudely. Advocates have reported waiting for several hours with a client because the physician delayed until his shift ended. Advocates should be prepared to question staff members if they feel a client is receiving inadequate or improper service.

The second important issue to negotiate is the financial arrangement. A few hospitals have special programs in which examination and treatment of sexual assault victims are provided free of charge. Most institutions, however, will not see a client until arrangements have been made to pay for services rendered. Even an ambulance used to transport a victim to the hospital may be billed to her personal account. In some private facilities, clients must present their insurance or Medicare/Medicaid numbers, cash, or a check in order to be treated. Medical institutions have an obligation to inform clients of anticipated charges and of available payment options. If no agreement can be reached, the facility should help the victim arrange an alternative site for treatment.

If a client is unable to pay for treatment and has no insurance, there are still options within public facilities. The Hill-Burton Act of 1946 requires any hospital constructed with or subsidized by federal funds to provide services at no cost to individuals who cannot afford them. Many clients are also eligible for local and state victim compensation, to help out with medical and other expenses. However, most of these funds are available only to victims who report the incidents to authorities (Stark & Goldstein, 1985).

The third major initial negotiation concerns the extent of intervention. No medical intervention can be undertaken without consent of the client, usually written, unless there is an immediate threat to life. A client who is unable to offer consent by reason of mental disability will need the consent of a parent or guardian, or a court-ordered consent, before nonemergency medical intervention. Separate consent forms may be required for the examination, for certain treatments, for collecting and releasing evidence, and for releasing information to any other agency. Even with consent, the client may terminate treatment at any time.[1]

THE MEDICAL INTERVENTION PROCESS

Treating Injuries

Examination for and treatment of injuries and physical complaints are the most important priorities of medical attention to the sexual abuse victim. Treatment

of serious injuries, including wounds, hemorrhaging, broken bones, and con-
cussion, and of dangerous conditions such as shock or respiratory difficulties,
takes precedence over other needs (Braen, 1980). Over fifty percent of 146 rape
victims one hospital treated had visible injuries from the assault, usually bruises
and marks on the face, arms, head, legs, and throat. Sexual injury, especially
tearing from vaginal or anal penetration, was found in nearly forty percent of
the victims (Burgess & Holmstrom, 1974). Internal injuries are often observed
in child victims who have been penetrated (Kerns, 1981). Bruising or irritation
in the genital area may be caused by fondling (Kempe & Kempe, 1984).

Whenever possible, the physical examination begins with a patient history.
This history should include existing medical problems, allergies, and medications
and any recent surgery, especially gynecological. For vaginally penetrated victims, the type of contraception used and the date of the last period are important,
for determining the possibility of pregnancy. Information about prior abortions
or past sexual history, however, might be used by a defense attorney in an
attempt to discredit the victim and should not be recorded.

If indicated, the genital, anal, and/or oral areas should be examined for evidence of bruising or tearing. If vaginal penetration has occurred, a pelvic examination should be performed. Special care must be taken not to further frighten
or cause pain to the client; the pelvic exam has been reported as the most difficult
part of medical treatment by a number of victims. Special positions, such as a
side position, are often best for children, as described by Warner (1980). The
pelvic examination may include a bimanual exam, for internal bleeding or for
existing pregnancy, and local surgery to repair large tears.

Even when physical injury from the assailant is not present, intense stress
may cause somatic disorders (Lindemann, 1944). Psychogenic problems include
nausea, motor restlessness, chest pains and heart palpitations, headaches, gastrointestinal distress, panic symptoms, and sleep disturbance. These disorders
can become extremely serious, developing into ulcers, a heart condition, or
migraines. A client should be encouraged to seek treatment if any of these
symptoms appear regularly or disrupt normal functioning. All disorders should
be carefully documented in harassment cases, so that the victim can file a work-
related disability claim or seek civil or other court action. Types of psychogenic
problems and treatment options are presented in Chapter Appendix 5A.

In addition, a range of existing conditions may emerge, or become more
severe, as a result of stress (Selye, 1975). These conditions include arthritis,
thyroid imbalance, kidney stones, dysmenorrhea, multiple sclerosis, shingles,
herpes, and heart ailments.

The existence of these symptoms following a stressful event, however, may
not rule out other origins. Each case must be examined thoroughly for evidence
of prior problems, of medication which masks or increases symptoms, or alcohol
or drug use. If substance use or abuse emerges as a problem, the client should
receive referrals and encouragement to seek treatment.

Collecting Legal Evidence of Sexual Abuse

Sexual abuses rarely take place in the presence of helpful witnesses. Therefore, many cases must rely on well collected and preserved medical evidence. The assailant can sometimes be identified by evidence like hair or skin found during the examination. The victim's injuries can validate charges of assault and substantiate verbal statements. Her emotional status and stress-related physical symptoms can provide the basis for civil action against all types of abusers. While medical evidence (or the lack of it) cannot prove or disprove sexual abuse, it can be extremely helpful in any legal action.

Consent to Collect Evidence. As with other medical interventions, the client's consent is usually required for the collection of evidence.[2] Consent to collect evidence does not require the victim to report the incident, nor should the physician turn the evidence over to the police without the victim's consent. If a client is unwilling to report an incident at the time, but there is a possibility that she may do so in the future, the evidence can be collected during the regular examination and stored on the premises until a report is made.

Purpose of Collecting Evidence. It is not the physician's responsibility to diagnose rape, abuse, or harassment. Whether or not an incident occurred is a matter for the courts to decide, not the medical staff. It is the physician's responsibility to collect evidence to substantiate the victim's story. Many sexual abuse victims have no external marks or injuries; in many assaults, penetration or ejaculation has not occurred. Lack of physical evidence should never be interpreted as "no assault" or "consent." The written records should never contain evaluations or remarks that could be interpreted by the courts as personal opinion, since the records are likely to become public (Gilmore & Evans, 1980).

Legal Requirements for Evidence. Careful handling of medical evidence is essential, as it must meet the same requirements in the courtroom as any other evidence. Evidence must be carefully labeled, including the victim's name, where and how it was obtained, date and time, and the name of the person collecting the evidence. This documentation is required for all evidence, including laboratory tests. Evidence must also be prepared properly for storage, including air drying clothing to eliminate moisture, since cases may take up to two years to come to court. All evidence should be kept together, and if the storage is done at the medical facility, it should be in a secure location. Throughout the process, *chain of evidence* rules must be strictly observed. The evidence should be handled by as few people as possible. Documents should indicate each person who has received the evidence, when, and from whom. Evidence should be turned over in person directly to the police, not sent by courier or mail service. Any deviation may eliminate the evidence from legal consideration.

The physician and other members of the medical team should be prepared to testify in court if called. Court testimony is not a diagnosis of sexual assault; it is a verification and justification of the medical record. Copies should be kept of all records turned over to law enforcement, so that medical personnel can refresh their memories before testifying in a sexual abuse trial. Braen (1980) and Klapholz (1980) give further advice about testifying.

Dimensions of Medical Evidence. Braen (1980) has identified four areas that should be reviewed in the examination for evidence of sexual abuse.

1. Whether the victim was capable of giving consent to intercourse. If there is evidence of mental deficiency, immaturity, or the influence of alcohol or other drugs, any sexual penetration may be legally defined as sexual assault. If the physician has any question about mental incapability, a detailed mental status exam or a request for records of any previous mental status exam is indicated.

2. Whether force was used. Evidence of forced sexual contact comes from a variety of injuries, sexual and nonsexual, and from the client's report of physical symptoms. Signs of emotional trauma and fear should be included.

3. Whether vulvar penetration occurred. In many states the act of penetration distinguishes first-degree sexual assault from other sexual abuses. Physical evidence of penetration may not be present, however, if the assailant did not ejaculate or if the assault occurred more than 24 hours prior to the examination. Lack of physical evidence does not mean that penetration did not occur.

4. Physical evidence from the assailant. There are several forms of physical evidence an assailant can leave on the victim and her clothing, and here the physician becomes a detective of sorts. In some cases the evidence can actually help identify an assailant; in a few cases it has helped clear an incorrectly identified assailant.

Types of Evidence. Most police departments around the country supply hospitals and clinics with a "rape kit," a prepackaged sterile evidence collection kit that makes the rape exam standardized and easy to perform. Typical contents of this kit are listed in Chapter Appendix 5B. Efforts should be made to locate this kit prior to evidence collection. A medical examination for legal evidence should include the items discussed in the following sections.

The Victim's Statement. The victim's story should be recorded in her own words. In some states the physician is required to obtain a full report of the circumstances of the assault, to be used as corroboration of her testimony in court. The victim's statement to a physician may provide important substantiation of an assault. However, if even a minor point on the medical statement diverges from the statement given to other authorities, such as the color of the assailant's clothing ("dark" or "black"), the defense attorneys may argue that the victim was confused or lying. Therefore, unless legally required, it is best to confine the recorded statement to the information needed to assess the extent of possible injury, the kinds of evidence to look for, and the treatment indicated. (See Chapter Appendix 5C.)

If the victim is a young child the statement might be videotaped or audiotaped, in order to avoid repeated questioning by others, who could be listening to the tape. Many have found the use of dolls or play figures very helpful in eliciting the required medical information from a child in a nonthreatening way (Sproles, 1985), enabling the child to establish her or his own terminology and describe events. This technique also avoids problems for shy or less verbally developed children.

Assessment of the Patient's Condition. The mental and physical state of the client at the time of the examination (and, if possible, at the time she arrived at the office or hospital) may be important evidence. Stains from blood, semen, or even her own crying should be described. If she is still wearing the clothing worn during the assault, photographs should be taken to substantiate descriptions of its appearance, and then the clothing should be removed carefully, air dried, and placed into storage.

The client's appearance and mental condition should be described factually, without judgmental statements. A disheveled appearance or lack of apparant interest in personal grooming may be a temporary result of shock and not indicative of the client's normal state. As discussed in Chapter 4, emotional reactions to trauma are never "typical." Calm, controlled reactions do not rule out extreme stress, and expressive, crying reactions do not rule out personal control. Phrases such as "uncooperative" or "hysterical" are not appropriate.

Description of injuries. Both external and internal injury may result from an assault. If physical contact has occurred, each area of contact should be inspected for external injury, including abrasions, bruises, or marks. Bruises on the backs of the forearms are consistent with efforts to fend off blows. A precise description of each injury, accompanied by drawings and/or photographs, is important to documenting injuries. In some cases, physical complaints of pain or forceful treatment by an attacker may not be accompanied by visible injury. Such complaints constitute legitimate evidence for an assault and should be entered into the medical record as reported symptoms (Burgess & Holmstrom, 1974).

Evidence of Penetration. Vaginal, oral, and anal areas should be examined for bleeding, tearing, or other evidence of penetration. If a foreign object was used, bruises or other injuries may be found. If the assault took place in a sandy or dirty environment, the vagina may contain sand or other materials. In a child, enlargement of the hymeneal opening, scarring, and fresh clots are consistent with penetration. A colposcope may aid in identifying less apparent injuries (Norvell et al., 1984). Lack of injury, however, even in children, should never be assumed to mean that penetration or other abuse has not taken place (Rimsza & Niggeman, 1984).

The opening of the vaginal canal during the pelvic exam offers the best opportunity for collecting samples for evidence of sperm or semen. To preserve evidence, the speculum should be lubricated with warm water (Braen, 1980). If the hymen is intact and the client reports that ejaculation occurred, a test of vaginal fluids for semen or sperm may be taken using an eyedropper inserted through the hymeneal opening.

Semen is indicated by a high level of acid phosphatase activity. Semen may be found in oral, anal, or vaginal cavities, but also may be found on the victim's body or clothing. A Woods ultraviolet light may be used to locate semen, which flouresces under this light. (Proper use of the Woods light requires dark adaptation.) Swabs should be taken of all penetrated areas even if semen is not visible. External samples, such as dried semen in pubic hair, should be carefully removed and preserved intact. Samples of semen may be used to determine the assailant's blood type (Mills, 1977), and with new DNA-matching techniques, identification may be possible by comparing an accused assailant's semen with that collected as evidence.

Sperm, if present, may be helpful not only in indicating ejaculation, but also in dating the assault. Sperm remain motile in the vagina and mouth for about six hours and in the anus up to two hours (Sproles, 1985); nonmotile sperm can be detected in the vagina and rectum for up to 24 hours (Braen, 1980). After 72 hours it may be futile to examine the vagina for sperm, although some physicians do so up to five days postabuse for the sake of thoroughness. Sperm can be identified from dried secretions on external body areas or clothing, even months or years after ejaculation, using acid phosphatase analyses (Sproles, 1985).

Evidence from the Assailant. Other small bits of evidence can help corroborate a victim's story and in some cases even confirm the identity of the assailant. Such evidence includes the following:

1. Pubic hair from the assailant may become caught in the victim's pubic hair or clothing. A comb is provided in most rape kits. A sample of the victim's hair, pulled to obtain the root end, should be included for purposes of comparison.
2. Scrapings or clippings of the victim's fingernails can reveal skin or blood samples from the assailant. Most rape kits contain a clipper for this purpose.
3. A pattern of bruises may be left by the assailant's hands, which can be compared to the size and linear extent of his fingers. Bruise patterns should be carefully measured and photographed.
4. Bits of material such as fibers from the assailant's car, home, or clothing may be found on the victim's clothes or body. Any unusual material should be included as possible evidence.

Aftereffects of Sexual Abuse. In some states the legal charges under which an assailant is tried are determined in part by the physical and emotional damage caused by the assault. Any aftereffects, especially injury requiring continuous care, sexually transmitted disease, pregnancy, or emotional disturbance, should be carefully documented.

Preventive Medical Care

Appropriate medical intervention anticipates future difficulties as well as treating existing problems. The medical consequences of most concern for victims of sexual abuse are sexually transmitted diseases, pregnancy, and psychiatric or psychosomatic disorders. Most sexual abuse examinations routinely include testing and preventive treatment for disease and pregnancy, and most clients readily agree to this treatment. Since a pelvic exam is not required for the treatments outlined below, a client who refuses other interventions but wishes preventive information and treatment can usually be referred to a specialized clinic or hospital for specific services.

When sexual contact or penetration has taken place, some victims are acutely concerned about the possibility of disease or pregnancy. Others may not yet have considered these potential problems. Care must be taken in approaching a client about future concerns, because the information may create further anguish. However, disease and pregnancy concerns are so important that every client should be informed about preventive care.

Sexually Transmitted Diseases and Other Infections. Estimates of the likelihood of contracting a disease after sexual contact are quite low, for example, 1 in 1,000 for syphilis (Braen, 1980). However, the importance of preventive care and followup treatment cannot be overstated. Some sexually transmitted diseases, notably chlamydia and gonorrhea, lead to pelvic inflammatory disease, which may cause permanent damage to internal sexual organs and sterility. Syphilis has a long list of potential long-term consequences, including neural and blood disorders, which are fatal. Acquired immune deficiency syndrome (AIDS) is believed to be always fatal. Herpes and venereal warts, while not life threatening, are painful and extremely disruptive to future sexual relationships. Even minor vaginal infections can cause physical discomfort. Since these diseases take time to develop after contact, and since followup with many victims is unreliable, acute postrape medical care usually includes some preventive treatment without waiting for symptoms.

The major diseases of concern are chlamydia, gonorrhea, syphilis, herpes, and AIDS. Some of these attack any mucous membrane, including the linings of the mouth and throat and the anus, as well as the vagina and cervix. Anyone exposed to oral or anal sexual contact, as well as vaginal contact, should be examined and treated. Contrary to earlier beliefs, children are not immune to sexually transmitted diseases, nor do they acquire them from nonsexual contact like toilet seats. In fact, many cases of child sexual abuse are only discovered after a disease is diagnosed (Kerns, 1981). A particular form of gonorrheal vulvovaginitis occurs in sexually abused female children, even when contact is external, because the immature linings of the vulva and vagina are especially susceptible to infection by gonorrhea (Horos, 1975). Tests and treatment are similar to those for adult gonorrhea.

The typical acute postrape examination begins with a test for existing infection (veinous blood sample for syphilis, culture test on vaginal discharge for gonorrhea) and ends with preventive treatment for syphilis and gonorrhea, for which massive doses of penicillin are recommended.[3] Persons who have shown prior sensitivity or allergy to penicillin, or who have severe allergy histories such as asthma, may be treated with alternatives like tetracycline. Rarely, penicillin may cause an immediate and severe drop in blood pressure called anaphylactic shock, which is life threatening. Therefore, the client should stay at the treatment facility for at least 30 minutes following penicillin injections in case a reaction occurs. Over the days following the injections, soreness around the site of the injections may be eased with massaging and warm baths. These injections should be sufficient to prevent any germs from causing either disease, but no treatment is foolproof, so most physicians recommend a followup test in six weeks.

Chlamydia is estimated to be three to ten times as prevalent as gonorrhea in the United States (Lumiere & Cook, 1983), but it has only recently been recognized as a serious disease. Its symptoms are mild and difficult to identify in most people, and because it is not well known, physicians may fail to recognize or provide preventive information to abuse victims. Furthermore, half of the women contracting gonorrhea also have chlamydia (Lumiere & Cook, 1983), so treatment for one disease may overlook the other. A slide test for chlamydia with immediate results is available and in use by most physicians. Recommended treatment is with antibiotics, usually oral tetracyclines or sulfanamides, for the client and all recent sexual partners. Although victims should request that a test for chlamydia be included in their six-week followup, treatment may be appropriate just to be safe ("Presumptive Treatment," 1988).

Herpes genitalis, or HSV–2, causes painful blisters that recur in 70 percent of its victims over time. Physicians may offer surface skin creams or aspirin to relieve painful symptoms, but no cure is yet available. Some success in reducing the level and recurrence of symptoms has been reported with Acyclovir, at least in the first attack. Clients contracting herpes should be referred for information and support to the Herpes Resource Center, 260 Sheridan Avenue, Suite 307, Palo Alto, CA 94302 (415–328–7710).

Little information has become available about a victim's chances of contracting AIDS or AIDS-related complex. While research indicates a person will probably not contract AIDS from a single contact, particularly when penetration and ejaculation have not occurred, the fear of AIDS can affect physical and psychological well-being. In most areas a free, confidential blood test screening for the Human Immunodeficiency Virus (HIV) antibodies associated with AIDS is available and is recommended because of its confidentiality. The local health department or AIDS helpline can provide information on testing and counseling centers. However, the test may not detect the antibody until at least six months after infection, and some clients may need support during the intervening months.

Less severe but still annoying infections may be transmitted or caused by sexual contact, including trichomonas, gardnerella (hemophilus vaginismus), pubic lice (crabs), scabies, and venereal warts. These create vaginal or penile itching or discharge, burning sensations during urination, or general discomfort. Acute infections such as monilia (yeast infection) may occur after antibiotic treatment for other STDs, since the bacterial environment of the vagina is altered by the system's response to the antibiotic. Treatments for these infections are generally very simple and require only one visit to a physician or clinic. Since most of these infections can be passed back and forth between sexual partners, all partners with whom intercourse has occurred since the abuse should also be treated.

Pregnancy. The chances of becoming pregnant after a single sexual assault are quite small, estimated at about one in one hundred when penetration and ejaculation occur (Braen, 1980). Menstrual cycle dates provide some guide to the client's fertility, but most experts recommend a followup test for pregnancy at three to six weeks in all fertile women victims (Braen, 1980; Klapholz, 1980).

Postabuse pregnancy can cause a distressing personal dilemma, particularly for a victim whose religious views clash with her desire not to bear the child of her assailant. None of the alternatives is without emotional and physical costs. For years the drug diethylstilbestrol (DES), commonly known as the "morning-after pill," was given fairly routinely to potentially impregnated victims who sought help during the first 72 hours. This drug apparently worked by making the lining of the uterus reject a fertilized ovum. However, more recent findings of cancer and other abnormal conditions in sons and daughters of women who had taken DES during their pregnancy have cooled enthusiasm for DES treatments (Klapholz, 1980). Although many believe the effects of short-term doses on nonpregnant women are minimal, concern has been sufficient to restrict or halt its use by a number of rape treatment centers. Another option, suggested by Klapholz (1980), is the immediate insertion of an intrauterine device.) Some models of the IUD have raised concern over increased infections and injuries leading to hysterectomies and death.

If a client becomes pregnant from sexual abuse, she needs immediate non-judgmental support, preferably including professional counseling, as she considers her personal options. Every helper needs to assess her own ability to support the client's decision and to assist the client in following through; if the helper cannot do so, the client must be referred to a more appropriate resource for help.

If the client chooses abortion, it is important that the decision to terminate be made by the client herself, that she is not just responding to external pressure (Lemkau, 1988). Furthermore, it is important to long-term recovery that she be clear about her reasons for choosing this option and that she decide that she has made the best decision for herself at this time (Quina et al., 1987). During the first 6–8 weeks of a pregnancy, a relatively simple vacuum curetage called menstrual extraction can be performed with local anesthesia on an outpatient basis. Although relatively safe, this procedure is not performed at all clinics because it is only about 90–95 percent effective in terminating pregnancy. At 6–15 weeks, suction abortion requires dilation of the cervix, and general or local anesthesia should always be applied. Suction abortion can be performed safely and effectively up through 15–20 weeks. From 14–26 weeks, saline instillation is the usual abortion technique. For guidelines and information regarding abortion, see Cooke and Dworkin (1981, chapter 6). With any procedure, the client should be accompanied by a supportive person throughout the process and allowed to work through her feelings about her decision.

If she does not wish to terminate the pregnancy, she may choose to release the baby for adoption. If so, she should be referred to a reputable adoption agency and good legal support. A client who chooses to raise the child will need a great deal of financial and emotional support and may need to seek out social services.

Psychogenic Difficulties. A variety of physical symptoms can emerge because of stress and are common after traumatic experiences, both in the acute and long-term phases. These symptoms may have psychological origins, having been brought on by acute stress, but they are real physical problems and deserve serious medical attention. Clients should be informed about possible psychogenic problems (Chapter Appendix 5A), advised to seek treatment should they appear, and given appropriate referrals.

RESPONSIBILITIES OF MEDICAL INTERVENERS

The Physician

The physical exam is intrusive and, for some, frightening. For young victims the internal exam may be their first. Forcible rape victims may experience the pelvic exam as a frightening reminder of the assault. Therefore the physician must be especially gentle and considerate during work with victims. Interviews with rape victims (Holmstrom and Burgess, 1978) have clearly demonstrated that the physician's gender did not affect their medical treatment, but that her or his attitude was very important. Tips include the following: (1) focus on the treatment, not the assailant or the reason for the treatment; (2) explain procedures clearly, especially why they are being done; and (3) show positive outcomes of treatment, how intervention will make the victim better. From an anthropological perspective, the exam might be viewed as a cleansing ritual, so that medical treatment is seen as a positive step toward returning to full health. Providing an opportunity to bathe or douche after the examination is completed expands this cleansing effect. A model protocol from the American College of Obstetrics is provided in Chapter Appendix 5D.

The physician also has an important legal responsibility with respect to sexual abuse. Since there are rarely any witnesses to sexual abuse, medical evidence is often crucial to prosecution. The physician, then, must be thorough and accurate in looking for evidence and careful to follow precise procedures, including documentation, to preserve that evidence. This responsibility includes knowing what *not* to say—opinions, unnecessary personal information—as well as the relevant data to include. Otherwise excellent prosecutions have been lost because the medical record was inadequate or inappropriate, hurting not only the client but future victims of her abuser.

In many cases, especially with children, the presenting complaint is not sexual abuse, but another medical or emotional disorder. The physician thus has a special responsibility in identifying sexual abuse from diffuse other symptoms. A child with urinary, anal, or vaginal rash or discharge should be tested for sexually transmitted disease and the possibility of sexual abuse should be explored. Sexual abuse should be considered in the history of any child who has suffered physical abuse or who is identified as a runaway. If one child in a family has been abused incestuously, all children in that family need to be examined, since incest abusers are repeat offenders.

Psychiatric problems may also indicate an abusive experience. Abused children may suffer night terrors, regressive bedwetting, changes in school performance, or social withdrawal (Kerns, 1981; Kempe & Kempe, 1984). Previous sexual exploitation may be a factor in cases of attempted suicide, depression, personality disorders, and sexual dysfunction. Even what appears to be a psychotic claim of assault may stem from a real experience, as we have witnessed in at least two incest cases.

Nurses and Other Staff Members

The other medical personnel who come into contact with a victim are extremely important in establishing comfort and ensuring comprehensive care. Perhaps the most important responsibilities are those of the nurses working directly with the client. The first contact a victim has with the medical system is frequently with a nurse, in the intake or triage session. While the time spent waiting for treatment is clearly affected by the seriousness of the injury, the number of other clients, and staff size, a sensitive nurse can make a difference by placing a high priority on sexual abuse crisis situations.

Nurses can provide a major source of support for victims during the physical examination. The team of physician and nurse working together allows a much greater check on accuracy and care in the examination and collection of evidence than one person working alone. Added personal touches such as describing procedures and providing physical support, or even as simple as holding the client's hand, are helpful and comforting.

Some medical systems employ a primary nursing model, giving one nurse the responsibility for coordinating each client's care. Gilmore and Evans (1980) have argued for a primary nurse model in the treatment of sexual abuse victims, pointing out the clear medical advantages of individualized assessment of needs and selection of the treatment team, and the emotional benefits of consistent interaction with a supportive primary nurse. (See McCombie, 1980, Appendix 1, for a primary nurse model.)

The Advocate

In most medical systems, even the most supportive group of physicians and nurses cannot meet all the needs of most victims. Thus an advocate serves an important function in the medical intervention process. The major roles are those of any advocate: supporting the client, helping her negotiate for the services she needs, keeping information, and preparing her for the examination. The specific functions the advocate should perform during medical intervention include the following:

1. Making the client as comfortable as possible, especially since the intervention may involve several hours' waiting. The advocate should try to obtain a private waiting room or area and use the time to help the client work through emotions that may interfere with the examination procedure. If she is tired, a comfortable resting place should be located; food and drink may be helpful at regular intervals. The advocate should see if a client has special needs, such as medication for allergies or seizures, especially if the wait is more than four hours. At least once every half hour, personnel should be reminded that the client should be seen as soon as possible.

2. Keeping information about the client's condition, including physical injuries, in case the physician fails to note them in his or her record.

3. Talking with the client about her needs and concerns, helping her prepare a list of written questions for the physician. The advocate should also prepare the client for the physician's questions by asking some of them in advance and writing down her answers. When was her last period? Where is she hurting? Are there any visible marks or bruises? Does she have any allergies or is she on any medication the physician should know about? If it seems appropriate, the advocate may gently broach the subjects of sexually transmitted disease and pregnancy, and help her consider her needs in advance of the examination.

4. Informing the client and, if necessary, the medical personnel about her rights as a medical consumer (Annas, 1975; Jackson, 1980). The advocate may have to insist that the client be accorded her rights, following guidelines established in Chapter 3. As always, the client should be provided with the information she needs, and her decisions should be respected and supported.

The Team Approach

Medical personnel working with sexually abused clients, particularly children, have advocated a team approach to medical intervention (e.g., Kempe & Kempe, 1984; Kerns, 1981). Recognizing the multiple complications of sexual abuse, including psychological, legal, social welfare, and various physical implications, these authors have observed the advantages of dealing with all aspects during one hospital visit, avoiding repeat trips, referrals, and retelling of the traumatic story. The multidisciplinary team can be customized for the individual client, providing coordinated intervention. One integral member of the team provides crisis counseling and advocacy throughout the treatment. A model medical team approach is described in Chapter Appendix 3A.

NOTES

1. An important exception occurs in cases of suspected child abuse, including sexual abuse. Medical personnel must report suspected abuse to the local or state agency responsible for the protection of children. That agency will investigate the report and probably will ask a physician to examine the child for detailed evidence.

2. The exception may be court-ordered examinations, as in cases of suspected child abuse. These examinations are especially difficult if the client is unwilling, and they probably require a team approach involving psychological and legal support.

3. Detailed information regarding recommended medical treatment is offered in McCombie (1980), Appendix 2.

RECOMMENDED READINGS

Cooke, C.W., and Dworkin, S. *The Ms. Guide to a Woman's Health*. New York: Berkeley, 1981.

Sproles, E.T., III. *The Evaluation and Management of Rape and Sexual Abuse: A Physician's Guide*. Rockville, Md.: National Institutes of Mental Health, 1985.

Warner, C.G., ed. *Rape and Sexual Assault: Management and Intervention*. Germantown, Md.: Aspen, 1980.

CHAPTER APPENDIX 5A: PSYCHOGENIC SYMPTOMS AND COMMON TREATMENTS

Symptom	*Treatment*
Vaginismus (muscle spasms)	Sex therapy (Chapter 8), progressive relaxation
Gastrointestinal distress	
Diarrhea, constipation, vomiting	Stress management, progressive relaxation
Weight gain or loss	Dietary restrictions
Pain (various causes), ulcers	Dietary restrictions, medication for ulcers
Headaches	Biofeedback, pain medication (temporary)
Muscle difficulties, including spasms, tightness, rigidity, chest and back pain, motor restlessness; cold hands or feet	Biofeedback, muscle relaxants (temporary), exercising (planned), progressive relaxation, massage, physical therapy, chiropractic treatment
Panic attack (agoraphobia)	Medication plus therapy (Chapter 8)
Breathing difficulties: dizziness, hyperventilation, asthma	Diaphragmatic breathing, breathing aids for asthma attack
Heart difficulties: pain, palpitations, arrythmia, racing pulse	Immediate medical attention (possible infarction, angina), relaxation, exercises, beta-blocking medication

Dental problems: clenching, grinding, jaw pain or tightness	Same as muscle difficulties, retainer for nighttime use
Sleep disturbance: confusion, disorientation, exhaustion, temporary psychosis	Relaxation exercises, exercising (planned), biofeedback, meditation, sleep medication (temporary)
Depression	Therapy (Chapter 8), plus close attention, antidepressants (severe cases)
Hysterical conversion reaction (e.g., numb limbs, vision change, hair loss)	Therapy focused on stressful event

CHAPTER APPENDIX 5B: TYPICAL RAPE KIT CONTENTS

Test	*Kit Contents*
1. Clothing collection	Standard paper clothing bags
2. Urine (for pregnancy test & drug screen)*	Two urine containers
3. Fingernail scrapings	Fingernail file or clippers, envelope or tube
4. Pubic hair trimming	Forceps, scissors, envelope
5. Pubic hair combing	Plastic comb, large paper towel to comb hair onto, envelope to put comb and folded towel into
6. Aspiration of vaginal contents	Vaginal speculum, aspiration pipette and bulb, test tube and stopper
7. Swab of vagina	Two glass slides (one frosted at one end), two cotton-tipped swabs, test tube and stopper, pencil for marking slide
8. Vaginal washing (if no specimen is visible in vagina)	10cc of saline, aspiration pipette and bulb (from Test 6 if not used)
9. Pap smear*	Cervical scraper, two clean slides, Pap smear fixative
10. Gonorrhea culture*	Thayer-Martin plates or Transgrow media, cotton-tipped swabs
11. Saliva for secretor status	Three cotton-tipped swabs and a test tube and stopper
12. Blood samples**	Three test tubes, tourniquet, nonalcohol swab to prep skin, syringe and needle

Other contents: Appropriate laboratory forms, rape examination forms, labels for samples, camera and film (optional).

*Specimens to be sent to the hospital laboratory.
**One sample to be sent to the hospital laboratory for serological test for syphilis. Other specimens are to be preserved for evidence.
Source: Warner, 1980, pp. 63–64.

CHAPTER APPENDIX 5C: THE VICTIM'S STATEMENT

The following items should be elicited from the victim during her statement and recorded in her own words.

Abuse Information

Physical description of assailant(s)

Specific sex acts that took place, including penetration or ejaculation

Geographic location of assault, such as on concrete, grass, or sand, so that physician can look for abrasions, splinters, stains, or particles.

Blows with solid objects, attempts to strangle, tight holds, or other acts that might leave marks. Marks existing prior to the assault should be noted.

Loss of consciousness

Drug or alcohol use, voluntary or involuntary, before or after assault

Maturity, if prepubertal, including breast maturity, since the victim may grow between the time of assault and the time the case goes to trial

Any change in evidence since the assault, including changing clothes, bathing, douching, urinating, defecating, drinking

Medical information

Medical history

Gynecologic history (confine to relevant information)

Current physical complaints

Sources: Braen, 1980; Klapholz, 1980; McCombie, 1980, Appendix 2.

CHAPTER APPENDIX 5D: PROTOCOL FOR BASIC SEXUAL ABUSE EXAMINATION

The following procedures meet the guidelines for examination of sexual assault victims published by the American College of Obstetrics (Warner, 1980).

1. Stabilize the client.
2. Verify consent and explain the procedures of each portion of the examination clearly.
3. Obtain relevant medical history.
4. Take the victim's statement about the abuse.
5. Assess and record the patient's condition at the time of the examination.

6. Perform the examination, locating and treating injuries, including local surgery to repair large tears, collection of evidence, and a swab test for existing gonorrhea.

7. Draw a venous blood sample to obtain the patient's blood type and to test for existing syphilis.

8. Collect evidence from fingernails, pubic hair, and so on.

9. Photograph bruises or wounds.

10. Order lab tests, if any.

11. Offer preventive treatment for STD and/or pregnancy, if indicated.

12. Air dry, label, and store evidence properly.

13. Write medical conclusions.

6

Legal Intervention

Several avenues for legal intervention are available after sexual abuse: police protection; criminal prosecution; civil action; federal lawsuit; and in many institutions, internal policies. Legal systems, however, are unfamiliar territory for most people, and confusing procedures, long delays, and unsupportive attitudes often deter victims from pursuing justice. In this chapter we will review the legal interventions that may be considered by victims of sexual harassment, assault, and incest and provide information about each option. Specific laws and resources vary with jurisdiction (state, district, institution), and the helper should become familiar with local systems.

The goals of legal intervention are (1) the safety of the victim and all other citizens, (2) punishment and rehabilitation of the offender, and (3) redress or restitution for harm to the victim. Any legal process is likely to involve a variety of professionals and to take months or years to complete. However, action toward these goals constitutes a healing process in itself for many victims. Although an acquittal or a mild sentence for the offender is upsetting, clients who pursue justice often report that they feel good about the fact that they made the effort to prevent others from being victimized.

LEGAL PERSPECTIVES ON SEXUAL ABUSE

The legal treatment of sexual abuse has been heavily influenced by the myths and attitudes described in Chapter 2, creating a "second victimization" by humiliation in the courtroom (Rowland, 1985). These historically have been codified into law, dating back to biblical writings, and have specific precedents in English common law (Brownmiller, 1975). While revisions during the past decade have reduced the impact of outdated assumptions on written laws, their effect is still apparent in the attitudes of legal authorities and victim treatment. Three of these assumptions are discussed here.

1. Women and children are the property of their father/husband/boss.

Brownmiller (1975) offers an excellent historical review of the property assumptions in laws concerning rape and incest. For example, in ancient Athens a father could "sell his daughter into slavery if she lost her virginity before marriage," even if by rape (Keuls, 1985, p. 5). Although women have achieved considerable independence in many legal statutes, some still reflect property assumptions. Perhaps the most obvious contemporary example is the "marital exclusion" for sexual abuse, still found in several states, under which a person cannot be charged with sexually abusing his or her spouse. The underlying attitude (Sasko & Sesek, 1975) is reflected in a Rhode Island judge's statement that "the marital relationship . . . implies a right to engage in sexual intercourse," which he thought was not sexist because the wife has the same rights (Henderson, 1984). This attitude of tolerance for actions by men toward their "property" often prevents justice for victims who have dated, or have been employed by, their abuser.

The identity of a father, husband, or boss also influences the treatment of the victim. The wife, daughter, or secretary assaulted or harassed by an important community member is less likely to find assistance. If that same man's wife, daughter, or secretary were abused by a stranger, however, she would likely be treated with more respect than other victims.

2. The victim's morality determines the crime.

In the past, laws traditionally framed sexual assault as different from other physical assaults. For example, in Wisconsin prior to 1975, a rape was a "crime against sexual morality." Even a violent rape was not a crime if the victim was considered an immoral person. Insinuations about the victim's sexual behavior, real or imagined, often formed the basis for deciding whether a crime had occurred. A common defense tactic was to taint the victim's moral character in the eyes of the jury, who then allowed the offender to go free (Borgida, 1981).

Thanks to intensive efforts nationally, "shield laws" are now in place in most states (Sales, Rich, & Reich, 1984), which generally protect victims from having irrelevant information about their personal lives, such as prior sexual history, introduced as evidence. Most clients no longer have to fear that their past will become public. However, there are still cases in which friends of an offender testify that the victim had approached them for sex or had told them the sex was voluntary. In spite of shield laws, perceptions of the victims' morality influence the kind of treatment they receive and affect juries' decisions (Holmstrom & Burgess, 1978). A case is less likely to be successful if the victim has engaged in prostitution, was drinking in a bar, wore "immodest clothing," or was born into a family known to the police for criminal behavior. Gay men and lesbian women are often automatically considered "immoral," and some experience further abuse by the authorities. The choice not to file a complaint by some clients is an understandable, although tragic, decision made because of a flawed system.

3. Women are not to be trusted.

Until the 1970s, in New York, Connecticut, and Iowa, "independent corroborative proof"—that is, a witness other than the victim—was required for prosecution on charges of rape, but not other crimes (Brownmiller, 1975, p. 371). These requirements have been removed, but again the attitude still haunts women victims, who are often treated with suspicion from the moment they lodge a complaint. Some police departments have required victims to submit to a lie detector test before they will file a complaint of sexual abuse, even though the results of the lie detector test will not be allowed in court. Unlike victims of other crimes, sexual abuse victims often endure repeated questioning and are warned that they can be punished for a false accusation. The combination of suspicious treatment and these terrifying warnings discourages many clients from following up on their initial complaints, which ironically is then perceived by the authorities as "proof" that they were lying.

IMPROVEMENTS IN THE JUSTICE SYSTEM

In spite of these discouraging scenarios, statutory and attitudinal changes have dramatically improved legal intervention for most victims. Sweeping reforms of laws and procedures for handling complaints have taken place in every state in the United States, bringing sexual assault in line with other crimes. A wider range of sexual abuses is now covered by federal and state statutes; civil precedents have been set by successful lawsuits; and internal grievance procedures have been established by most universities, corporations, and other large institutions, allowing greater justice across the continuum of sexual abuses. Specially trained individuals, often policewomen and women attorneys, are often assigned to handle sexual abuse cases, dramatically improving the treatment of victims. Educational efforts have enlightened many participants in the justice system, from police officers to jury members to legislators, resulting in heightened sensitivity to victim needs and experiences, and more successful outcomes throughout the legal system. In fact, Stark and Goldstein (1985) point out that "the movement urging reform of rape laws is so active that information published on the status of the legal rights of rape victims is in danger of being outdated by the time the publication is in print" (p. 384). This caution should be applied to the specific laws and procedures referred to in this chapter.

TYPES OF LEGAL INTERVENTION

In this section, various avenues for justice are reviewed for each of the major types of sexual abuse, highlighting the requirements for legal claims and the important issues to consider in each case. Of course, specific actions will depend on the circumstances, but this range of options provides the client greater choice.

Sexual Harassment

Sexual harassment is generally defined as unwanted sexual attention, ranging from offensive verbal behavior to physical sexual assaults. Fitzgerald (1987) has identified five levels of sexual harassment:

1. Gender harassment (generalized sexist remarks and behavior)
2. Seductive behavior (inappropriate and offensive, but essentially sanction-free sexual advances)
3. Sexual bribery (solicitation of sexual activity or other sex-linked behavior by promise of rewards)
4. Sexual coercion (coercion of sexual activity by threat of punishment)
5. Sexual assault (gross sexual imposition or assault).

Most people who are being harassed merely want to stop the offensive behaviors and to prevent interference with their employment, school, or right to obtain services. Many try to ignore the harassment, believing that their unresponsiveness will signal the offender to end the abuse. However, one survey of office harassment victims found that 75 percent of the women who used the silence strategy found that the harassment continued or actually increased (Farley, 1978, p. 22). Therefore, victims of even minor harassment should consider some form of action. The message must be clear and succinct: The actions are unwanted; they are inappropriate; and they must stop. The options for action include the following:

1. Offensive jokes or comments by workers or students should be reported to their foreman or principal, and if possible to the owner of the property. Threatening comments or gestures should be reported to the police. A court-ordered temporary restraining order may be imposed on an individual threatening violence, and charges such as disorderly conduct may be appropriate.
2. Harassment by someone the client knows, such as a coworker, may be resolved in one of two ways. The first is verbally informing the offender that his behavior is not welcomed, and asking him to stop it. A written record should be kept of the conversation and his response. The second way is sending a formal letter to the harasser, stating clearly that specified behaviors are offensive and why, as described in Chapter Appendix 6A.
3. Most large companies or institutions have an internal grievance process for complaints of sexual harassment. Employees belonging to a union may find that the union covers work-related cases, while abuses by college students are usually covered by a student judiciary.
4. Various federal, state, and local regulations prohibit sexual harassment, giving victims

the right to sue an institution covered by those regulations in federal, district, or state courts. Several legal precedents have established the right of a sexual harassment victim to use the same avenues open to victims of sex discrimination (Ross & Barcher, 1983), supported by a 1986 Supreme Court decision in *Meritor Savings Bank* v. *Vinson* (Tatel, 1986). Specific federal statutes are outlined in Chapter Appendix 6B.

5. Any individual victim can file civil lawsuits against the harasser and against others who failed to provide protection, seeking reparation for specific losses and compensation for pain and suffering. Significant civil sexual harassment cases are reviewed in Center for Women in Government (n.d.).

6. Professionals such as physicians, therapists, or lawyers are prohibited under ethical codes from engaging in any sexual contact or relationship with a client, under any pretext. If the offender is licensed or professionally accredited (lawyers, physicians, psychologists, some social workers, dentists, optometrists, chiropractors, and others, varying from state to state), sexual contact with a client can result in loss of licensure and thus the ability to practice in the state. The state licensing board or professional association (e.g., the local bar association, medical society, or psychological association) can provide more information. Responsible agencies and their phone numbers are available from the state or local consumer protection service. A victim of professional misconduct may also sue the perpetrator in civil court. Pope and Bouhoutsos (1986) provide excellent guidelines for either form of complaint.

7. A client who is fired or can no longer continue work as a result of sexual harassment may be eligible for unemployment compensation (Ross & Barcher, 1983). Stress-related psychogenic medical conditions that result from sexual harassment may be grounds for Worker's Compensation (Alliance Against Sexual Coercion, 1981). An employee who is fired or demoted after filing a harassment complaint may file a union grievance or civil lawsuit for reinstatement and lost wages.

Evidence. Documentation of sexual harassment is an important requirement for success in any of the above options. The client should keep a written record of the abuse, with each incident spelled out in detail and the date, time, and place noted. A journal or diary kept for other reasons that contains these incidents is excellent. A copy of a letter sent to the harasser is acceptable evidence, even if the offender fails to respond. Clients may try to seek out others who have been harassed by the same offender, including former employees or students, to develop a class action or group complaint. Performance evaluations made prior to the abuse, such as an employee file or grade reports, may be important in establishing that the victim was otherwise in good standing. As detailed in Chapter 5, evidence of stress-related medical or psychological conditions is important for recovering damages from the offender or obtaining other compensation.

Sexual Assault

Most states broadly define sexual assault as nonconsensual contact with any sexual body area (pubis, buttocks, female breast), penetration with any object into vagina or anus, or oral contact with a penis or vagina.[1] Nonconsent is defined as an inability to consent, through force (including intimidation or the element of surprise) or through the victim's incapability of making such judgments (by reason of age, mental handicap, or the influence of drugs or alcohol).[2]

Options for sexual assault victims include the following:

1. The most common option is a criminal complaint. Depending on the specifics of the assault, additional charges may be brought against an offender (physical assault, assault with a deadly weapon, possession of illegal firearms, sodomy). If the offender is under the age of 18, except in extremely violent cases, he will be charged and tried through the juvenile justice system, so the process and the outcomes will be somewhat constricted compared to the normal criminal procedures.

2. In most police districts an anonymous police report may be filed. A victim, or in some locations a third party such as an advocate, can provide all of the information available about the assailant and the assault, without giving the name or address of the victim. While this report cannot serve as the basis for any prosecution, police can use the clues to identify a pattern of assaults or resolve subsequent assaults. Police discourage the anonymous report option, however, because they cannot act on the information that they gain from such reports.

3. Civil action may be taken to receive compensation for physical and psychological harm, even if criminal prosecution is unsuccessful or not possible (Carson, 1986; Rowland, 1985). Victims have successfully sued their sexual abusers, the owner or employees of the place where the assault took place (e.g., for failure to maintain safe conditions), and other responsible people for failure to intervene (Stark & Goldstein, 1985).

4. Colleges and universities have student judiciary systems, to which assaults committed by a student can be taken for internal justice. A jury of student peers reviews the evidence and usually makes recommendations to the president of the school for implementation. The most severe penalty these bodies can recommend is suspension of the offending student from the school permanently. Recent court battles over the jurisdiction and procedures of student judiciaries have made this route less desirable for criminal offenses, although removing the offender from the victim's environment, even for a semester, can be helpful.

Evidence. Since the criminal penalties for sexual assault are severe, usually from five years to life in prison, the evidence is critical. Among the evidence needed are the medical reports and evidence described in Chapter 5, material evidence obtained from the scene of the crime or the defendant, and testimony from witnesses to the assault or witnesses to the victim's condition after the assault. The outcome, however, usually comes down to the victim's word against the defendant's, since there is rarely direct confirming evidence.

Marital Sexual Assault in Excluded Jurisdictions

As described earlier, in some states a spouse cannot be charged with rape. Some local prosecutors have successfully challenged this exclusion by proceeding with test cases. If criminal charges are not possible, several options may still be considered.

1. In situations involving physical force, a criminal physical assault complaint may be filed. An alternative shelter should be located for an abused wife and children if needed, and a court-ordered temporary restraining order obtained to prevent further contact. Local battered women's shelters can help a client pursue these options.
2. The client should consider filing for marital separation or divorce, so that criminal sexual assault charges can be lodged if future abuses occur.

Child Sexual Abuse and Incest

Although the statutory age varies from state to state, from thirteen to eighteen, any sexual contact with a person under age is automatically considered nonconsensual and thus is criminal sexual assault, regardless of the victim's role. The courts need only to establish that the sexual contact took place with the offender. While incest statutes, which prohibit sexual contact between blood relations, might be invoked as additional charges, cases of sexual abuse within family units are usually charged under the general sexual assault statutes. Special family service agencies will be involved, however, and courts may mediate a noncriminal solution, such as mandated family counseling.

Any suspected abuse of a minor child must be reported to and investigated by the district or state child protective services, even if the victim or the offender reveals the abuse during private, confidential treatment. Factors such as an offender voluntarily seeking help are usually taken into consideration in determining the appropriate course of treatment or punishment.

When the offender is a member of the child's family unit (including a stepfather), steps should be taken to protect the child from future abuse, preferably removing the offender from the home, or if necessary finding an alternative placement for the child. In some states a separate court handles family matters, and a range of options, including family counseling in place of incarceration, may be mandated. Many judges prefer to leave the family intact wherever possible and to direct intervention toward reconciliation or reintegration of all family members, in order to minimize further disruption of the child's life.

Some adult survivors of childhood incest have won monetary awards from their abusers in civil lawsuits for long-term emotional harm (Cleary, 1984; Yunker, 1986), although the statute of limitations may prevent this option in some states.

PURSUING JUSTICE

Of the options explained in the preceding section, three have been chosen for more description: institutional grievances, civil lawsuits, and criminal prosecution. For each of these three interventions, we provide a guide for helping a client decide which options may be appropriate. Then we outline the procedures involved and offer tips for the client pursuing that intervention.

Institutional Grievances

In general, institutional grievances are the least expensive and, in some cases, the least distressing of the options, particularly in cases of sexual harassment. However, punishments are usually limited to minor disciplinary actions, such as a letter in a personnel file, temporary suspension from student or job status, or a demotion or lateral job move for the offender, and no formal criminal record results. For the victim, an award for lost income, reinstatement of a job, or correction of an evaluation or grade may result. If the case is unsuccessful, the victim may be viewed as a "troublemaker" and punished with job loss or mistreatment.

When is an Institutional Grievance the Best Option? The first requirement is that a grievance procedure be available that covers the situation. To learn about institutional coverage, the client should explore union, company, or school policies (by contacting her ombudsperson, personnel department, employee assistance program, or affirmative action representative) and federal, state, county, and city regulations.

Second, the limited outcomes available through internal grievances should be sufficient to meet the client's psychological and financial needs. If not, other options, including criminal complaints, should be considered as well. Finally, the client should consider the consequences of filing an internal grievance if the offender is found not guilty, and be prepared to accept them.

The Institutional Grievance Process. Specific procedures depend on the institution or regulatory agency, but in general the following steps are taken:

1. A formal, written complaint, charging the offender with specific actions, is filed with the appropriate internal grievance office. A private attorney may be engaged (at the victim's expense) if the institution allows external legal representation for the complainant.
2. The offender is informed of the charges and may seek representation from his union or a private attorney.
3. A committee or board, usually representative of various constituents of the institution, hears the testimony of the complainant, the defendant, and other witnesses and examines the documentation. The hearing committee may decide on actions to resolve the complaint, or it may only be in a position to make recommendations to the president or chief officer for disciplinary actions.
4. Most grievance procedures have built-in appeal processes available to both complainant and offender.

Tips for Institutional Grievances. The following should be considered before pursuing an institutional grievance:

- The client should seek others who may be able to join in a class action suit against the offender or institution.

- Most institutions require procedures to be followed exactly, or complaints are dropped on technicalities.

- The district Equal Employment Opportunity Commission office should be informed of the grievance, so that it can monitor the process and outcome.

- Any settlement must include a clause protecting the victim against subsequent harassment and retaliation. Some offenders have sued their victims for libel or slander after out-of-court settlements in which records of the offense are sealed and therefore made unavailable to the victim.

- It is extremely important that clients have a support system and advocacy throughout the process, to cope with the everyday stress of continuing to work or cooperate in an unsupportive environment.

- Additional action may be pursued through a civil lawsuit, or through federal or state courts under Title VII, Title IX, the Civil Rights Restoration Act of 1988, or other regulations. For medical needs and counseling, Workmen's Compensation or other disability claims should be filed.

- Regardless of the outcome, the client may wish to join or help form a women's network or support group, to assist others in similar situations.

Civil Actions

In civil courts, a victim may obtain financial remuneration for expenses incurred because of an assault or harassment, including medical and psychological treatment, prior or future lost wages, compensation for pain and suffering, and legal fees. Anyone who has the energy and time, and in some cases the attorney's fees, can pursue a legal suit through the civil process. A civil claim does not have to involve criminal wrongdoing; rather, the complainant must be able to demonstrate (1) that the defendant was responsible for a wrongful outcome, (2) that the requested monetary or related awards to the victim are appropriate. The targets of civil action should be selected carefully and must be reasonable to the situation. If not, the defendant can countersue the complainant for engaging in a "frivolous lawsuit" and may be able to collect his legal defense fees from the victim.

When Is Civil Action the Best Option? Civil lawsuits offer a victim considerable control over the process. On the other hand, the consequences are limited to monetary or in-kind payments, and no criminal record results. The cost of obtaining good legal representation must be factored into the civil justice process. Furthermore, upon filing a civil suit, the victim's name and personal information become a matter of public record. Several factors should be evaluated: the potential financial gains, including legal costs and the ability of the offender to make any court-ordered restitution; the stress to the victim; and the length of the process—up to ten years in some cases.

Civil action is not advised without good (not just adequate) legal representation, preferably someone with civil rights experience.[3] Lawyers will often
consent to work for an agreed-upon percentage of the settlement if they see a
case has potential for substantial monetary gain; however, the client is then at
the mercy of that lawyer, who may also decide to drop out if the case becomes
difficult or lengthy. Ross and Barcher (1983) recommend against using this
arrangement; rather, legal costs should be charged to the offender as part of a
judgment or settlement. Court fees and out-of-pocket expenses such as hiring
expert witnesses are charged to the complainant if the case is unsuccessful, so
these costs must be considered in advance.

The Civil Complaint Procedure. Civil trials may be heard by a judge alone
or by a jury at the option of the defendant. The judgment is two-part: (1) whether
the complaint is true and (2) to what extent (in dollar amounts) the complainant
has been demonstrably harmed by the offense. The following process is typical:

1. A suit is filed in civil court that names the defendant(s) and stipulates the basis for
   the claims and the outcomes desired.

2. The defendant(s) and major witnesses are informed of the action (usually by subpoena,
   a formal notice delivered by a sheriff). Each defendant may engage a personal attorney
   for representation. Institutions usually have a staff attorney who handles legal defenses.

3. After months of preparation, the trial is heard in court. The jury (or judge) decides
   whether the complainant was wronged and, if so, determines the restitution.

4. Either party may pursue appeals in higher courts. It is not uncommon to find an award
   drastically reduced on appeal or a reduced settlement negotiated in order to avoid the
   costly appeal process.

5. At any point, negotiations between the two parties may take place for an out-of-court
   settlement.

Tips for Civil Actions. The client pursuing a civil suit should know the following:

• Statutes of limitations and filing deadlines exist and should be consulted and adhered
  to closely.

• The client and attorney should decide in advance who shall answer any letters or calls
  related to the case, and be consistent. It is usually best, although costly, to have the
  attorney fill this role.

• Offers for out-of-court settlements must be considered carefully in terms of the adequacy
  of the award, prevention of subsequent sexual abuse to the victim and others, protection
  from countersuits or retaliation, and the benefits of resolution to the victim.

• If the amount involved is not large, the option of small claims court may be preferable.
  Court fees should be included in the proposed settlement.

Criminal Prosecution

Criminal action can only be taken when four conditions are met: (1) a specific criminal law has been broken; (2) the defendant has been apprehended; (3) the prosecuting attorney's office is willing to carry the case to trial; and (4) the victim is willing to testify as a witness to the crime. The process is long and arduous, and legal maneuvers, such as a behind-the-scenes agreement, may halt the prosecution. The victim has virtually no control over the criminal prosecution after an initial complaint is filed. However, punishment and a permanent criminal record for the offender are powerful potential outcomes of criminal prosecution, for the victim and for society.

Perspectives on the Criminal System. Two assumptions influencing legal systems in the United States are important to consider for understanding the legal process and and the client's needs.

1. The offender is presumed innocent. Our system is based on the idea that an accused person is presumed innocent until proven guilty beyond reasonable doubt. The offender is protected by a number of regulations governing procedures of grievances and arrests, beginning with the following terminology: he must be referred to as the ''defendant,'' ''accused,'' or ''alleged abuser'' until found guilty. The offender often seems to have more rights than the victim. The victim must be cross-examined and questioned, while the offender may not even have to testify. The defendant's morality, including other instances of abuse, is rarely allowed to be questioned,[4] while the victim's moral and sexual discretion may be scrutinized. If a police officer or prosecutor commits any technical violation of ''due process,'' the case may be dropped. Finally, during the long criminal process, most sex offenders are free on a bail bond, causing continuing terror and potential harassment for the client.

2. Crime is against society. Laws and regulations are created to protect society, not the individual victim. Thus the prosecution and punishment of criminals is controlled by an array of authorities, who decide how, when, and to what extent to pursue justice. The victim becomes merely a witness to the crime, whose testimony is essential but who may not even be informed about the process or its resolution. In this system, the victim's only choice is whether to testify or provide information. Since empowerment is a critical post-abuse psychological need, too often victims opt for their only form of control, albeit negative, and drop out of the process.

When Is Criminal Prosecution the Best Option? Anyone who has experienced unwanted sexual contact may file a criminal complaint if the statute of limitations has not expired. The capture of the offender, however, does not guarantee prosecution. Because prosecutors are elected officials, the decision to pursue a complaint is often based on whether they believe a trial is likely to be successful.

The process of criminal justice moves very slowly, taking up to two years to bring a case to trial, with additional time for appeals. During this time, the victim may be called in to testify, usually on very short notice, at several different hearings, and often must repeat her story to police, detectives, physicians, and attorneys. For some of the proceedings the assailant is present. The victim may engage a personal lawyer for advice, but the prosecutors's office maintains control and presents the case. These circumstances discourage many victims from continuing to participate in criminal proceedings.

Convicting an offender for sexual assault of an adult requires that the prosecution prove, beyond a reasonable doubt, that (a) the sexual contact took place; (b) the contact was nonconsensual; and (c) the accused assailant committed the act. Defense attorneys will usually try to counter on these points: a lack of medical or other corroborating evidence for sexual penetration or contact, claims that the victim had consented to sex, and alibi witnesses who claim the accused was somewhere else at the time of the assault. (For other defenses, see Stark & Goldstein, 1985.) Defense attorneys also make an effort to damage the victim's credibility, to cast that "shadow of doubt" even on minor points like the color of the defendant's pants. ("Were they dark or brown? You gave conflicting statements!") The victim's ability to handle cross-examination as a witness is often an important consideration in deciding whether to carry a case to trial.

The Criminal Complaint Process. Calling the police to report a crime sets off the following steps in the complex criminal process:

1. The victim contacts police in the jurisdiction where the incident occurred. Arriving officers have the responsibility to (a) protect the victim; (b) apprehend the assailant, if possible; and (c) collect material evidence from the scene of the assault. They will seek immediate medical treatment for a victim suffering physical injury, calling an ambulance if necessary. Otherwise they will probably transport the victim to a hospital for collection of medical evidence. They will likely request a description of the assailant(s) in order to apprehend them as soon as possible. The victim may request a female officer; many police also offer to contact the local rape crisis agency (Sales, Rich, & Reich, 1984).

2. In the days immediately following the initial report, one or more detectives should investigate the complaint, taking the victim's statement and searching for evidence. If a suspect is apprehended, the victim will be asked to select the offender out of a police lineup, which includes other people of similar build and physical appearance. Although the offender cannot see the victim, this can be a terrifying moment, but a solid identification is essential to the case. Failure to identify the offender from a lineup does not signify the end of the case; the wrong person may have been apprehended.

3. If a suspect has been apprehended and identified, and the detectives believe they have collected enough evidence, the case is turned over to the prosecuting attorney's office, where the victim will again be interviewed. The defendant engages a private defense attorney if he has the financial resources, or a public defender is provided at no cost.

4. Within a few days, a formal hearing is held to determine whether there is "probable cause" (enough evidence) to pursue the complaint, and to determine bail or other conditions.[5] The victim usually must testify at these hearings and may be cross-examined, but additional requirements vary with the jurisdiction. Defendants should be warned to avoid the witness, even if they are family members or neighbors.

5. In some jurisdictions the evidence will be subjected to a hearing by a grand jury, made up of ordinary citizens, who review the evidence and talk to the witnesses. They do not judge guilt or innocence, but only whether the evidence is adequate to justify the criminal charges.

6. Over the next few months, preparations for the criminal trial take place on both sides. During this time the defendant's attorney may request several court appearances in attempts to throw the case out on technicalities. In some cases a trial begins with one of the attorneys requesting a delay. These tactics rarely succeed legally, but they intimidate and inconvenience the victim, who must appear each time. For women who must obtain child care, leave school or work, and find transportation to and from court, the process may be too costly to continue.

7. At any point, the prosecutor and the defense attorney may arrange a plea bargaining agreement, whereby the charges are exchanged for less serious ones; or the penalty is reduced, in exchange for a guilty plea. In most courts this decision can be made without consulting or informing the victim. Plea bargaining may be the best option for a weak case, ensuring that some conviction is recorded on the defendant's criminal record. In other cases, however, the light sentence (often probation) accorded the defendant seems unjust given the seriousness of the crime. Recently some jurisdictions have given victims more input in plea bargaining (reviewed by Stark & Goldstein, 1985).

8. After several months of pretrial activity, the criminal trial should take place. From the selection of jurors to the verdict, the trial may last hours, days, or weeks, depending on the complexity of the case. The prosecuting attorney presents the state's case against the defendant and calls various witnesses, including the victim, to testify before the open court while facing the defendant.[6] Each witness may be cross-examined by the defense attorney, who may utilize brutal and confusing tactics. The defense attorney then presents witnesses for the defendant, and perhaps the defendant himself, and the prosecutor cross-examines each in turn. The case closes with a presentation, often dramatic, from the attorney for each side. The judge may offer specific cautions to the jury before it adjourns to a private room for deliberations.[7]

9. Juries may deliberate for several days before they reach a decision. If all jurors vote not guilty, the defendant is acquitted and is immediately set free; the charges are removed from his criminal record, and no further criminal prosecution for this case is possible. If the vote is split, the case is temporarily halted, and the prosecuting attorney has to decide whether or not to pursue the case in a subsequent retrial. If all the jurors vote guilty, they may also recommend a level of punishment (e.g., leniency, life in prison, the death sentence).

10. If the jurors vote for a verdict of guilty, the judge will set a date for sentencing. In this formal court appearance, the judge will hear arguments from both sides about the most appropriate punishment and, taking the jury's recommendation into account, set the punishment. Victims should be prepared to hear a much shorter sentence than they would have wanted; many convicted sexual offenders are not required to serve any sentence beyond time already spent in jail. Crowded prisons and generous parole policies almost certainly guarantee that only the most dangerous offenders will spend the full sentence in jail.

11. The defense is likely to pursue various avenues of appeal of a guilty verdict, based

on technicalities of the trial, new evidence, or claims of unfair treatment by the judge or prosecuting attorney. These appeals will likely continue for several months or years and may result in overturning the initial conviction. The judge may allow the offender to remain free on bail while appeals are pending.

Tips for Criminal Complainants. In deciding whether to file a criminal report, clients should be advised to consider these issues:

• A victim may exit from the legal process at any time by refusing to testify or provide information. No one can force a victim to testify except in very unusual cases. However, any refusal to cooperate may forfeit the case. The reasons for discontinuing a case should be made clear, as an offender whose charges are dropped may attempt to sue his victim for slander.

• If the case has little chance of resulting in a criminal conviction, other options, such as a civil complaint, should be considered.

• If a victim encounters harassment or abusive treatment by police officers or attorneys, she may request the local American Civil Liberties Union office to intervene and/or file a complaint about the inappropriate behavior.

• The victim should organize her thoughts as soon as possible, by writing down every detail she can remember. She should not show these notes to others, but should review them privately before each interview.

• Some defense attorneys practice inappropriate tactics, such as interviewing victims on false pretenses, outside the normal process (Sales, Rich, & Reich, 1984). The client should never speak to the defense attorney or to any stranger requesting information without first clearing it with the prosecuting attorney.

• Preparation for and practice giving testimony and responding to cross-examination are extremely important. Preparation programs and tips are often available through rape crisis centers and victim-witness advocacy programs.

• Support should be sought from friends, family, and a special advocate during this process, especially to accompany the victim to the courtroom.

• Victims should learn about their rights in the criminal process and should exercise them. (See Chapter Appendix 6C.)

SPECIAL LEGAL PROTECTIONS

Victims who are handicapped by age or disability may be able to obtain additional assistance from the criminal justice system. Examples of these are offered here; local agencies and court personnel should be contacted for other options.

Children

Recognizing the dismal record for justice in child sexual abuse cases, many jurisdictions have attempted to incorporate new ways to assist children who have been sexually abused. Although videotaped testimony, specially trained counselors who obtain testimony during taped play sessions, and closed-circuit television witness stands have all proven helpful to obtaining child victim testimony, the Supreme Court has thus far rejected all alternatives to facing the abuser and being cross-examined (*Coy* v. *Iowa*, 1988). Many juries are still affected by the belief that young children cannot distinguish truth from fiction, so defense attorneys may attempt to damage a child's credibility.

Social workers, counselors, and court personnel are overtaxed by enormous caseloads, and individual cases may not get the most appropriate treatment. Children are frequently removed from their homes without warning, and sometimes sent to an abusive foster home. Long delays may prevent helpful counseling. The abuser may lose or quit his job and cease economic support for the family. Too often, the negative consequences impact the children. Involvement with child victims demands sensitivity to members of the family and ongoing advocacy, to "fill in" gaps left by the overworked system.[8] Women Organized Against Rape (1981) offers an excellent guide to family/juvenile court.

The Elderly

Crimes against the elderly have a special impact. Age-related physical handicaps make the elderly more vulnerable to crime in the first place. Injury is more likely, and healing takes longer, causing greater medical needs and expenses. For a person on a fixed income, financial losses have a more serious impact. Those elderly already suffering from problems such as hearing loss or reduced mobility may have difficulty participating in the standard judicial process.

Some states have enacted laws that increase the punishment for any criminal whose victim is over 60 or 65 years of age or disabled. Larger police departments often have specially trained "senior citizen units" to work with elderly victims and help them obtain additional sources of assistance (Stark & Goldstein, 1985). Every state has an office on aging, which can provide, or refer victims to, homemaker services for food and companionship. Some will also assist in replacing personal property and obtaining financial aid.

The Disabled

In addition to the services described above, disabled crime victims may be specially covered under statutes regarding sexual assault. In many states, a victim who has a mental handicap or a physical disability that affects communication is considered by law to be unable to give consent. For these victims, the requirement for demonstrating sexual assault is that the perpetrator (a) had reason to know the victim was disabled, and (b) had sexual contact with the victim. Many cases involving disabled victims are unsuccessful in court, however, because jury members may be prejudiced against their ability to understand the truth. (See A. Asch, 1984, for a review of these attitudes.) Persons institutionalized for psychiatric or mental disability are particularly vulnerable to abuse without recourse because of these prejudices.

Some jurisdictions now provide special advocates for mentally disabled victims. Another option, particularly useful when a victim is abused while in the care of an institution, is a civil lawsuit against the abuser and/or the institution, perhaps brought by family members on behalf of the victim. Awards covering future physical and psychological care of the victim are possible outcomes.

INTERVENTION ROLES AND RESPONSIBILITIES

Training for police, lawyers, and court personnel is available from the staffs of rape crisis centers and other professionals. Such training has clearly made a difference in the effectiveness with which offenders are apprehended and prosecuted, the gathering and utilization of evidence, and the ways in which victims are treated throughout the process. The rates for both reporting and conviction for sexual assault have increased dramatically over the past few years, as have the numbers of successful civil judgments in favor of sexual harassment victims (Ross & Barcher, 1983). However, the low overall rate of conviction for sexual abuse shows that more work is needed.

Special training in issues relevant to sexual abuse offenders and victims is strongly recommended for any professional, at any level, working on these cases. Additional special training in issues concerning children, the elderly, and the disabled is helpful for any legal intervention, not just sexual abuse.

Four major helping roles can be identified in the process of legal intervention after sexual abuse: those of the police officer or initial investigator, the judge or hearing officer, the expert witness, and the advocate.

Police Officers and Initial Investigators

The initial investigator is perhaps the most critical individual in the entire process of justice. Many cases are lost because the victim refuses to subject herself to a disbelieving or abusive investigator. Many other victims, however, attribute their long-term recovery to the kind, supportive responses of these authorities. One difference is the basic attitude about sexual abuse and about victims. As described earlier in this section, educational programs are generally quite successful in promoting supportive attitudes through increased sensitivity and awareness. Another difference, not as easily taught, is whether the investigator steps outside his or her role. The investigator is not the judge or jury, but is there to carry out specific responsibilities (protecting the victim, collecting evidence, and if a police authority, apprehending the offender). Whether the case will "look good" in court is not for them to decide. A third difference, at least with institutional grievance officers, is the investigator's primary alliance: to the institution, which wants no legal costs or publicity, or to the victim.

Successful institutional programs have given their grievance officers a charge to help victims, not cover up incidents.

As with physicians, victims report that the sensitivity of police and other investigators is more important than their gender. However, many victims, men and women, feel more comfortable talking to a woman. Male officers should understand that requesting a female officer is not a statement about their skill or sensitivity, and try to accommodate the victim's request.

The approach taken by the investigator toward the offender is also very important in the prevention of future abuse. Any suggestion that the victim deserved her fate, or that the charges are false, sends a clear message that the offender can continue to abuse. One police captain we worked with provided an extraordinary model. Although it seemed that the case would probably never go to trial because the victim had been drinking heavily with several men, the captain apprehended the offender and informed him he was taking the crime seriously, and warned him to stay away from the victim. He also told the offender's friends that they were also responsible for making sure no further harm came to this woman or to other women in his community. He subsequently was promoted to chief of police, a positive note for the entire community.

Prosecutors, Judges, and Hearing Officers

Criminal Prosecutors. Many victims have felt that the person who should have been the most supportive—the prosecutor—caused the case to be lost through negligence or lack of preparation, or even by being hostile. Victims complain of having to tell their story repeatedly, of not being informed about important decisions, and of impersonal treatment. Much of the problem lies with the structure of the system. Prosecutors often employ newly graduated attorneys with less experience; the attorneys are shifted from case to case and may only be assigned to a case the day it goes to court, and they are not likely to be assigned to the same case for subsequent hearings.

Many larger offices have attempted to overcome this problem by assigning sexual abuse cases to a small subset of attorneys who, to the extent possible, remain with a case from start to finish, minimizing the need for the victim to repeat her story and maximizing their sensitivity. Others have worked to assign cases earlier and more systematically, to avoid the problem of unprepared attorneys. The goal is a high conviction rate, and such changes are likely to produce a higher rate and more positive public attitudes.

Courtroom Personnel

In the trial process, jurors are affected not only by the witnesses' testimony and attorneys' arguments, but also by the behavior of court personnel, especially the judge. A wide range of sexist behaviors have been documented in courtrooms (Blazevic, 1987; Crites & Hepperle, 1987), such as a sheriff making comments about a victim's appearance, a judge referring to a victim by her first name and the offender by his title ("Jane" and "Dr. Jones").[9] The judge also is responsible for preventing actions that might prejudice the case or result in a mistrial, for intervening when cross-examination of the victim crosses the line into abusive treatment, and for providing direction to the jury as it makes its decision. Finally, the judge is ultimately responsible for assigning the sentence for convicted offenders, affording an opportunity for rehabilitative treatment as well as more serious punishment. Some states have undertaken special training for court personnel, and judges have responded to the call to leadership in providing equity in the courtroom.

Hearing Officers. Although not subject to the same legal restrictions or jury process, hearing officers in institutional grievances also carry responsibilities for creating a fair, equitable process. The hearing officer may be employed by the institution against which the complaint is filed, making the role particularly sensitive. Historically, however, institutions have lost more by attempting to cover up incidents or ruling against victims than they have gained—in public opinion as well as dollars. Hearing officers must be educators for the institutions they serve, as well as carrying the responsibilities for the roles described above.

Expert Witnesses

In recent years, courts have begun to listen to the testimony of psychologists and other mental health professionals about the devastating effects of sexual abuse on the victim's mental health. This testimony may be used to increase the jury's understanding of the seriousness of the crime, to establish the extent of damage to a specific victim, or to clarify the typical responses to sexual assault in order to establish the normality of a victim's reactions. In order to admit expert testimony, three factors must be established: that the testimony has scientific validity, that it will help the jury understand the case by providing something beyond everyday knowledge, and that it will not be prejudicial (Frazier & Borgida, 1985).

Expert testimony has proven very helpful in a number of cases, but there are numerous legal issues still not resolved. For example, it is possible that evidence of rape trauma syndrome may hurt the victim's credibility rather than help her. Frazier and Borgida (1985) review this and other relevant legal issues for expert testimony on the rape trauma syndrome.

Advocates

Victims need someone to clear a path through the legal process, someone to help them understand their options, plan for testifying, and in some cases speak for them. Intervention can be as simple as insisting on a private waiting room for the victim before and after testifying, or as complex as testifying on behalf of a minor child. Advocates need a combination of an understanding of the workings of the legal system, knowledge about the specific laws or grievance procedures to be addressed, and access to special assistance programs. Rape crisis centers and victim-witness assistance programs perform a range of advocacy roles. No matter how skilled or educated, any victim can use one or more legal advocates.

Another advocacy role is providing *support*. The legal process is the longest, most emotionally draining aspect of postabuse intervention. The client needs consistent, long-term support. No one should have to go to a hearing or trial alone. If possible, friends, family, and other supportive persons should rally together and attend court sessions in as large a group as possible. The sight of a courtroom full of supporters can provide the strength for a victim to carry through the frightening and painful task of testifying. As with other forms of support, the most important rules are to be clear about limits, consistent, empathic, and willing to see the client through to the resolution of the case.

NOTES

1. Sexual assault statutes generally incorporate degrees of seriousness, with corresponding degrees of punishment, following one of two models: a) degrees are defined by type of act—first degree involves penetration of mouth, anus, or vagina and second degree is sexual contact without penetration—or b) degrees are defined by extent of injury or harm to the victim—first degree involves bodily harm, including pregnancy or serious emotional disturbance, and other degrees indicate less long-term injury—but any sexual contact is considered sexual assault.

2. If the person was under the statutory age at the time of victimization, he or she is considered unable to give reasoned consent, and the only requirements are to prove that the sexual contact took place and that the accused assailant committed the act. Mentally and emotionally disabled victims are also protected from the consent requirement. Some states also assume that a person under the influence of alcohol or drugs is unable to provide consent, and these states need only prove that the offender knew that the victim was intoxicated. These latter cases are often unsuccessful in court, however, because jurors consider victims' testimony about events that took place while they were intoxicated to be unreliable.

3. A union member filing a work-related grievance against a member of management may be able to receive legal representation through the union.

4. The offender is protected from "double jeopardy"; that is, he cannot be tried twice, and prior abuses cannot be raised in the courtroom unless they resulted in a conviction.

5. During the pretrial period, only the most violent offenders are incarcerated. First-time offenders or those with "responsible" employment may be released on personal recognizance (no bail required). Large bail amounts are deceptive; offenders may post only 10 percent of the announced figure.

6. The judge may require other witnesses to leave the courtroom during the testimony of the victim, to prevent any collaboration on stories. Some victims have been shocked to see their mother or a friend leave the courtroom just as they take the witness stand. All witnesses should be prepared with explanations of the process and the reasons for it.

7. Warnings to the jurors, such as the previously common "Rape is the easiest crime

to charge, and the hardest to prove" or comments about the severity of putting a man in prison "for the rest of his life," discouraged guilty verdicts (Brownmiller, 1975). These warnings are no longer considered appropriate.

8. Many courts rely on court-appointed advocates, guardians, and counselors to recommend actions regarding child victims. These advocates generally interview and mediate with each interested party, but always for the best interests of the child. For more information about the highly successful Court Appointed Special Advocate program, contact the National CASA Association, 909 NE 43rd Street, Suite 202, Seattle, WA 98102.

9. Differential titles for the victim and defendant may be used as a defense tactic, to make the victim seem less credible and the offender seem more credible. It is the responsibility of the prosecutor to object to such terminology and the judge to determine which terms are more appropriate.

RECOMMENDED READINGS

Ross, S.D., and Barcher, A. *The Rights of Women*. New York: Bantam, 1983.
Stark, J., and Goldstein, H.W. *The Rights of Crime Victims*. New York: Bantam, 1985.

CHAPTER APPENDIX 6A: A LETTER TO A SEXUAL HARASSER

Mary Rowe, a labor economist, has suggested an excellent tactic for a first step for many harassment situations (Rowe, 1981). Recognizing that some offenders do not realize their behavior is harmful, she recommends that victims write a letter, formally addressed and delivered (in person or by registered or certified mail) to the offender, which spells out the unwanted behavior in detail, including the date(s) it occurred, identifies the behavior as unwanted, and requests that it be stopped. The victim should sign and date the letter and, of course, keep a copy. This relatively nonconfrontational approach gives the offender the opportunity to change without consequence, but still serves as legal documentation should the behavior continue. A sample format is provided by Sandler (1983), as follows:

Part 1 tells the facts of what happened, without evaluation, as seen by the writer. It should be as detailed and as precise as possible, with dates (or approximate dates), places, and a description of the incidents the writer has experienced with that person. Part II describes how the writer feels about the events described in Part 1, such as dismay, misery, distrust or revulsion and includes the writer's opinions or thoughts about what happened. Part III consists of what the writer wants to happen next. This part may be very short since most writers usually just want the behavior to stop: *I want our relationship to be purely professional from now on.* (p. 1.)

CHAPTER APPENDIX 6B: FEDERAL STATUTES REGULATING SEXUAL HARASSMENT

Under federal regulations against sex discrimination for employees of many firms and for students, several avenues of protection from sexual harassment are available. If the statutes apply to the case, the process is heard before a federal judge. The major statutes are as follows:

1. Title VII of the Civil Rights Act of 1974, which covers employees in firms with more than 15 employees and holds the employer responsible for educating the work force and maintaining a harassment-free environment;

2. Title IX of the Education Amendments of 1972, which covers participants in any educational program receiving federal funding, such as financial aid programs, and by which a school or college may lose its federal funding if the discrimination is not halted;

3. The Civil Rights Restoration Act of 1988, which protects students in any educational institution receiving federal funding, with penalties similar to those under Title IX; and

4. Similar state statutes which protect employees (often including those of firms with fewer than 15 employees) and students in any state-supported school or college, and by which institutions may be sued through state courts.

Information on these statutes, although slightly dated, is found in Ross and Barcher (1983); current regulations are available from any district Equal Employment Opportunity Office. Information regarding academic institutions can be obtained from the Project on the Status and Education of Women, 1818 R Street, N.W., Washington, DC 20009.

CHAPTER APPENDIX 6C: VICTIMS' RIGHTS

In any criminal case, victims have certain rights, but the justice system may not be informative or helpful to those who wish to avail themselves of these rights. The American Civil Liberties Union has published a series on individual rights in the justice system, including *The Rights of Women* (Ross & Barcher, 1983) and *The Rights of Crime Victims* (Stark & Goldstein, 1985). These books are excellent guides for those pursuing sexual harassment or sexual assault cases, respectively.

J. Stark and H.W. Goldstein identify six fundamental victim rights, offering details on each. These are:

1. The right to participate in the criminal justice system. The victim's level of participation in the process varies by law and practice across jurisdictions, but should include access to information about the status of the case, opportunities for input on plea bargaining, statements about the impact of the crime on the victim in sentencing or parole hearings, and timely return of personal property held as evidence.

2. The right to assistance for expenses resulting from the crime. Most states now have some funds to compensate victims for medical expenses, transportation and other needs while attending court, and loss of wages directly caused by the victimization and subsequent judicial action. Witnesses may be paid a small fee each day they appear in court, and many courts have adopted special victim/witness assistance programs to ensure that the necessary applications are submitted to obtain these fees.

3. The right to receive restitution for property lost or damaged in the criminal act. As part of a plea bargain or sentence, or in lieu of a sentence, a court may order the defendant to make financial payments to the victim (through the court as intermediary) for property damaged or lost as a result of the crime. While this option in no way compensates for the psychological or physical harm to the victim, it should be viewed as an important supplement to any settlement.

4. The right to recover damages through civil court suits. Whether a case is won or lost in court, the victim has the right to pursue financial awards through civil court actions. Examples of successful civil actions, including some that make explicit the rights of victims to share in royalties a criminal may earn from writing about a crime, are described in Stark and Goldstein (1985).

Further information on pursuing civil lawsuits is available from the Washington, D.C., Rape Crisis Center, P.O. Box 21005, Washington, DC 20009.

5. The right to be free of intimidation. Attempting to prevent or discourage a witness from testifying or continuing in a case is against the law. Since fear of reprisal is a major reason given by victims for dropping out of a case, this right, and the power of enforcement behind it, is extremely important to the justice process.

6. The right to seek alternative avenues for resolution of a dispute. In sexual abuse, especially when the victim knows the assailant personally, criminal prosecution may be an uncomfortable option. Even after a criminal charge has been filed, the victim has the right to pursue an alternative settlement out of court, such as compensation for damages. Agreements to drop charges if the assailant seeks counseling are frequently used in family situations and in cases where the offender is a juvenile. In many locations, arbitrators are available through community organizations to help mediate such cases.

Part III

Counseling Survivors of Sexual Abuse

7

Promoting Recovery

For many survivors, recovery from sexual abuse takes years. While as few as 5 percent of victims seek help immediately after an assault (Koss, 1985), nearly 50 percent eventually seek intervention for psychological aftereffects (Ellis et al., 1981; Koss, 1985). A number of specific problems have been identified for rape and incest survivors who are more than one year postabuse: fear, mistrust, sexual difficulties, depression, guilt, and marital and relationship problems (Becker et al., 1982; Burgess & Holmstrom, 1979; Kilpatrick et al., 1979; Miller et al., 1982; Nadelson et al., 1982; Quina-Holland, 1979). Burgess and Holmstrom (1979) found that three-quarters of rape victims continued to have significant psychological symptoms six years after their assault. Emotional and social difficulties are found in adulthood for victims of childhood sexual abuse (Huckel, 1985; Tsai & Wagner, 1978), particularly when the abuse was incestuous (Courtois, 1988; Lundberg-Love, 1987). Any sexually abusive incident can produce dramatic long-term effects.

THE RECOVERY PHASES

In this chapter we will describe the recovery phases and then offer several approaches to intervention during these phases, matching them to client needs. As described in Chapter 4, the acute phase of crisis and stress is frequently followed by an avoidance phase, when the survivor regains stability by denying or evading the emotional impact of the abuse. Time and distance from the actual abusive experience allow greater freedom to explore feelings previously too raw to expose. Greater openness to trying new approaches, combined with a growing long-range perspective, make the recovery phases exciting and promising times for effective resolution, potentially very rewarding for client and helper.

The Reemergence Phase

A second crisis often marks the transition from the avoidance phase to a phase of readiness for long-term resolution. This reemergence crisis may take place just weeks after the initial trauma, or years later. It is especially common for child victims to experience reemergence in adulthood, when they are emotionally and physically stronger (Tsai et al., 1979). The two most important factors determining when the transition occurs seem to be the survivor's psychological readiness and the presence of external reminders or stressors that cannot be ignored.

For some, the need to come to terms with the abuse merely overtakes the need to repress its symptoms. For most, however, the trauma reemerges suddenly, without warning, when the survivor encounters some reminder of the experience, such as a movie scene or a discussion, or sees someone resembling the assailant. The anniversary of the abuse, even without conscious recognition of the timing, may trigger a reemergence crisis.

The onset of the transitional crisis has been referred to as the *time bomb effect* (Sutherland & Scherl, 1970), because of its suddenness and its impact. The emotional effects may be as intense as those of the acute phase. At this point the survivor is likely experiencing posttraumatic stress disorder (American Psychiatric Association, 1987; see Chapter Appendix 4B), even though time has elapsed since the traumatic event. Clients experiencing a reemergence crisis should be treated according to intervention guidelines for the acute phase, with initial concerns for safety and medical attention, taking into account the potential for suicidal responses.

Most clients do not understand why this crisis is taking place. The time bomb effect is extremely confusing to the victim, who believes she has "recovered," or put the incident behind her. A common first concern is "Why is this happening now? It was so long ago." Education about the phase perspective, including the adaptive reasons for the previous avoidance, should be explained. Above all, the reemergent client needs "permission," through support and validation, to reexperience the trauma. If the client understands that this stress is temporary and believes that she will not always feel so badly, she can see her symptoms as a normal, healthy sign that she is emotionally strong enough to overcome her trauma. This crisis signals that she does not have to deny her feelings any longer and that she is ready to take back control over her life.

The analogy of a splinter buried deep in a finger may help to explain this reemergence phase: the splinter may not hurt, but it is waiting for tissue around it to reach a point where it can fester up to the surface. When it does, it will hurt almost as much as it did when it first went in, but that pain also signals that it is ready to be removed. Festering is the first step to recovery for the wound; next it can be opened, cleaned out, and allowed to heal.

Posttraumatic stress reactions to incest, rape, or harassment must be distinguished from other psychological crises. If a client indicates that the stress reactions are frequent, or if the sexual abuse is only one of several unrelated issues creating anxiety, she should receive counseling for a wider range of problems. A client with dependency behaviors such as alcohol or drug abuse, or eating disorders, needs to receive immediate attention on those issues as well. A transitional crisis may be triggered by a recent trauma, such as a divorce, that has left the survivor vulnerable to her prior traumas. If a client is experiencing a more immediate life stress, again such as divorce, her energy should be channeled into resolving that problem, with appropriate support resources. If she is reacting to the earlier sexual abuse trauma at the same time, she must be helped to understand the connection between the two trauma responses.

If considerable time has elapsed since the original incident, the time bomb effect may be particularly hazardous because in her current anxiety the client may not see the connection to the prior abuse. Furthermore, without the information that the client's history includes sexual abuse, the helper may incorrectly perceive her emotional reactions as a symptom of psychopathology. All helpers should be aware of signs of posttraumatic stress disorder and consider the possibility that stress symptoms may signal a reemergence crisis due to an earlier victimization, even in clients who do not reveal or remember that they have been sexually abused.

The Resolution Phase

From the transitional crisis of the reemergence phase, most survivors move forward into a period of active recovery, characterized by openness to memories and efforts to relieve their pain. Genuine resolution is possible at this time, removed from the immediacy of the stressful experience. This is an important time for therapeutic intervention, particularly counseling. Clients often need help in accepting feelings of anger, helplessness, and vulnerability; in redefining personal space and sense of self; and in establishing or revising relationships on a more equal and mutually beneficial footing. Bassuk (1980) calls this process rape work, although the issues are common to those for all forms of sexual victimization.

Long-term reactions to sexual abuse are often quite negative and self-blaming. These reactions have been "brewing" over months or years, while the victim, fearing rejection, has told no one else. Self-directed negative attributions, fed by others' responses and cultural myths, have further diminished her self-esteem and confidence in her ability to cope in the world. Helplessness about the future is also common; many wonder, "Will I always feel this way?"

Resistant clients could be reminded of the person with a severe toothache who will not go to the dentist because dental work hurts. Resolution work may be painful and difficult, but relative to the long-standing agony and destructive-ness of unresolved abuse, it is short and only hurts for a little while. Most survivors are amazed and delighted at the relief they experience. In a few short weeks the success of their resolution work overwhelms years of deeply felt emotional pain.

It is unrealistic to think of resolution as a permanent state. As described in Chapter 1, a key framework is to view resolution as a process of growth. The path is not always unidirectional; the client may move back into avoidance or crisis phases and forward into comfortable resolutions during different successive periods of her life. The work by Kegan (1982) suggests that a normal resolution process resembles a spiral: even as the person moves toward better mental health through improved relationships and self-knowledge, she also experiences cycles when emotions are confused and changing. At times intense work may be needed, perhaps in a therapy or support group setting; at other times emotional issues seem resolved and energy can be concentrated on other life spheres, such as a career or children. Hartman (1987) views the fact that abused clients move into and out of her self-help groups as a positive sign of growth rather than a negative trait. In long-term intervention, the helper and client should continually assess their goals at regular intervals and not hesitate to shift the level and focus of intervention to meet the client's needs.

HELPING ROLES FOR RESOLUTION

Clients have a variety of needs during resolution work. Social and emotional support and encouragement, empathic and patient listening, education, self-help groups, and resources for self-understanding such as reading materials and work-shops are all helpful, especially where these include help from family and friends. In addition, most clients also benefit from a therapeutic relationship with a counselor and with an advocate, with whom their process can be checked.

Many survivors attain satisfactory recovery on their own, without counseling. Nevertheless, effective counseling can reduce the length of the painful resolution period considerably, and can help the client develop self-esteem, understanding, and a positive outlook in addition to coping with the trauma. Seeking counseling does not indicate that a client is inadequate or unstable; rather, it demonstrates her courage to work to achieve greater mental health and to resolve difficult issues. In making referrals, the helper must be certain that the client understands the positive reasons for counseling, so that the client does not assume that she is perceived negatively by the helper.

Although Chapters 7 through 9 are designed to offer techniques and approaches to trained and qualified counselors working with victims, the information should also be helpful to survivors or to helpers in other roles. Negotiation with the client in the open and honest manner described in Chapter 3 is crucial before proceeding with the counseling approaches offered in these chapters. The client's overall support network and those others she wishes to involve must be considered part of the resolution process, and they may need assistance and intervention as well.

Advocacy during resolution includes monitoring the therapy process, helping the client to evaluate whether the counseling she is receiving is appropriate for her and whether it is helpful. There have been too many cases in which a distraught victim seeks counseling after years of pain, only to encounter blaming attitudes or even sexually abusive treatment. Since feelings of vulnerability are often heightened by the ''patient'' role, others must encourage and assist her in evaluating the progress of her counseling. An advocate should be prepared to provide options, including that of seeking a different counselor, if a therapist is not working in the best interests of a client.

COUNSELING APPROACHES

The format and structure of counseling should be based primarily on the goals of the intervention. This section reviews common counseling approaches in order to help clients and counselors evaluate the relevance of these approaches for each situation, with an emphasis on matching client goals to intervention approaches. For the client looking for a counselor, or for the counselor choosing the approach to take with a client, guidelines for the decision process are provided here.

Intervention Formats

Counseling can be formatted around such widely varying models as a single weekend marathon session involving a family unit in intensive therapy, or hour-long weekly meetings over a period of months or years. The frequency of the sessions may range from once every week or two, to twice a week for critical periods, to the daily sessions preferred by psychoanalysts. Two general categories of psychotherapy help illuminate the format selection issues for potential clients and counselors: brief and long-term. Interventions falling within these formats differ in their time course, methodology, and most importantly, their goals (Small, 1971).

Brief Psychotherapies. ''Brief'' is intended to indicate the time limits placed on these interventions, but in fact therapists have called approaches ranging from 1 to 25 or more sessions brief (Small, 1971). The time course depends on the techniques applied by the therapist and on the complexity of the target problem. For example, the brief intervention models presented in Chapter 9 range from 5 sessions for adult survivors of child molesting to 18 sessions for incest survivors.

Brief interventions are generally focused on one issue, usually provided by the client as the ''reason for coming for help'' (Mann, 1981, p. 25). The goals of brief psychotherapy are also focused: to eliminate or relieve symptoms or to solve a problem, in order to restore healthy functioning (e.g., Bellak & Small,

1978; Wolberg, 1965). The therapist is an active figure in brief intervention, defining at least some aspects of the process. In some time-limited frameworks, the client's motives or life history are not reviewed, and long-standing character traits or complicated life issues are explicitly avoided. As summarized by Small (1971), brief psychotherapy (1) maintains a focus on the current reality, (2) targets specific symptoms or emotional conflict, and (3) teaches clients their own coping techniques.

Brief psychotherapies are most appropriate for clients who have "strong ego resources," that is, good previous adjustment, ability to relate, and high motivation (Butcher & Koss, 1978), and whose problem is focused around a specific incident. Fuhriman et al. (1986) offer a checklist for assessing a client's appropriateness for time-limited psychotherapy. The majority of sexual abuse clients, who are generally functioning well except for problems arising from the specific trauma, are appropriate for such a limited intervention. In addition, brief therapies offer fairly immediate relief from many painful symptoms of abuse. For these reasons, the models described in Chapter 9 are brief interventions.

Long-Term Psychotherapy. A less structured, more process-oriented format may be necessary for, or preferred by, some clients. The typical time course for intensive psychotherapy, which is weekly meetings over several months to a year or more, allows for in-depth personal insight and perhaps a restructuring of personality (Small, 1971). Roles, relationships, and ego functioning can be explored in an unhurried therapeutic setting that does not define specific topics or schedules in advance. Intensive psychotherapy is appropriate for any client wishing to explore a range of issues, but it is especially valuable for those who are experiencing a complex range of problems, those who have completed a brief intervention and wish to continue the counseling process, and those for whom long-term growth is a specific goal.

Dual Interventions. Many clients, particularly in the early recovery phases, benefit from experiences with both formats: for example, brief psychotherapy, to gain control over the predominant symptoms of stress and anxiety, may be followed by intensive psychotherapy to work through relationship and role issues and promote long-range personal growth. For reemergent clients, brief targeted interventions are often required before longer-range work can be effective, since stress symptoms can interfere with deeper analyses. Some counselors combine brief intervention for specific issues arising from sexual abuse, such as an incest therapy group, with ongoing intensive therapy for overall personal growth.

Intervention Structures

Client goals may be accomplished in any structure, but some structures may be more beneficial for a client than others. In most cases the choice depends on the extent of presenting problems, the nature of the abuse experience, and of course the client's own preference. Considerations include the client's self-esteem, adaptive skills, readiness to work on the issues, and intensity of emotional trauma; the level of physical and psychological violence involved; the length and number of victimization experiences; whether the abuse is ongoing; and compounding issues such as familial needs. The following description outlines specific advantages and drawbacks of the five most common structures for sexual abuse survivor counseling.

Individual Therapy. Individual therapy brings together client and therapist to build a therapeutic alliance concentrated on the client's personal issues. The safe, trusting relationship that develops in one-to-one work is especially valuable for a client who has basic needs in self-esteem, trust, and intimacy. A client who is not able to function because of severe depression, anxiety, or fear may find that feelings of stability are more readily achieved in individual work. Clients with inadequate social or communication skills may need to develop more productive skills before other therapeutic work can be successful.

Individual therapy is also often preferred for personal reasons. Some clients simply prefer the privacy found in the individual therapist-client relationship. A victim of extremely violent abuse may feel uncomfortable revealing her story to anyone other than a single trusted therapist. Some clients fear others' reactions to their family backgrounds, sexual relationships, social status, poverty, drug addiction or alcoholism, or psychiatric or medical histories. Before any other counseling structure is considered, the client's wishes should be ascertained, and her wishes should be respected where possible by offering individual therapy if desired.

Family Therapy. Members of a family, or a small group functioning as a family, may enter therapy together. In sexual abuse the primary client is frequently the victim, and the goals are to reestablish her as a fully respected member of the family. Involvement of other family members may be considered any time the client's feelings about the abusive situation could be resolved with their help, or with the opportunity to let them know about her pain. Family therapy should only be selected if the client and all the unit members agree to participate, and then only if the benefits to the client are apparent. Courtois (1988) has pointed out that the traditional family therapy model, which focuses on intrafamilial relationships and assumes that all members participate in a system, is not sufficient for the sexually abusive family, where the abuser's individual responsibility and concern with intergenerational patterns are critical.

Incest often hurts other family members in addition to the victims; the mother and siblings each react with their own pain. In order to evoke genuine change in family functioning, the abuser needs to see that pain and recognize his responsibility. For these reasons, effective family therapy can be the best weapon an incest survivor has against continued abuse and long-term emotional difficulties. It is the sentence of choice by many judges for incest offenders. Family therapy, however, can be harmful if the other members do not participate or if the victim is blamed or continues to be persecuted.

At an appropriate point within individual therapy, a client may wish to involve her partner or family members. The presence of the counselor can ease the difficulty of revealing an earlier sexual abuse to those from whom it has been kept secret. Partners and parents who already know of the abuse may need to express their own pain and issues in the safe environment provided by the counselor. Joint counseling can strengthen specific relationships, such as mother-daughter bonds, that have been damaged by an abuse. Working through these issues as a unit can promote a better long-term relationship for all parties.

Group Therapy. Therapy groups bring together several individuals, usually unknown to each other prior to counseling, who share common goals, experiences, or difficulties. Individual issues are raised in the context of group goals, such as understanding and recovering from sexual victimization. Working with other survivors has a number of advantages in the resolution of sexual abuse. The presence of similar others gives people a sense of not being alone in the world. Each survivor sees a range of normal people with experiences and problems like her own, among whom she is not unusual. She can share her thoughts and feelings without fear of seeming deviant and receive validation from others who share her experiences. Group discussions offer the opportunity to see patterns in behavior and reactions, particularly for clients with extensive self-blame and guilt responses. By observing how others handle their problems, group members can become aware of alternative ways of coping. A cohesive group spirit helps foster the support, trust, and intimacy that are important to the resolution process.

In a group, the individual's needs are spread out through the whole group, rather than placed onto a single therapist. This is less frightening for the needy client, who often fears "swallowing up or being swallowed up by" too much individual dependency. Shared intimacy also keeps group members from feeling individually responsible for solving anyone else's problem. Furthermore, the group members can feel good about themselves for helping each other. Contributions to another's well being in a reciprocal relationship can greatly enhance self-esteem. For these reasons, group work is often effective. As few as five sessions can move some clients well into resolution.

Caution must be exercised in bringing groups together, however. First, clients should be carefully screened for readiness for group work, which requires adequate levels of personal stability and social skills. Individual work is more appropriate for clients with extensive complicating factors, including other psychological problems. Second, widely disparate types of people or experiences may not mix well in a group. For example, incest and nonincest rape victims may have very different needs. For the present purposes, it is best not to group men and women together (Burden & Gottlieb, 1987). A minority client, whether by race, culture, or sexual orientation, should never be placed alone into a majority-different group unless the facilitator is willing and prepared to work to resolve potential problems. (See Brody, 1987, for her approach to mixed groups.) Introducing a new client into an ongoing group is also risky, because the group's dynamics have already been established and may have moved beyond the new client's needs. Finally, there are times when a group might be the best approach but is not available. Although mothers in incest families need group structures and (given the number of victims) there are plenty of potential members, such a group has not often formed because of a lack of participants.

Support Groups. Many individuals do not need intensive counseling, but rather a source of a consistent understanding and support. These goals can be met in a group in which individual issues are raised and discussed by interested people who share some points of view, with or without the presence of a counselor. Sharing a common experience allows group members to respect each other and to share knowledge. Knowing that there are others "looking out for her best interests," the individual member can gain the courage and skills for handling her problems, moving forward with her growth, or tackling onerous tasks. Seeing others coping with a similar trauma offers the critical element of hope for a better future (Yalom, 1970).

Support groups are often pragmatic, focused on situational or environmental coping. Therapeutic emotional benefits may occur, but as a by-product rather than as a goal. Effective support groups teach their members how to give and receive support productively, and can be very useful in concert with ongoing individual therapy. Their members, however, need to be functioning at an adequate level of emotional health and should be somewhat homogeneous, as with a support group for women managers, for whom problems like sexual harassment are common. P. R. Silverman (1980) offers suggestions for organizing and facilitating successful support groups.

Support groups can also serve as a helpful followup for survivors who have in large part resolved the abusive impact and who wish to educate themselves further about gender and violence issues. Some support groups that began with a self-educating function have produced tangible results, including workshops for others, books relating personal perspectives (McNaron & Morgan, 1982), and dramatic presentations. Several models for consciousness-raising groups for women are found in Brody (1987).

Inpatient Treatment. In limited cases, when a client is under severe stress and is exhibiting extreme behaviors such as debilitating depression or severe anorexia or is exhibiting suicidal tendencies, treatment intervention may take place in the restricted surroundings of a hospital or psychiatric facility. State laws restrict the conditions under which a client can be committed for inpatient treatment and the duration of nonvoluntary treatment, so it is important to be aware of the local laws and court policies on committal if a severely disturbed client is not willing to seek intervention. Inpatient therapy may involve medication of the client to reduce anxiety, depression, or psychotic symptoms; it should only be considered as a last resort.

PHILOSOPHICAL APPROACHES TO TREATMENT

In this section we will review three philosophical positions for analyzing and assisting in recovery from sexual abuse. While most counseling benefits derive from the quality of the counselor-client relationship itself, these philosophical approaches are essential to helpful intervention with sexual abuse survivors. The first position is that the goal of treatment is to give power and control to the client; the second is that the therapist should adopt a holistic approach to each client, considering all aspects of her life, and should be flexible in selecting from the wide range of therapeutic techniques available to help sexual abuse victims; and the third is that gender and power issues should be subjected to the explicit analysis and treatment provided by the feminist therapy approach. Therapist-powered, restricted, or sexist perspectives shortchange the client and for some may be quite harmful.

Empowering the Client

The therapist's priorities must always be those of the client, that is, to educate the client and significant other people in her life, to help the client construct a healthy world view, and to allow the client to direct her own future toward productive outcomes.

While the therapist is working to give power and control back to the client, the reality that sexual victimization may occur again must not be denied. Recovery that takes place within a realistic framework may help the client reduce her vulnerability to future abuse, but makes no promises about the future (Bassuk, 1980). Empowerment does not mean simply gaining physical or social power. Rather, the skills and experience of each individual can serve as strength from which to build empowerment. These strengths include learning to trust intuition and other generally undervalued skills (Gilligan, 1982; Greenspan, 1983). Learning to trust "gut feelings" such as a stomachache or a generalized discomfort may empower a survivor in future potentially dangerous situations (Hartman, 1987).

The Holistic Approach

Each client is a complex person, with a potential range of long-term reactions to assault that includes somatic/medical, cognitive, emotional, and spiritual components. In anticipation of that complexity, the counselor must be able to look at the whole person and to be flexible in approaching each individual. It is important to be willing to utilize more than one form of treatment, or to work together with others, such as a minister or physician, wherever it will benefit the client.

An holistic assessment considers all aspects of the client's life. Lazarus (1986) systematizes the assessment process by considering seven basic life areas (called BASIC-ID): behavior, affect, sensation (e.g., somatic complaints), imagery (including of self), cognition, interpersonal relationships, and drugs/biology (including smoking and dietary habits). Each of these areas may impinge on other areas; for example, high coffee consumption may increase both somatic and affective symptoms of anxiety. These seven areas are a helpful guide to maintaining a holistic perspective.

This approach also demands that the therapist be multiskilled, or be willing to work together with other therapists. Each therapeutic approach has its advantages. For example, behavioral therapies can in a short time remove some important blocks that prevent the client's movement toward recovery, like phobias. Cognitive restructuring of the abuse experience often provides the key that opens deeply locked doors to understanding and changing patterns like self-blame. Contemporary psychodynamic therapy can help the client gain personal freedom by removing internal barriers in a supportive and personalized exploration of herself and her relationships. In their eclectic integrated psychotherapies, described later in this chapter, Norcross (1986) and Prochaska (1979; 1984) systematize the process of integrating multiple treatment approaches.

Feminist Therapy Approach

Women's experiences form the basis of feminist theory and therapeutic intervention, and cultural and economic analyses of the status of women are consciously incorporated into understanding the client's needs. The philosophical tenets, found in Rawlings and Carter (1977) and adapted here for sexually abused clients, include the following:

- All clients are equally valued, regardless of social status, race, or gender. Individual autonomy and responsibility are necessary for healthy adjustment and can be developed in a beneficial therapeutic relationship.

- Pathology is assumed to be caused primarily by social, not personal, influences. This value is critical for helping sexually exploited clients, where blame must consistently be placed externally on the abuser. The therapeutic goal is not to adjust to unhealthy social conditions, but to change the status quo to allow all persons a free and full life. When clients believe sexual abuse is not an acceptable social condition, working to eliminate abuse becomes a highly therapeutic experience.

- Relationships of friendship, love, and marriage should be equal in personal power. For the abused client, obtaining rights within personal relationships creates an empowering future. These relationships should include other women, who are important sources of emotional support, especially through shared understanding.

From these philosophical guidelines, Rawlings and Carter (1977) offer specific strategies for feminist psychotherapy, presented in Chapter Appendix 7A. Key to these strategies is that "whenever possible, the personal power between the client and therapist approaches equality" (p. 58). (More information on feminist therapy is found in Brody, 1987; Brodsky & Hare-Mustin, 1980; Greenspan, 1983; and Robbins & Siegel, 1983.)

SELECTING THERAPIES

To help shape the counseling process for sexually abused clients, this section provides a brief outline of the major theoretical treatment approaches in terms of the special advantages and disadvantages each brings to survivor counseling. (Additional helpful guidelines for selecting the most appropriate techniques for general cases are found in Prochaska, 1984, and Norcross, 1986.)

Psychoanalysis

As conceived and practiced by Sigmund Freud and his followers (e.g., Deutsch, 1944–45), psychoanalysis has been devastating to victims of sexual abuse because of concepts like narcissism, passivity, masochism (including rape fantasies), and the "seductiveness" of young girls as part of normal femininity. As discussed in Chapter 2, Freud's claim that hysteria, a personality disorder linked primarily to women, was the result of incestuous fantasies has adversely affected a half-century of incest and rape treatment.[1] Factor (1954) wrote of his victim-client's "unconscious complicity," caused by her "erotic transference in which analyst, father, and rapist were condensed" (p. 244).

As a result, psychoanalytic treatment from this traditional belief system may be viewed cautiously or avoided by sexually abused clients. Furthermore, therapists may have to help the client overcome prior treatment by a traditional, psychoanalytically oriented therapist. Many women share the experience of Irene, who sought help for the aftereffects of incest only to be told she was to blame, not only for the incest, but also for her father's alcoholism, because of the guilt he was suffering over her seduction.

There are benefits inherent in the psychoanalytic approach, however, particularly for survivors of childhood sexual abuse. Its emphasis on early experiences as a shaping force in later relationships allows a client to examine current dynamics in the historical context of abusive relationships. The therapeutic process of talking by the client often leads to heightened personal awareness of the experience and its multiple effects (Prochaska, 1979). Techniques such as dream analysis can help a client recall incidents that have been "forgotten"; concepts such as repression and displacement may help her understand why she has forgotten, and why she had any other confusing reactions.

Contemporary Psychodynamic Therapies

The psychodynamic theories that have been developed recently, particularly those developed within the feminist therapy movement, provide a growth-oriented therapeutic environment. Chodorow (1978) explored the early relationships between mother and child, to produce an object relations theory of the dependence-independence struggle and of gender roles and beliefs. J. B. Miller (1986) focuses on adult relationships in light of cultural power imbalances between men and women and promotes a healthy view of the values she sees as characteristic of contemporary women. The therapeutic approach includes a review of the personal history of the client; a perspective on past and present relationships; and examination of defense mechanisms and displaced reactions such as anger and denial. These approaches are particularly helpful to clients for whom direct access to painful memories and their connections to current relationships are difficult. The focus on intra-and interpersonal dynamics promotes long-term growth: development of self-esteem, discovery of more effective patterns for relationships, valuing of personal strengths. Feminist psychodynamic therapies provide important therapeutic techniques and goals for clients who have time, and for whom indirect methods of personal inquiry are appropriate. (More information can be found in Alpert, 1986, and from working papers in the Stone Center Series, available at cost from The Stone Center, Wellesley College, Wellesley, MA 02181.)

Behavioral Therapies

Modification of maladaptive behaviors is the goal of behavioral therapies. Intervention is focused on observable behaviors and physical symptoms. Maladaptive behaviors are assumed to arise from a reinforcement history; for example, fear of open spaces can be traced to a client's having been assaulted in a park. The behavioral therapist sets up a plan, using empirically demonstrated techniques, to help the client develop a more satisfactory set of behaviors through increased self-control. Behavior modification techniques include desensitization, relaxation, and biofeedback (Wolpe & Lazarus, 1966).

The advantages of behavioral techniques for sexual abuse survivors include relatively rapid results in the degree of control the client regains. Behavioral therapy is particularly effective with psychogenic stress disorders like headaches or chronic pain, phobic reactions, and sexual dysfunctions (Becker & Skinner, 1984) and for developing social skills like assertiveness (Linehan & Egan, 1979).

Cognitive Therapies

Several techniques fit under the rubric of "cognitive." In general, cognitive therapies assume that the individual's self-labels, problem-solving strategies, emotional reactions, and/or rational thinking processes have gone awry. The resulting irrational belief systems include feelings of worthlessness, "awfulizing" (focusing on worst-case scenarios), and unrealistic overgeneralizations (Ellis & Bernard, 1985). Treatment involves restructuring those damaging attributions or cognitions, particularly in terms of gender role issues (Wolfe, 1985). Once the client relabels herself or reframes her experience, and learns more effective problem-solving strategies, other feelings and perceptions will fall into place. Beck and Greenberg's (1974) treatment for depression features this cognitive restructuring approach, as does the approach taken in Chapter 8 to overcoming guilt, Walker's (1984) treatment of learned helplessness, and Wolfe's (1987) work with women's issues.

Cognitive therapies are particularly effective with features of the postabuse experience that are influenced by verbal (spoken or internal) messages, such as expressions of self-blame or fears of overwhelming vulnerability. Cognitive-behavioral techniques, practiced through homework assignments, self-reinforcements, and behavioral monitoring, are valuable in developing self-acceptance (Wolfe, 1987), stopping obsessive thoughts (Rimm & Masters, 1974), and teaching problem solving (Goldfried & Davison, 1976), all common emotional tasks for sexual abuse survivors. Approaches such as rational-emotive therapy,[2] which encourages self-discovery and thinking through problems in a highly logical fashion (Ellis, 1973), also allow a sense of control over the therapeutic process.

Humanistic, or Client-Centered, Therapy

Humanistic therapies are focused on therapy as a process, rather than on a specific goal or objective, and attend to the phenomenological view of the client as primary to that process. The relationship between the therapist and the client allows for expression of the client's self and life in an environment of respect, of being heard at deeper levels, and of safety. The problems focused on are often those associated with self-image and self-esteem, particularly the self-concept that has never been allowed to develop or that has been shattered through a traumatic experience (Prochaska, 1979). The connection with the experience of sexual abuse victims is clear. The therapist assumes an involved and reflective role with the client's thoughts as they are verbalized. This "mirror" process allows a client to see for herself the troubling discongruence, to recognize the devastating impact of abusive experiences, and to begin to heal from them. Catharsis, or emotional expression, which is an important part of victim recovery, is also important to the humanistic therapeutic process.

Eclectic Integrated Psychotherapies

"Eclectic" refers to any combination of theoretical approaches (e.g., psychoanalytic and behavioral) applied to a single intervention. A majority of therapists actually use more than one approach in their practice (Larson, 1980), and over a third of them prefer the eclectic approach (Norcross, 1986). Systematic eclecticism has emerged in the past few years as a a way of helping clinicians provide the most efficacious combination of treatments (Norcross, 1986; Prochaska & DiClemente, 1984).

Eclecticism has the advantage of bringing together the insights and skills of individual theoretical "schools." The therapist can focus on the overall process of change (e.g., Prochaska, 1984), rather than forcing the client's issues and behaviors into a single theoretical framework. A systematic eclectic approach can be applied to time-limited therapy (Fuhriman, et al., 1986), or to long-term treatment (Lazarus, 1986). Lazarus (1986) offers a model of systematic eclectic treatment for anxiety, from his multimodal approach. He assesses key aspects of each client, using the BASIC-ID system described earlier. After problem areas are identified, techniques are selectively applied to some or all of them.

Existential Therapy

The questions raised by survivors of sexual abuse and other victimizations are often existential: "What kind of world would allow this behavior?" "What meaning can I make from this experience?" These questions can lead to resignation and a deep sense of futility, and they should not be brushed aside. Spawned by existential philosophers such as Jean-Paul Sartre (1956) and advocated as a psychotherapeutic approach by Rollo May (May et al., 1958), existential therapy focuses on clients' questions about the meaning of life, on anxiety raised by efforts at adjustment in a society that is dishonest and often cruel (Tillich, 1952). The goal of intervention is an appreciation of self-honesty and the development of personal control, as well as harmony within the social reality. The social reality is made explicit, and the client's feelings of frustration and helplessness are validated. The existential strategies of validation and shared concern can guide clients through and beyond potentially blocking questions.[3]

Transactional Analysis

Transactional analysis (popularly called "TA") focuses on styles, or scripts, acted out in relationships. Some of these life scripts are healthy, but many incorporate low self-esteem, hostility, and poor coping strategies (Steiner, 1974). While the effectiveness of TA-based therapies depends on the therapist, some of the popular books written for TA can be helpful with sexually abused clients, who often suffer from self-esteem, relational, and coping problems. At a superficial level, a client can be asked to read *I'm OK—You're OK* (Harris, 1969) or *Games People Play* (Berne, 1978) and analyze her own behavior in light of the scripted roles she reads about. Such exercises can provide a stimulant to further therapeutic work.

Adlerian Therapy

Alfred Adler (1929) focused his psychoanalytic theory on instinctual drives for aggression and power. His concept of the "inferiority complex" raises issues particularly relevant for those survivors who turn to self- and other-destructive activities after abuse. Adler's approach is to help the client recognize goals such as self-destructiveness and counteract them through revaluation (Prochaska, 1979).

Self-Help

The self-help movement is relatively recent in the history of psychological treatment and is based in part on the willingness of survivors to speak publicly about their experience. The lack of available treatment has always been a problem for people with "unusual" or unspoken life difficulties. Thus, people with similar experiences can be helpful to each other in ways that do not require professional assistance. Self-help groups may be formed without a therapist, or with a leader/ therapist who shares the common experience and serves as a model for other group members (e.g., Swink & Leveille, 1986).

Self-help implies that the individual takes an active role in seeking out whatever she believes will help herself the most. This may include reading, social support, or personal growth experiences. She is free to select her own options, but is guided by the experiences and wisdom of others who share her history.

Many sexual abuse survivors have taken their recovery into their own hands. A few individuals have written about overcoming their own personal traumas; others have formed small support groups of similar others to talk about their experiences. Among the self-help books for sexual abuse survivors are some impressive and personally meaningful works, notably Bass and Davis (1988), *The Courage to Heal*, and Poston and Lison (1989), *Reclaiming Our Lives*. Other self-help resources are listed in Chapter Appendix 7B,[4] and specific resources are provided throughout Chapter 8. Greenspan (1983) incorporates self-help into her approach to therapy for women, while Hartman (1987) describes a self-help therapy group for women seeking to leave abusive relationships.

NOTES

1. Originally, Freud believed hysteria was the result of actual incestuous assaults. His famous reversal, adopting the position that hysterical women merely fantasized about incest, has now been demonstrated as having been politically motivated and as inaccurate (Masson, 1984).

2. Relevant publications and professional training are available through the Institute for Rational-Emotive Therapy, 45 East 65th Street, New York, NY 10021.

3. Carlsen (1988) conceptualized therapy as a meaning-making process, based on cognitive-developmental theory. Using dialectical strategies and other practical cognitive activities, she approaches therapy as a way to turn crisis experiences into motivation for growth.

4. Rosen (1987) has raised important concerns about the undocumented and untested claims made by many self-help books published by the popular press, and Starker (1988) has extended that concern to the large proportion of therapists prescribing self-help books as adjunctive therapy. Clients should be advised of the wide range in quality and safety of the advice available, and all material prescribed should be reviewed in advance by the therapist.

RECOMMENDED READINGS

Greenspan, M. *A New Approach to Women and Therapy*. New York: McGraw-Hill, 1983.

Miller, J. B. *Toward a New Psychology of Women*. Boston: Beacon, 1986.

Prochaska, J. O. *Systems of Psychotherapy*. 2nd ed. Homewood, Ill.: Dorsey, 1984.

CHAPTER APPENDIX 7A: FEMINIST THERAPY STRATEGIES

The following strategies are adapted from Rawlings and Carter (1977):

1. Before therapy begins, the counselor tells the client what her own values are regarding women's roles and specific issues such as sexual abuse.

2. The client is kept fully informed and allowed to know about information in her files, including diagnostic labels (which are not normally used in feminist therapy) and any test results.

3. Autonomy is nurtured and encouraged. However, "it is not sufficient merely to encourage women to develop themselves. They must also be given sufficient personal support and help in analyzing emotional and social barriers to their goals" (Rawlings & Carter, 1977, p. 59). Thus feminist therapy is often done in groups, as described in Brody (1987).

4. Sexist expectations of oneself and others, including cultural expectations, are exposed through explicit sex role analysis (see Brodsky & Hare-Mustin, 1980).

5. The therapist "usually takes what the client says at face value . . . [and] confronts contradictory behavior. The therapist assumes that the client is her own best expert on herself" (Rawlings & Carter, 1977, p. 61).

6. The therapist serves as an equal and as a role model (Gilbert, 1980).

7. The client is given the tools to become her own therapist.

8. Social action is encouraged for clients (Adams & Durham, 1977) and for therapists.

CHAPTER APPENDIX 7B: SELF-HELP RESOURCES

The following are recommended resources on self-help groups and materials. Information about local self-help groups should be available at local mental health centers.

Books, Directories

Powell, T. J. *Self-Help Organizations and Professional Practice*, (1987). Available from the National Association of Social Workers, Silver Spring, MD 20910.

Scheffler, L. W. *Help Thy Neighbor*. New York: Grove, 1984.

Information

Incest Survivors Anonymous, P.O. Box 5613, Long Beach, CA 90805. Phone (213)422-1632 or (213)428-5599.

National Self-Help Clearinghouse, 33 West 42nd Street, New York, NY 10036.

National Alliance for the Mentally Ill, 1901 North Fort Meyer Drive, Suite 500, Arlington, VA 22209.

8

Emotional Aftereffects

Several emotional and behavioral reactions are experienced with considerable regularity by survivors of sexual abuse: grief, depression, guilt and self-blame, rage, terror, mistrust, low self-esteem, fears about control, body image distortions, intimacy and sexual difficulties, and self-destructive behaviors. In this chapter these reactions are examined and techniques are offered for helping a client recover from each. As in the acute phase, there are individual variations in the expression of emotional aftereffects among abuse survivors. The client's history, including personal attitudes, reactions of others, and extent of abuse, will play a role in shaping the resolution process. Intervention must be accommodated to each client's symptoms and needs. In addition, the extent of intervention in a client's resolution must depend on the counselor's training and experience and the client's willingness to participate. Although anyone can gently guide a survivor through to resolution, helpers are cautioned not to attempt therapy without the appropriate training, experience, and credentials.

GRIEF AND LOSS

Permeating all survivor reactions is a sense of loss: loss of tangibles like family, job, or possessions *(tangible losses)*, and also losses of security, self-esteem, and wholeness *(emotional losses)*. Both are often extensive after sexual abuse. The grief created by these losses is comparable to grief over other tragedies—death of a loved one, amputation of a body part (Rando, 1986). The client and therapist must appreciate the significance of each loss and the depth of grief over those losses.

The process of recognizing and mourning losses typically fits into the analytic grief framework, including phases similar to those described by Kubler-Ross (1970) for dying patients. For sexual abuse survivors, these phases are *denial* (avoidance), while the client represses the intense emotions created by the grief; *depression*, when the client can no longer deny the grief and is overwhelmed by sadness, with accompanying self-blame; *anger*, as the client recognizes that she has been victimized and has a right to be enraged; and *integration*, putting the grief into its proper perspective as a traumatic life experience from which one recovers. Grief counseling recognizes these phases and gently guides the client through them. Both depression and anger are significant responses and may require intensive work. Other helpful guidelines for grief counseling are provided by Rando (1986).

Tangible Loss

Harassment victims may be fired or leave a job, withdraw from school, or be closed out of a desired career path. Rape victims frequently move away, and friends and lovers may abandon them. Incest victims may lose their family support or be forced to leave home when they report their abusive situation. Returning to the former life, or regaining tangible losses, may not ever be possible.

Letting go of these losses may be very painful. The acquaintance-rape survivor may have fantasies that her assailant will return and apologize for hurting her; the fired secretary may want her abusive boss to recognize his error and rehire her. Even as adults, incest survivors often continue to seek out the approval of a rejecting parent, usually without avail. The counselor can help the client (1) recognize her losses and experience her feelings as a normal process of mourning; (2) examine the disruption and stress created by the losses, allowing her to rest when needed; and (3) find options for gaining or building a new life. The client needs to work through all options and to be prepared for failure in attempts to recapture lost relationships. She may have only one option: to let go of her dreams, mourn them as losses, and redirect her energy into building new, supportive relationships.

With tangible losses the needs are pragmatic, such as support and skills for moving, finding another job, changing schools, or resuming work or study at the same location with a new awareness. Returning to a residence in which an assault has taken place may require protective steps, such as new locks on doors and windows. Finding a new job may entail developing a new resume and practicing interviewing skills; changing schools may mean making choices about where and when to transfer. With more sweeping losses, such as family rejection, the impact is potentially more devastating, as the client has to develop new, trustworthy relationships,[1] ones which will not have a history of shared experiences. Suggestions for helping a client develop healthy substitutes for lost emotional bonds are offered in Chapter Appendix 8A.

Emotional Loss

The psychological factors constituting emotional loss—loss of security, self-esteem, and a sense of wholeness—are often more subtle and destructive than the tangible losses. While appreciating the healing effect of time, the counselor can ease the client's process through her grief by helping her

1. accept the reality of the assault, through disclosure and then detailed retelling of her experience and its impact on her sense of self;

2. place feelings of depression, self-blame, helplessness, and anger into a context of normal responses to abnormal events, providing models to help her believe that she, like others, can recover;

3. learn why she feels as she does, including the effects on her of societal myths and attitudes;

4. find alternatives to negative self-perceptions, alternatives that absolve her of any personal responsibility for the abuse while providing a sense of control in her life;

5. direct blame and the resultant anger to the appropriate external targets, the abuser and those who have betrayed her over the abuse;

6. channel anger into positive, abuse-free goals with satisfying results, such as helping others.

DEPRESSION

Loss and grief are often accompanied by some level of depression. The process of mourning involves a natural period of sadness, often with a generalized low energy level, reduced concern with outside demands or options, and withdrawal from social activities. Many sexual abuse survivors coming out of the relative stability of the denial phase are confused by such a depression, feeling they should be "over this by now" or "coping better." Clients should be encouraged to accept some depression, recognizing it as a normal and temporary process. A client needs companionship as much as possible during and immediately following any period of depression.

A major depression, however, requires stronger action. Major depression is often marked by disruptions in eating and sleeping patterns, lethargy, confusion, inability to make decisions, and suicidal ideation. Any severely depressed client should be closely monitored, and as a last resort, hospitalization may be added to intensive therapeutic efforts to prevent physical harm. If a client expresses self-destructive thinking, or has a plan and method of suicide in mind, treat the situation as a crisis. (See Chapter Appendix 4A.)

A range of treatments has been offered for severe depression; particularly effective are behavioral and cognitive therapies. Behavioral approaches attempt to alter mood by reducing the frequency of depressive behavioral symptoms and increasing the frequency of active coping behaviors. The client is asked to keep a daily record of activities and reinforcers, which in itself may promote a sense of positive control. Other tactics include recording and reinforcing any increase in active behavior, breaking large problems into small steps, with reinforcements at each small step (applied by the therapist, a partner or family member, or by the client herself), and modeling or reinforcing safe, physical ways to express feelings. Games or activities with increasing physical impact and accompanying verbal cues can be an effective way to elicit expression of suppressed anger. Such physical exercise may also induce endocrine system changes, counteracting depression. Even minor exercise, such as taking a short walk, can produce marked changes in willingness to continue constructive therapy.

Cognitive approaches target distorted interpretations of the abuse experience—negative attributions, self-blame, selective attention to negative thoughts, and overgeneralizations (Beck, 1972). The client is asked to monitor her thoughts for specific interpretations and then evaluate them. Those thoughts that are idiosyncratic or unhealthy are given more realistic interpretations, and the client is taught to increase attention to positive messages. Myths and unhelpful attitudes, such as the rape and sexual myths discussed in Chapter 2, are exposed and discussed. The therapist may have to raise these faulty beliefs in order to elicit such a dialogue, because the client may be too frightened by her thoughts to discuss them openly. Finally, positive imaging, or fantasies of what *can* be, is used to help the client grasp a sense of a better future. These and other techniques may be found in Beck (1972) and Beck and Greenberg (1974).

The client is also likely to need support for changing the elements of her environment that trigger or maintain her depression—lack of career opportunity, or dependency on an abusive spouse or unhappy family situation. Such support can be found by joining a support group or through increasing social contacts with friends who have a positive outlook on life, while decreasing the amount of time spent with those who are negative.

Antidepressant medications may help reduce the clinical syndrome of sleep and appetite loss, lethargy, lack of interest, and helplessness in conjunction with psychological interventions (Weissman, 1980). Individuals respond differently to the various types and doses of antidepressants, however, and most antidepressants interact with alcohol and other drugs. Thus the client must be carefully evaluated and monitored if antidepressants are prescribed. Furthermore, clients must be fully aware that beneficial effects take from one to four weeks to develop, so that they do not get discouraged and interpret their lack of progress as a failure in themselves.

GUILT

The origins of survivor self-blame have been outlined in Chapter 4 as part of an acute response to trauma. With supportive feedback and more realistic appraisals of the experience, after most traumas, guilt feelings decline over time. After sexual abuse, however, stereotypic attitudes and beliefs encourage the incorporation of self-blame and guilt in the survivor. Those survivors likely to suffer the highest levels of guilt in the long-term reaction are those

- who were abused by someone they knew, especially close friends or relatives (Katz, 1987). Family abusers often openly blame child victims for their own abuse, reinforcing guilt feelings.
- who are sensitive to others' feelings and strive for harmony in relationships. After sexual harassment or acquaintance rape, for example, the sensitive person is more likely to assume she did not "make the relationship work well," or did "something to arouse him beyond his control."
- who used no strategies to avoid or escape from the assault. In situations where submission was the most reasonable response, survivors often wish they had tried some form of escape or avoidance, even at the risk of death.
- whose self-blaming tendencies are reinforced by others, who point out her mistakes, question her judgment or actions, or otherwise cause self-doubt.
- who have never told anyone about their experience. Silence leads to isolation and feelings of being "the only one," enhancing self-blame.

Self-blame is a stumbling block to resolving sexual abuse (Katz & Burt, 1988). As long as the survivor feels guilty, she is not free to work fully on self-esteem and anger. Well-established guilt patterns tend to be difficult to modify, especially in incest survivors, for whom most of the enhancing factors are present. Clients with deeply held self-blame often counter efforts to reassure them with "but I should have. . . . " Some clients can intellectually accept that the responsibility for abuse in general belongs to the perpetrator, but will cling tenaciously to self-blame: "My situation was different."

Self-blame often centers on actions immediately prior to an assault. From "I shouldn't have gone into his office alone" to "I shouldn't have been hitchhiking," behavioral self-blame is resistant to change. Miller and Porter (1983) have found that survivors using behavioral self-blame show better functioning in some areas during the first two years after a rape. They suggest that attributing victimization to a behavior that could be changed leads to better long-term resolution. Casting an assault as the result of one's own actions makes the abuse seem like an avoidable experience, which may have some self-protective benefits during the denial phase. However, using behavioral self-blame as a form of denial may not be helpful in the long-term resolution of sexual abuse (Katz & Burt, 1988). A more appropriate goal for long-term resolution is an understanding that while behavioral changes may reduce chances of future victimization, no one has the right to abuse another person, regardless of prior actions.

Cognitive restructuring techniques are extremely helpful in resolving guilt reactions. A return to the reality of the assault is often necessary: what the client was doing at the time, what she thought would happen if she did try to escape, and most importantly, how frightened she was during the assault. To help the client assess these facts, the counselor may have to: (1) reflect back what she has said, making connections for her if she doesn't see them: "It sounds to me like you did not try to run because you thought that he would catch you and hurt you more"; (2) counter assertions of "I could have" or "I should have" with information from her experience: "From what you've told me about his anger, that probably would not have been a good response, and you probably knew it at the time"; and (3) suggest that she interpret her actions in the context of the terror that she was experiencing: "Perhaps in normal times you could have outrun him, but remember how paralyzed you felt by his violent change of behavior. You were in shock, and it's hard to create new responses when you are in shock." Most clients need reassurance that their behavior was understandable and "normal," given the circumstances.

Intervention should serve another function: helping the client regain a sense of control of her life by recognizing that she made a choice for survival, even though she had no choice about the abuse itself. If a client can view her responses—including submitting—as reasonable choices under the circumstances, she can ease her self-blame over not making the "best" response or achieving an escape.

The counselor should state frequently and unequivocally that no matter what the client did, she did not ask to be abused, any more than she would ask to be robbed, fired from her job, injured, or murdered. The focus must consistently be shifted away from sexual, seductive, or "bad girl" images and onto the assailant's responsibility. Group exercises are particularly effective in countering guilt feelings (Tsai & Wagner, 1978), as described in Chapter 9.

If the client is normally an aware, vigilant person, she may feel that the abuse occurred to her because she let down her guard or violated her own standards. A review of her standards will determine whether they are realistic. If not, a more reasonable set should be developed that would include acceptable levels of risk in exchange for her freedom to move about in the world. If her behavior did violate her own standards, such as going to a bar alone, she should be encouraged to be angry at the abuser for taking advantage of her vulnerability. She must recognize that none of us is perfect and that her behavior does not excuse the abuser for his actions. It may be helpful to ritualistically apologize to, and forgive, herself for the behavior she feels bad about, and then to restructure the bad experience as a learning experience.

ANGER

Anger is essential for postabuse resolution. However, for most survivors, anger is not easy to develop nor to target at the abuser. Expressing rage is especially difficult for most women, who are socialized from childhood not to express any negative emotions. When feelings of anger do emerge, they tend to be either diffuse, directed at the wrong targets, or self-directed—none of which are helpful. Incest survivors often rail against their mothers for unspecified acts of neglect or failure to protect, and harassment survivors fault their peers for not helping them out. In Quina-Holland's (1979) interviews, only one-fourth of rape survivors expressed any anger toward their rapists at all. In addition, forming a clear image of the abuser, usually necessary for targeting anger, is frightening in itself. Finally, anger at the abuser conflicts with any behavioral self-blame serving as psychological protection.

Process therapy was developed by Schaef (1984) to deal with women clients' emerging consciousness of oppression, including sexual victimization, and the rage brought forth by the awareness. Schaef makes two primary assertions. First, the concern of the counselor should be with the process of therapy and with validating and facilitating the client's feelings, rather than with the specific content. For example, if the client describes self-hatred, those feelings should not be denied or counteracted but allowed free expression. In doing so, she can explore her feelings and the reasons for them, and move on. Process work can be facilitated by "body work" (e.g., breathing and relaxation exercises) to remove blocks to expression such as numbness or tension.

Second, Schaef asserts that since our culture rarely allows women to express even minimal anger, women clients are likely to harbor years of suppressed rage. Thus, when anger over an incident (such as sexual abuse) is first expressed, it is often accompanied by a lifetime of rage. These powerful feelings of rage are themselves terrifying: clients fear that they may "go off the deep end" and never be able to control or stop their feelings once they are released. Thus their anger often initially takes diffuse or inappropriately directed forms. Schaef has found it better to encourage women clients to express their diffuse rage first, in a safe setting. Once the client becomes less frightened or overwhelmed by her own rage, the specific targeted anger can be expressed more easily and with less associated terror over her ability to recover.

Neither of these two tenets is easy to achieve for therapists who have been trained to listen to specific content and to intervene when emotions seem to be rising. Much of Schaef's work is done in groups, where the shared experiences facilitate the individual client's awareness while the group support encourages trust and overcoming fear of abandonment. Schaef's approach is particularly suitable for sexually abused clients who have difficulty getting in touch with their anger. However, counselors should not attempt body work or rage therapy without special training and experience and a commitment to the full process. Eliciting rage and then pulling back from the client, for example, can be more destructive than never allowing its expression.

Schaef (1984) describes four stages in process therapy through which most of her clients pass. Since her approach is nondirective, she sees this as a natural progression, from "being a victim" (in a general sense) to articulating a new, empowered world view. Initially, her clients express a range of feelings, often vague, while struggling with their experience. Validation of all feelings, good and bad, at this stage helps a client learn to trust her own perceptions and thus increases self-confidence. The therapist intervenes only to explore with her client the reasons for her feeling as she does. As her self-esteem rises, the client begins to express self-blame and self-pity. In this second stage, the therapist should support these expressions, allowing the client to focus on her feelings of being a victim. As a deeper rage begins to emerge, often in a turbulent therapy session, self-blame and self-pity will decrease by themselves. Allowed free expression in a supportive environment, with restraints only to assure safety, the client comes in touch with her deepest emotions and fears.

Once this initial rage has been expressed and the client is no longer afraid of her own anger, she should be helped to direct her anger toward the appropriate external targets, especially the abuser. Permission to target another person for feelings of rage, and safety from that other person while the rage is being expressed, are often necessary. When the specific rage has been experienced fully and the client is no longer directing blame or anger toward herself, the energy associated with the rage can be channeled into more positive goals. Helping others is especially beneficial for many survivors, as it both utilizes energy and increases self-esteem.

LOSS OF TRUST

Sexual abuse often leads to feelings of betrayal, especially when the victim had trusted or loved her abuser. Fear of future betrayals often makes a survivor wary in all relationships. Coping with betrayal and learning to trust are two prominent tasks for the resolution process.

Deliberate betrayal is used by "con rapists," who nurture their target's trust and attack after she has let down her guard. Sexual harassers also usually engage their targets in some kind of relationship prior to their abusive behavior. Incest usually involves several kinds of betrayal: not only does the abuser take advantage of familial and emotional ties, but the survivor feels betrayed by others as well, especially by her mother. Even when family members do not know of the abuse, the survivor often feels that they failed to prevent or contributed to the abuse. Fathers often deliberately displace their victim's feelings of betrayal onto others, telling the child that the sex is necessary because the mother is not "doing her job."

After sexual abuse there are often secondary betrayals. Friends may question the survivor's behavior; a lover may end the relationship; family members may react with anger instead of support. In new relationships, revelation of the prior abuse may bring subsequent betrayals. The new partner may reject her, or he may find her story arousing and attempt to replicate the sexual fantasy he has created around it. After secondary betrayals, mistrust generalizes to a much wider range of people.

Other spheres of a survivor's life, such as her sense of competence, may be affected by betrayal. For example, sexual harassers often target young students or employees, who are initially praised and encouraged to work on "special projects." When such a victim learns that the real intentions are sexual, she loses more than an important mentor; if she refuses, she may be fired or flunked, while if she cooperates, she becomes nothing more than a mistress, and the "special project" continues only at his whim. Victims of this kind of offense often come to believe their abusers and doubt their own ability.

Betrayal often leads the survivor to doubt her own judgment, particularly her ability to distinguish harmful from helpful people. Date rape survivors often take a year or more to begin dating again, and even then they are nervous and mistrusting. Childhood sexual abuse can preclude healthy adult partnerships, as the betrayed child becomes mistrusting or cynical. Some decide never to trust anyone again.

Four counseling goals emerge with betrayal. The client needs to (1) recognize the betrayal she feels and mourn the losses created by those people who betrayed her; (2) regain trust, in herself and in others; (3) examine the effects that betrayal has had, directly through others' treatment and indirectly through feelings of worthlessness; and (4) rebuild healthy self-esteem.

Reestablishing trust can be very difficult, because it also requires renewing trust in one's own judgment, with no guarantees. One counseling task, then, is to review past and current experiences with trustworthy people, as a contrast to the betrayal. Some clients need to become more discriminating in their relationships, learning how to distinguish between trustworthy friends and nontrustworthy acquaintances. The therapist is especially important to these clients as a model of a trustworthy friend (Gilbert, 1980).[2] Others need to learn that not all people behave in accordance with their trustworthy values. The knowledge that abuse can occur may be recast in a different belief system, as new information can be used to make decisions in future relationships. A related task is to develop techniques to counteract feelings of vulnerability, such as asserting personal needs in relationships and insisting on trusting her own intuitive or "gut" perceptions.

When people who had been kind and loving commit sexual abuse, the reaction is particularly complex. Such a betrayal usually involves a sudden change in the abuser's behavior, so that it is unpredictable and unrelated to past actions. If the survivor has continued to love or care about her abuser, as often occurs in familial situations, love and abusive treatment become even more confused. Clients need to clarify the distinction between positive feelings for the abuser and the horror felt at his abusive behavior, and to recognize and accept the conflicted emotions that are created. If subsequent abuse is likely, the client should end contact except under highly restricted circumstances in which the client is in control. Even in apparently safe circumstances, such as adult incest survivors visiting their elderly abuser, specific avoidance strategies need to be taught in order to help the client feel she is in control.

Destructive tactics used by an abuser, such as attempts to undermine the victim's self-confidence, as well as unsupportive acts from friends and family, must be identified and responded to with anger focused on the psychological abuse. Above all, clients need to accept that they are better off without friends and family who are capable of betrayal.

FEELINGS OF DEVIANCE

Feelings of being different or "marked" arise after most traumatic experiences. Merely being the focus of attention, however kind, may foster a self-image of deviance. Survivors of sexual abuse frequently report that they feel like strangers even with close friends.

Corollary feelings of being weird or "crazy" may arise. It is common to hear, "If they knew about the real me, they would think I'm awful." These feelings are reinforced by friends and family who distance themselves physically or verbally ("I would have tried to escape" or "Nothing like that ever happened to me!") or who express disgust at the degrading acts involved.

Feelings of deviance need to be confronted early in the counseling process. Their existence should be placed into a normative context: such feelings are common for all types of survivors and do not indicate psychological disturbance. A counselor who has had a similar experience can share how she felt. Others find it helpful to say, "If I had been in your situation, I would have felt the same way." This open validation lets the client know that someone cares and helps her verbalize her experience.

Social patterns that isolate the client need to be interrupted by helping her find others with similar experiences. A support or therapy group can be helpful, or the client can read about others' experiences. Such conversations and readings also help the survivor identify and label symptoms not previously associated with the sexual abuse.

Seeking counseling may itself create feelings of deviance. Yalom (1970) described clients first entering therapy as feeling "unique in their wretchedness, that they alone have certain frightening or unacceptable problems, thoughts, impulses, and fantasies" (p. 10). Unless serious disturbance is noted, it is critical to tell a new client, "You are not crazy." Reassurance of normalcy, especially from an "expert," is often one of the greatest benefits of counseling.

TERROR

Anxiety and fear usually diminish considerably during the acute postabuse phases. (See Chapter 4.) However, some fear reactions become attached to specific environment stimuli or circumstances that remind them of the abuse, creating specific phobias. A few survivors experience more continuous fear about the world around them, ranging from timidity to agoraphobia to constant terror. These terror responses must be distinguished from anxiety over the counseling process itself. Temporary anxieties are normal and usually are put to rest as soon as the client becomes comfortable with the therapist. Terrors require substantially greater intervention.

Specific Phobias

A phobia is a strong, consistent fear reaction to a specific place or thing—
elevators, spiders, airplanes. The intensity of these fear reactions is what defines
them as a phobia: the person is debilitated in the presence of the stimulus,
experiencing a range of physiological symptoms (heart palpitations, shaking,
dizziness) and behavioral responses (fleeing, screaming). Phobic reactions are
considered to be learned responses, emanating from some trauma the person has
experienced or from an association with potential trauma.

Some minor phobias almost always result from sexual abuse: a woman raped
in her home at knifepoint has to remove all sharp objects, even for cooking; a
man accosted as a teenager in a shopping center restroom avoids shopping in
large stores. The link between these reactions and the sexual abuse are usually
recognized by the client. In fact, the avoidance pattern may serve a psychological
protective function and may not need to become a focus of intervention unless
it interferes with normal life or the client wishes to pursue it.

Other phobic reactions, however, are more disruptive: a woman harassed on
her job becomes afraid to go to work; the Black victim of a White assailant
cannot ride on a bus if a White man is a passenger. Survivors of abuses in their
own homes, especially incest, may spend much of the night driving or walking
around outside. These disruptive avoidance patterns may not be linked in the
client's mind to the abuse; in fact, the existence of such a general phobia is a
cue for the therapist to explore the possibility of a prior sexual abuse in a client
who has not disclosed or who may have repressed such abuse.

Interventions for phobias are usually behavioral. The client needs to recognize
her fear as a learned response and, if possible, to link it to its source. Then
behavioral techniques can be used to reverse the learned association and replace
it with a nondisruptive reaction. Of these techniques, discussed extensively by
Wolpe and Lazarus (1966), the best choice for a sexually abused client is probably
a combination of relaxation techniques and systematic desensitization, which
allows the fear to dissipate or be extinguished as the feared stimulus is moved
closer. Any desensitization should be carried out with the client's full awareness
and at the client's pace, allowing her control over the process. Gentleness and
sensitivity are essential; abrupt techniques that maximize fright, such as implosive
therapy, are unwise for the client who has experienced major trauma.

Panic Attacks and Agoraphobia

Severe trauma may elicit a dramatic, nonspecific terror reaction—a panic
attack, characterized by one sufferer as "the worst nightmare you can imagine,
multiplied by a thousand times. You really think you're going to die." The
experience of one or more panic attacks creates anticipatory anxiety, and thus
the external world becomes a conditioned stimulus for a "fear of fear," or

agoraphobia (Chambless & Goldstein, 1982). Not all persons suffering a panic attack become agoraphobic, but those who interpret the attack as meaning they are "crazy" or "about to die" are more susceptible to developing further symptoms. Sufferers begin to confine themselves to a restricted "safety zone," often their own home, and this enhances feelings of being "crazy."

The experience of sexual abuse, particularly during susceptible periods such as the teens or early adulthood, may increase vulnerability to agoraphobia. According to Chambless and Goldstein (1982), high stress may trigger the initial panic attacks. The social environment is also important. Overprotectiveness from family or partner, a normal response to abuse, often reinforces the sufferer's belief that she cannot sustain a normal existence without help.

Treatment of panic attacks and agoraphobia is often successful with a combination of therapeutic approaches. Whether panic attacks are precipitated by a hormonal or metabolic imbalance or are sympathetic nervous system responses to trauma, many professionals believe they have a physiological basis or component. Thus, some recommend medication along with psychotherapy, using propenalol (Inderal) or antidepressants such as imipramine to block the exaggerated sympathetic nervous system symptoms of heart palpitations or racing, dry mouth or choking, or dizziness (Sheehan, 1983).[3] However, there are also learned associations perpetuating the intense traumatic response, which respond well to behavioral techniques such as flooding, including careful exposure (often in groups) to the frightening situation (Chambless & Goldstein, 1982). Finally, the confining, passive social roles for women (Fodor, 1974; Kravetz, 1980) and the actions of others who reinforce the fearful behavior must be acknowledged. This awareness develops particularly well in support groups, where clients examine common patterns and learn assertive approaches to change (Brehony, 1987; Fodor, 1974).

Terrorized and Terrorizing Patterns

The *terrorized client* is likely to have a history of long-term abuse, such as incest, or to have been the victim of a violent assault. Their abusers have often used particularly degrading or frightening tactics. Stern and Stern (1985) have described three ways in which terrorized clients commonly express anxiety: *dissociation and personal depreciation*, corresponding to Kubler-Ross's (1970) denial; *exacerbation of terror*, when normal experiences can become terrifying confrontations; and *resigned dread*, expecting a terrible disaster to befall at any moment, often immobilizing the client.

The dissociative state creates further terror for a survivor, who may literally watch the world "go flat" during periods of stress: other people acquire a distant, two-dimensional quality like actors on a television screen. This experience feeds back into her belief that she is deviant, or "crazy." There is a danger of misclassification of the client as schizophrenic or as having a dissociative disorder and of improper medication (Lundberg-Love et al., 1987; Stern & Stern, 1985).

The counselor should work with the client to learn about the protective purposes served by this dissociative state and to develop less disruptive coping techniques. To appreciate how her dysfunctional coping strategies arose in the first place and to recognize that the terrorizing experience is finally over, the client may need to return to the experiences that are causing her terror. Most likely, during the abuse the inability to escape was so overwhelming that the victim selected the only coping mechanism available: mental or emotional avoidance. She removed her mind from the situation, imagining being somewhere or someone else or thinking of the ongoing assault as unreal: "This is a play, and soon the actors will act normal again." As the client comes to see her dissociation as a learned strategy to a previously inescapable situation, she can work to replace that strategy with more appropriate patterns of response to normal stressors.

Perhaps the most difficult terror response to deal with is *terrorizing by the client* (Stern & Stern, 1985). The survivor who has learned to expect fearful outcomes may induce confrontations in order to relieve the anxiety produced by the anticipation of terror. She may "bait" others with unrealistic demands that cannot be met, and then attack them for failure. The end of a relationship, even if caused by her own action, "confirms" her belief that everyone treats her badly. Clients with these patterns should be treated as manipulative, so the therapist does not get drawn into the terrorizing cycle. (See the section on borderline symptoms in this chapter.) At the same time, the client needs a tremendous amount of structure and patience from the counselor and others in her life, so that trust can build to a point where the terror can be expressed in helpful ways.

Stern and Stern (1985) point out that counselors tend to want to make their clients "feel better," including prescribing medication to reduce or mask anxiety symptoms. Instead, terrorized clients need help in getting in touch with their real feelings and a reliable base of reality from which to explore the regions that frighten them. Because the terrorized person is so fragile during this process, it is essential that the primary counselor be a responsible professional and that medication not be used as a substitute for effective counseling. The volume edited by Stern (1985) contains some helpful resources for guiding specific expressions of terror.

LOSS OF SELF-ESTEEM

Most psychotherapists agree that a positive and integrated sense of self is necessary for mental health. Self-esteem comes from a rewarding environment, in which activities and risks result in accomplishments and recognition. Inherent in self-esteem are a sense of personal worth and an expectation of control over the outcomes of behavior. The intentional degradation and disempowerment of sexual abuse negate both.

Self-esteem problems are often compounded by events following an incident. The evidentiary and legal processes emphasize the degrading aspects of the assault (for example, photographing the victim naked), and control is taken over by legal and medical personnel. Friends and family may impose embarrassment and isolation, further lowering the survivor's sense of self-worth.

The long-term impact of sexual abuse often depends on the person's self-esteem prior to the abuse. Clients with a high prior level of self-esteem have several advantages. (1) A history of more successful experiences helps the client to see life in a generally more positive light, and the *relative* impact of this abuse will be less, although the emotional effect may be as great. (2) An integrated sense of self is not as easily fragmented into "good" and "bad" parts, nor dissociated from the reality of the abuse. (3) A prior sense of having control over oneself enables a client to see the victimization as atypical and unjust and the fault of the assailant rather than herself. (4) An integrated sense of self indicates the client has the flexibility and the inner resources to adapt to the demands of resolution. (5) The high self-esteem client starts with a greater belief that she can succeed in this resolution effort. Intervention can thus focus on rebuilding and recapturing her former healthy self.

For the same reasons, the client whose self-esteem is initially low is likely to experience greater difficulty after abuse. Women in our culture already tend to suffer from low self-esteem (Rivers et al., 1979; Sanford & Donovan, 1984). Thus for most women clients an important part of the therapeutic process is building, for the first time, a healthy sense of self-esteem. Low self-esteem may be a consequence of ongoing negative messages from a parent, partner, or coworker. Extremely low self-esteem may indicate a prior history of abuse (Walker, 1984). When low preexisting self-esteem is evident in a client, counselors should be prepared to deal with unsupportive family or friends and with earlier unresolved abusive experiences.

To promote self-esteem, the client needs a sense of having control throughout the counseling process, and a progressive sense of success dealing with other problems, however small. The counselor should help the client build a rewarding environment of support and encouragement, inside and outside the therapy setting. Herman (1981) found that for incest victims, support from mothers was important to the development of self-esteem, and we have noted a similar importance for support within intimate relationships. Thus conjoint or family therapy to improve mother-daughter and other close relationships may be helpful.

Sanford and Donovan's (1984) *Women and Self-Esteem* can serve any client with self-esteem issues, either as a self-help book or as readings assigned during counseling. This easy-to-read, engaging book covers the social reasons for low self-esteem among women and normalizes those feelings. Based largely on cognitive-behavioral approaches, Sanford and Donovan provide a set of homework exercises designed to stop negative thoughts and unrealistic expectations, develop more healthy emotional interpretations and expressions, and build a more healthy self-esteem. Specific chapters on relationships, motherhood, work, depression, body image, and sexuality may be utilized as bibliotherapy at appropriate times during the counseling process.

CONTROL ISSUES

The feeling of being utterly unable to predict or control events is another nearly universal trauma experience. One common response is a generalized paralysis, a continuing helplessness that affects other realms of life: "If ultimately I have no control, why bother?" Such learned helplessness increases vulnerability to subsequent victimization. A second common response is to attempt to compensate for loss of predictability by increasing control over future events. Some survivors move to a safer residence or change jobs. Some develop new strengths: a harassment survivor goes to law school and becomes a civil rights lawyer; an incest survivor becomes a public speaker on the topic.

Other survivors adopt less healthy resolutions, maximizing control over themselves through strict behavioral regimens ("I won't date again") or emotional denial ("I won't ever love anyone again") or compensating with control over others. Manipulative behaviors are common in clients raised in dysfunctional families, particularly when the abuser has taught or modeled manipulation. Incest histories are overrepresented in clients with symptoms of a borderline personality (Barnard & Hirsch, 1985) and multiple personalities (Chance, 1986). Occasionally, angry survivors attempt to regain a sense of control by victimizing others.

Learned Helplessness

Seligman (1975) induced a reaction of "helplessness"—the loss of all motivation to attempt escape—in lab animals subjected to repeated unavoidable shocks. A similar reaction has been observed in survivors of multiple abuses, such as incest, battering, or marital rape (Peterson & Seligman, 1983; Walker, 1984), of a single severe trauma such as a violent rape, or of ongoing exposure to a system that supports victimization such as harassment among unsympathetic coworkers. After sexual abuse, helplessness takes various forms: (1) a general passivity in threatening situations, based on the feeling that one is not strong enough to overcome others' power; (2) a belief that one is a victim by nature, as in a religiously committed incest victim who blames her plight on "evil" within herself; (3) a tolerance of sexual exploitation by males because of their nature as "animals," as "hormonally driven"; or (4) a resigned sense that "I can't beat society," that rape and violence are inescapable in our culture.

Learned helplessness can generalize to a variety of situations, including those over which the survivor previously felt she had control. Helplessness increases vulnerability to subsequent abuse, as survivors believe they are unable to prevent or escape it. A frequent result is depression (Seligman, 1975). Thus learned helplessness must be seen as a potentially life-threatening pattern.

Seligman found that he had to physically drag his helpless animals through an escape route before their passivity was overcome, but voluntary control behaviors then usually reappeared. Walker (1979, 1984) has provided a look into perhaps the clearest human treatment analogy, the battered wife. Walker recommends giving immediate control to a client in a violent relationship by getting her physically removed from the source of her helplessness. Once physically safe, counseling can focus on teaching "escape competence" by showing the client ways to control her life. NiCarthy's (1982) *Getting Free* offers helpful techniques with empowering exercises for leaving an abusive relationship.

Seligman and his colleagues also observed that the interpretation a person applied to her or his misfortune affected the development of learned helplessness (Abramson et al., 1978; Peterson & Seligman, 1984). The helpless client is most likely to attribute misfortune to internal causes ("I should have known better than to stay late at the office"), to see her misfortune as a stable trait ("I had this problem in my last job, I always give out these messages"), or to generalize her plight to global circumstances ("I will never be able to find a harassment-free job"). The client's explanatory style should thus be targeted for intervention, altering the interpretation in order to alter or prevent feelings of helplessness. The intervention should stress the abuser's responsibility for his abusing action, the victimization experience as a temporary state not caused by personal traits, and a recognition that less abusive situations or people do exist ("This doesn't happen in every office, I just had two unfortunate experiences"). In addition, the helpless client often needs to develop a personally satisfying set of goals for the future. The therapist may need to model successful behavior-consequence relationships—positive confirmation when the client reaches out to assist another person or assert herself in an appropriate setting—in order to recognize and appreciate the predictability that comes with a normal environment.

Patterns of helpless behavior that are likely to enhance vulnerability, such as withdrawal or silence about abuse, should be targeted for active change through specific techniques for regaining control of a situation (for example, in harassment, providing instructions for filing a complaint and assistance in writing a letter). Viewing patterns of helplessness in others, through support groups or volunteer work in a shelter agency, can be helpful in recognizing one's own patterns. However, the counselor must avoid sending a message that the client's behavior is causing the abuse.

Emotional Denial

Excessive control over oneself often results when the fear and pain of sexual abuse are too devastating to experience directly. Woititz (1983) has described self-controlling reactions among adult children of alcoholics that are similar to patterns seen in abuse victims, particularly among incest survivors who have been raised in uncontrollable, often alcoholic, environments: (1) lying to themselves and others about their real feelings, denying pain or problems; (2) judging themselves harshly; (3) "[taking] themselves very seriously, [and having] difficulty having fun" (p. 37); and (4) overreacting to situations that they perceive as out of their control. Eventually, many clients run out of ways to stop the emotional pain, sometimes seeking help only because they feel they are "losing control.'' Some perceive only one option: exercising the ultimate self-control of suicide.

Self-controlling patterns must be identified and appreciated as responses to the prior abusive situation. Clients who have adopted a defensive posture of denying feelings need to reexperience their emotions in a safe environment; this is much like the experience of discovering and expressing rage described earlier in this chapter. Therapists may use a range of techniques to elicit these emotions, but with two requirements: the client must never be left without support and ''safety'' while expressing them, and the client must never be forced into the experience. Losing control to the therapist may be experienced as another abuse.

Clients also need to see how excessive control has been, or might be, destructive. Although initially frightening, learning how to be less controlled can be a very positive experience. For many, it is not easy to become less rigid, judgmental, and intolerant of change, for these qualities all serve protective functions. It is best to start with minor changes, agreed upon in advance, such as staying in bed an extra few minutes on Sunday morning or taking a trip that has not been planned. The client can be encouraged to admit to minor errors without becoming angry at herself. Each change can be noted and reinforced by discussions of new feelings of self-tolerance, acceptance, and self-love.

Controlling Others

Manipulative patterns are frequently learned from dysfunctional family patterns of dishonesty, indirect control, and unpredictability. For the abuse survivor, manipulation takes on special importance as a means of gaining back some predictability through controlling others. While manipulative behaviors may serve a protective function in the disordered family environment, they interfere with the development of new healthy relationships. They also consume an extraordinary amount of energy, from the manipulator who must figure out others' potential responses before each of her own actions, and from others who are caught up in the cycle of trying to accommodate her needs.

A manipulative client will often attempt to use the same tactics in the counseling relationship, to control the counselor through excessive demands (''My last counselor talked to me whenever I called''), guilt (''You're just like my father; I knew I couldn't trust you'') or blaming (''This is all your fault for telling me to change''). When manipulative patterns are recognized, they must be confronted by the counselor, in the context of acceptance and understanding. An agreement to try to change the behavior may be a condition of continuing the therapy. In return, the client needs an open and honest environment in which the consequences of behavior are direct and predictable, and a good model of nonmanipulative behaviors on the part of the counselor. The client may need to look at her history of being manipulated by others in order to understand that these control patterns have been learned, and that they can be unlearned and replaced.

If the client's social environment outside of therapy continues to be manipulative, as is often the case with younger clients who live at home, or if she continues contact with parents or others who treat her in a manipulative way, she can learn how to recognize and respond to manipulative behaviors in others. As she begins to differentiate herself from that environment, she may choose to leave or to continue the relationships with a reduced emotional investment when manipulation is being used.

Borderline Symptoms

According to the American Psychiatric Association (1987) *Diagnostic and Statistical Manual of Mental Disorders*, 3rd ed., rev. (DSM-IIIR), Borderline Personality Disorder is a diagnosis characterized by emotionality, chaotic relationships, excessive fear of being alone, identity diffusion and problems with interpersonal boundaries, impulsiveness, and/or suicidal behaviors. Borderline symptoms seem to be prevalent among incest victims and other individuals with disturbed family backgrounds (Barnard & Hirsch, 1985; Courtois, 1988), supporting an interpretation of these behaviors as a desperate effort to maintain control.

Borderline clients can be extremely manipulative, attractive, interesting, and difficult to treat and are likely to form intense dependencies on their counselor, as they have with others in their lives. Any variation on the part of the therapist, such as changing an appointment or taking a vacation, may be perceived as abandonment and may precipitate a crisis or anger reaction. Linehan (1987) has observed five common behavior patterns among her borderline clients: emotional vulnerability, feeling as if one's life is an open wound; self-hate and self-rejection; giving the appearance of being highly competent while experiencing feelings of incompetence and anger at having to live up to others' standards; learned helplessness and a passivity toward change; and a "crisis-of-the-week" orientation to life, a pattern of overreacting to less serious problems following multiple overwhelming emergencies.

Linehan (1987) offers a dialectic group therapy model for borderline clients. Group members are given explicit information, data, and theories about characteristic symptoms of the disorder and about group process. Expectations for the therapist and all group members are structured and upheld, and reasons for violations are explored openly. The therapist may alternately serve as a teacher, consultant, soundboard for reality testing, source of reinforcement, or model. Clients work on skills for interpersonal communication, modulating emotional reactions, and accepting and tolerating distress. Throughout, the therapist offers validation of each client's pain and suffering, concrete strategies for improving relationships and solving problems, and instruction and modeling of more appropriate relationships. Kroll (1988) discusses case studies and individual treatment approaches.

The therapist working with borderline clients must be prepared to deal calmly, openly, and directly with problematic client patterns such as inappropriate demands, suicidal behaviors, or manipulative attempts. Therapist boundaries must be set from the beginning and maintained.

Elizabeth, an attractive and charming young woman, came to see Dr. Wilson because her first therapist "wasn't any help." With probing, she confided that she had carried a knife into therapy several times. The source of her anger was her therapist's request to cut down on the number of evening phone calls.

Dr. Wilson set up the following conditions for working with her: no phone calls unless it was indeed an emergency; overwhelming emotional upsets precipitating a potential for suicide would result in her being taken to the hospital emergency room; and no weapons or drugs would be tolerated. During her next session, the fact emerged that Elizabeth had been forced to sleep with her parents for the first eight years of her life.

Multiple Personality Disorder

A more severe way of achieving control over the trauma and fear of repeated sexual abuse is to dissociate into more than one personality. Multiple Personality Disorder is less frequent than other disorders, but is more difficult to diagnose and to treat. The DSM-IIIR defines Multiple Personality Disorder as

the existence within the person of two or more distinct personalities or personality states (each with its own relatively enduring pattern of perceiving, relating to, and thinking about the environment and self). At least two of these personalities or personality states recurrently take full control of the person's behavior (p. 272).

These personalities, from two to over twenty in number, may begin in childhood and have "varying degrees of distinctness and complexity, many with different habits, values, and ways of expressing themselves" (Courtois, 1988, p. 156). Although they begin as protective mechanisms to avoid pain, they may become disinhibiting mechanisms to allow the individual to commit aggressive or sexual behaviors that she or he would not ordinarily act upon.

Courtois (1988) suggests that a client who experiences blackouts, time distortions, memory lapses, or other forms of amnesia may have Multiple Personality Disorder, and she offers a series of questions to assist in diagnosis. Treatment generally proceeds slowly, as the various personalities are located and identified and the client is helped to recognize the personality dissociation as a coping strategy. Braun (1986) offers approaches to treating clients with multiple personalities.

Abusive Control

A history of sexual abuse is found among a substantial proportion of men and women who sexually abuse others, especially among men (Courtois, 1988; Groth, 1979; Petrovich & Templer, 1984). Some survivors have told of fantasies of forcing sex on others. While no causal relationship has been clearly identified, some abusive fantasies or behaviors may be another desperate form of trying to acquire control over their own frightening memories. However, it is a form with serious consequences, for the abusers and for their victims.

The counselor working with an abusive client must report any act of abuse already committed against a child to the appropriate child protective agency and inform the client of that responsibility even though it may cause the client to leave therapy. The lines of responsibility for reporting a client who confesses desires to abuse, but has not acted on them, are less clear and still under debate, but if a client names a target and has a specific plan in mind, the therapist may be required to warn the target and/or the police. See Beck's (1985) discussion of the *Tarassoff v. Regents of the University of California* Supreme Court decision regarding the therapist's duty to warn. Thus the facts of the case must be gathered carefully and the legal aspects reviewed and strictly observed, prior to engaging in long-term therapy with a confessed abuser. Such intervention is beyond the scope of this book, but helpful resources may be found in Groth (1979) and Abel et al. (1976).

If the client suffers from a more general feeling that she or he has the potential for abusing, the first step is to help the client recognize that she or he is already displaying a strong ability and will to control such actions, by seeking counseling. Other ways in which clients demonstrate control in their lives can be reviewed, following a model developed for counseling men who batter their wives.[4] For example, men who attribute their interpersonal violence to uncontrollable anger are helped to see that "you didn't hit your boss, you waited until you got home and hit your wife, so you can control your anger." Second, the client needs to believe that sexual abuse is harmful, and that his target will suffer—as he has suffered from his own abuse. Achieving such empathy for the victim is especially difficult for men who have repressed their own emotions, so finding and expressing feelings of pain may be necessary. For male clients who are potentially abusive, beliefs that men must be sexually dominant in order to be masculine, and that women and children are permissible targets of hostility, must be a focus of change.

BODY IMAGE PROBLEMS

Many survivors feel differently about their bodies after sexual abuse. Some attribute the abuse to an attractive or seductive appearance. In an effort to make themselves less likely targets in the future, they may gain weight, change their style of dressing, or cease to keep themselves clean. Changes in body image may also appear: loss of clear personal boundaries (Rowan & Rowan, 1984), hate and disgust over sexual body parts (Swink & Leveille, 1986), and distortions in self-perceptions, which at their most severe involve anorexia or bulimia. Others may overeat or indulge in compulsive behaviors, in an effort to fill the emotional void they experience (Swink & Leveille, 1986).

Any client with body image problems needs to understand that physical appearance does not cause or prevent sexual abuse, so that body issues can be worked on outside the context of fear. Clients with unclear or distorted body images benefit from appropriate physical exercise, including karate, weightlifting, dance, or any other activity that demands attention to body parts and boundaries. These exercises carry an important additional benefit of increasing physical strength and confidence in overcoming subsequent physical force, and they can counteract depression.

Eating patterns often change after sexual abuse. Lundberg-Love (1987) reported that one-half of her incest survivor clients were overweight, while others report a high proportion of incest survivors with bulimia or anorexia (Swink & Leveille, 1986). The tendency toward eating problems is already marked among women, especially young women. A majority of college women express dissatisfaction with their weight or figure (Douty et al., 1974), and preoccupation with dieting continues throughout the lives of most women. The sexy body shape idealized in the media and fashion industry is ironically often used as an excuse for sexual assault: "He couldn't help himself, her body turned him on!" Survivors of sexual abuse may experience a severe distortion of their own body image, as they seek to avoid looking thin or sexy, hating their bodies while being encouraged by society to emulate the sexy body type.

The overweight client who is unhappy with her weight may need assistance not only in losing weight through a health-oriented program, but also in examining the causes of her weight gain and the social factors that are reinforcing her behavior (Brown, 1987; Orbach, 1978). Discriminatory treatment and self-esteem are important issues for overweight clients to resolve.

Weight loss among anorexics and compulsive purging among bulimics can constitute serious dangers to health, necessitating hospitalization. However, as with overweight clients, effective treatment must go beyond medical attention and diet. Wooley and Wooley (1980) argue for a comprehensive, integrated therapeutic program that deals with the client's sense of control over herself as well as her diet. Brown (1987), Orbach (1978), and Wooley and Wooley (1980), while differing in specific approaches, all stress the importance of considering self-esteem, social expectations and attitudes towards "fat" women, and cultural images of women and beauty in treating the woman client with body image distortions. Boskind-Lodahl (1976) offers a group treatment approach to anorexia/bulimia that explicitly incorporates feminist consciousness raising.

INTIMACY AND SEXUALITY PROBLEMS

Sexual abuse survivors experience a range of disruptions in relationships with parents, siblings, and partners. General anxiety or confusion leave many unable to deal with the emotional demands of relationships. Disruptions may be heightened by preexisting problems in relationships, such as poor communication or a lack of concern. Fear and rejection of sexual contact are common, as the survivor experiences flashbacks of terror or panics over a loss of control (Warner, 1980). It is common for survivors to withdraw from sexual relationships, even with supportive partners, for weeks or months after an abusive sexual experience. When they do return to intimacy, it is often with hesitation.

Ellen, a widow, was raped on a date five years ago. For the past year, she has been seeing a kind, gentle man who himself was sexually abused as a child. She describes their relationship as "a strange dance with intimacy—when I move forward, he moves backwards. I step back when he moves in." They are in therapy together, but they are both cautious.[5]

When the first sexual experience is abusive, or when love has always been defined by sex, as often occurs in incest, the impact is more pervasive. Sexual abuse may disrupt normal developmental tasks such as acquiring an adult body image, resolving confusion about sexual orientation, coping with shame and guilt over sexual thoughts, and finding a satisfying and responsible sexuality (Rowan & Rowan, 1984). Intimacy, love, and sexuality can become confused, in this and subsequent relationships. The survivor who grows up to expect abuse needs to learn alternatives to victimization.

Assessment of disruption of these areas should include the client's

1. History of intimate relationships, including family members, partners, and close friends. Successful prior experiences with intimacy provide a base from which to discriminate good from abusive relationships and a potential goal for post-abuse recovery. Clients without satisfying past relationships will have to formulate new goals.
2. Current intimate relationships, assessed for quality and level of intimacy. If a client is in an ongoing relationship, the partner's level of support and willingness to help or participate will be important in the resolution process.
3. Specific symptoms of disruption. Commonly affected are concepts of intimacy and sexuality, current relationships, sexual self-image, and sexual function. Techniques for dealing with these specific symptoms follow.

Concepts of Intimacy

With a parent, sibling, friend, or lover, an ideal relationship would include emotional honesty, trust, and mutual respect. Adult relationships would share equal power and responsibility; sexual relationships would be fulfilling for both partners. When prior relationships have been manipulative, untrustworthy, unbalanced in power, or sexually abusive, however, adult relationships may mirror these histories. Some survivors accept powerlessness or abuse in relationships as normal; some develop unrealistic ideals, refusing to tolerate any deviation from perfection in others. When love has only been available through sex and submission, the survivor may use sexuality to acquire or maintain intimacy, without discretion. Children abused by a parent are especially vulnerable to this confusion, because their experience with alternate models of intimacy without sexuality is limited.

Cognitive restructuring can help the client to develop new concepts of intimacy, both ideal and realistic, and new goals for relationships. A caring counselor can provide feedback for intimate relationships even when a client lacks other intimates, as well as clarification of unacceptable behaviors for future relationships. The counselor should offer a relationship in which the client can "test out" new concepts of intimacy without fear of sexual abuse or betrayal.

The client may try to enact a confused concept of intimacy in the counselor—client relationship. She may attempt seduction or act out sexually during the counseling process, or she may assume that the therapist—like others—wants sex, and she may become confused if a sexual demand is not made. The transference that normally develops during the therapy process can thus be either an opportunity for the client to develop a new model of trust and intimacy without sex or an opportunity for further abuse. Providing a healthy model of a nonsexual intimate relationship must be the only option for the counselor. In addition to being ethically unacceptable, a therapist who responds to sexual vulnerability by engaging in a sexual relationship reinforces the client's confusion between sex and love and leads to more complicated and difficult problems in future resolution attempts.

Relationships

The ability to resolve problems in existing intimate relationships depends to a great extent on the willingness of both parties to participate, although a partner's refusal to participate may signify a direction the problem-solving should take. Miller and Williams (1984) recommend joint therapy for couples whenever possible. As with any couple, specific concerns and dissatisfactions must be identified. Next, the counselor should help the clients distinguish problems associated with the abusive trauma (e.g., withdrawal of affection) from longer-standing patterns in the relationship. Postabuse problems are likely to diminish as the client and her partner (or parent or friend) gain greater appreciation of normal stress reactions, the amount of time required to overcome a trauma (at least a year in most cases), and each other's responses to the abuse. In order to achieve such understanding, the counselor may have to teach better and more direct communication skills. Suggestions for partners and family members are found in Chapter Appendix 8B.

If problems have preabuse origins, long-term family or marital therapy may be called for. Women frequently need assertiveness skills, while their male partners need help with opening up and sharing their emotional responses (Carlson, 1981, 1988). Some relationships may be too severely disrupted to continue, particularly when others refuse to participate. In these cases, clients need to work on decisions about the future of the relationship and to prepare for the adjustments created by ending it.

When physical or emotional abuse within a marriage or other ongoing relationship is detected, the counselor is obligated to label the relationship as abusive and to pursue alternatives to the existing pattern. If violence has occurred and the client is in physical danger, the situation should be treated as a crisis and the client should be removed from the danger as rapidly as possible.[6] Patience is essential in guiding clients to emotional resolutions of abusive relationships.

Sexual Self-Image

Whether or not a client is sexually active at the time of sexual abuse, the experience may affect her self-image with respect to sexuality. This image, in turn, may cause extremes in subsequent sexual behavior. Postabuse sexual patterns often include asexuality, promiscuity, and submissiveness in sexual relationships, or some combination thereof. For example, after her acquaintance rape experience, Donna alternated between complete avoidance of physical contact (so she would not be seen as "teasing") and undiscriminating promiscuity (believing rape "couldn't happen" if sex was already available). Unpleasant postabuse sexual experiences are often reported by these clients, along with guilt or self-hate for engaging in these relationships.

The connection between sexual patterns and self-image should be made explicit, preferably through the client's own self-discovery process. Then, the client needs to formulate a healthy ideal for future sexuality, including new goals for sexual and nonsexual relationships. Unproductive or unrewarding relationships and the feelings they cause can serve as learning experiences for these redefined goals and ideals. Training in assertive techniques for taking charge of oneself in relationships is frequently helpful.

It is not unusual for children to enjoy some physical pleasure during sexual contact, although they are usually very frightened by the abuser. The resulting mixture of pleasure and shame may affect adult sexuality. These clients need to recognize that their feelings of pleasure were normal and did not lead to or cause the exploitation. Therapy should separate the abusive from the sexual components of the abuse and focus on the former. Similar problems may arise with adult victims. Women often find they lubricate vaginally during sexual penetration, a response they have always associated with sexual arousal rather than with the body's protective system. Some abusers force their victims (particularly males) to have an orgasm, raising a complex set of emotional self-doubts. Common sexual myths need to be dispelled with these clients, who must be reassured that pleasure is *not* synonymous with sexual response and that erections, lubrication, and other responses *can* occur without pleasure. Once clients appreciate that, they are better able to focus on the violence of the abuse and to overcome feelings of guilt and complicity.

Some clients experience confusion over sexual orientation, particularly after same-sex abuse. Baisden (1971) noted that child sexual abuse survivors frequently experience problems accepting their sexuality, regardless of their orientation. Whether the client is heterosexual, lesbian, gay, or bisexual, the counseling goal must be the client's clarity and comfort with self-definition.

"Curing" or changing sexual orientation should never be the goal and should never be attempted. A bisexual client should not be asked to redefine herself or himself as heterosexual or homosexual, or be treated as "confused." When confusion or concerns about sexual orientation are expressed by the client, possible reasons from both within and outside the context of the sexual abuse should be explored. Current concerns (e.g., dissatisfaction with relationships) should be separated from abuse issues and worked on independently. Frequently misconceptions, such as the psychoanalytic idea that early same-sex experiences cause homosexuality, have caused the client's anxiety, and correction of these myths is a primary step toward resolution. Further discussion of these issues is found in Chapter 10.

Sexual Dysfunction

Sexual relationships are subject to extensive disruption after sexual abuse. Burgess and Holmstrom (1979) found that two-thirds of the rape survivors they interviewed experienced sexual difficulties immediately after their assault; a year later, more than half continued to experience sexual difficulties (Nadelson, 1982). Up to 40 percent of rape survivors may have chronic sexual dysfunction (Becker et al., 1982; Burgess & Holmstrom, 1979). These dysfunctions occur even in loving, supportive partnerships.

Several kinds of dysfunctional sexual responses are commonly observed after abuse (Rowan & Rowan, 1984): flashbacks or panic attacks during sex; pain, discomfort, or vaginismus (tightening of vaginal muscles); and anorgasmia, the inability to experience orgasm. Sprei and Courtois (1988) discuss disorders of desire (inhibition and aversion) and of arousal. Clients presenting with physical pain should be referred for a physical examination by a competent physician, since they may be suffering from an infection or internal damage such as a tear in the vaginal wall. (See Chapter 5.) The client's sexual history is important to determining whether the dysfunction is specific to the abusive experience or a longer-standing problem. For example, a client may never have experienced orgasm because of inexperienced or uncaring partners. (See Kaplan, 1974; 1979.) Some dysfunctions, particularly flashbacks, can be controlled by teaching the client relaxation techniques and by systematic substitution of positive images of the loving partner as alternatives to frightening images. The partner's patience and help are essential in overcoming these terrifying intrusions.

Sexual dysfunctions such as vaginismus or anorgasmia may require more intensive intervention. Becker and Skinner (1984) have described a behavioral therapy that has been quite successful with sexually abused clients. Their ten-week program includes ways to help the client develop control over the fear and anxiety that are interfering with sexual pleasure. Nichols (1987) discusses sex therapy with lesbians.

ROLE OF RELIGION

Clients are likely to come into psychotherapy with a set of religious beliefs. These beliefs may be unique and idiosyncratic, but they nevertheless help shape the survivor's view of a healthy personality and may influence the therapy process. In most cases, the client's beliefs and faith in a higher power are integrated in a healthy way into a sense of personal meaning. However, there are some important issues to consider with the religiously raised or committed client, issues made especially urgent by sexual abuse.

Therapy is often perceived as being in conflict with religious belief: many religions teach that clients should "place their problems in God's hands" rather than looking inward for sources of strength. Some survivors who have sought help from clergy or other religious leaders have only been told to pray (sometimes for forgiveness, sometimes for the abuser), which for many of them is not sufficient (Sargent, in press). Some religious leaders (and followers) discourage therapy, viewing it as denial of faith. If possible, a supportive individual should be found within the religious group, who can serve as a helpful adjunct to therapy by talking with the client about strengthening her belief system in conjunction with developing a healthier sense of self.

When religious leaders or beliefs are not helpful, the client may need to resolve her feelings about therapy as an alternative. In these cases the client is likely to experience conflict and guilt and may be ostracized by her church-based support group. The counselor should be sensitive to the possibility of these conflicts in the initial assessment of the client's relationships. It is often sufficient to help the client recognize that the outcomes and benefits of therapy do not have to conflict with religious beliefs and in fact can strengthen them.

In the worst case, resolving religious conflicts may involve an active change in the client's beliefs, or some form of confrontation with the client's church or religious support group. Such a change is not to be taken lightly, as the religious beliefs may form an essential part of the client's emotional life and identity. Furthermore, the counselor must be absolutely convinced that a change is in the best interests of the client and not motivated by the counselor's own belief systems. In these situations the counselor should proceed cautiously and seek more information from individuals who know about the particular religion or group. Fundamentalists Anonymous can offer resources and a support group for clients attempting to resolve negative experiences with religions.

From the client's perspective, perhaps the most common religious issue is a loss of an earlier faith that being faithful and "good" would protect the individual from others' hate. This issue is similar to the destruction of nonreligious belief systems described in Chapter 2 and necessitates a change in belief systems if it is to be resolved satisfactorily. This loss of faith can be a frightening crisis and may involve forms of grief. As with other existential crises, the client should be allowed to examine these doubts without judgment and assured that it is normal to raise such questions. It is helpful to work toward a more mature belief system, in which simple concepts of "good-bad" are replaced by a more complex view of a world in which others' actions cannot be controlled. The book *When Bad Things Happen to Good People* (Kushner, 1981) can be very helpful to a client experiencing these doubts.

A related issue arises when the religion has taught the client that individuals who act in bad ways are motivated by some deep source of evil. Clients who have been raised in some religions, whether currently practicing them or not, may adopt a religion-based shame ("I did something to make God mad"). The client seeking meaning after sexual abuse may create a link to past "sins"— this is punishment for having an abortion, being angry at her mother, not going to church. Clients exhibiting these forms of self-blame will need to explore their concepts of good and evil, causality, and God (or other higher power) as a source of punishment. It is helpful to stress the "evil" (using the client's terms) of the abuser, shifting accusations of sin and fantasies of punishment from the client to the abuser.

A third, very powerful issue for incest victims is the links between God and father, Jesus and brother. Sargent (in press) and Weiner (1989) have discussed the powerful effect that images of God as an omnipotent father have on their incestuously abused clients. The impact of this image may be exaggerated by associations of good with the Virgin Mary. Religion itself becomes a frightening experience, overwhelming the victim with feelings of powerlessness and abandonment. Some survivors create their own comforting image of God (including maternal images); others reject religious images altogether. The client who wishes to resolve religious beliefs can review writings that offer alternative images and pursue active analyses of gender bias in traditional images. Above all, she must be helped to trust her own image and judgment (Sargent, in press).

SELF-DESTRUCTIVE BEHAVIORS

The prevalence of incest and other sexual abuse of teens and young adults who are runaways, prostitutes, and drug and alcohol abusers is estimated to be from 40 to over 80 percent (Bianco, 1984; James & Meyerding 1977: Weber, 1977; Weisberg, 1984). Reports of survivors who inflict serious physical harm on themselves, directly through self-mutilation and indirectly through eating disorders or medical neglect, and of survivors who later attempt suicide, provide additional evidence that sexual abuse creates a serious potential for self-destructive behaviors.

Teenage Runaways and Prostitution

While some interpret running away during teen years as "acting out" in rebellion against parents (especially the mother), the sexually and physically abusive family histories of these children suggest other reasons (Silbert & Pines, 1981). Running away may be a desperate escape attempt rather than a rebellion, and prostitution may be the only way to survive on the streets (Weisberg, 1984). By the time they reach the street, these children's bodies and psyches have already been so objectified and degraded that prostitution does not seem very shocking or foreign.

The immediate needs of these clients are safety (sometimes from violent pimps), shelter, medical attention, and treatment for drug or alcohol abuse. With the high rates of AIDS among teen prostitutes, the possibility of HIV infection must be considered, although testing must only be done at the client's request and in a confidential manner. Because of their well-learned lack of trust for adults and the inability of most child protective systems to care for them adequately, intervention with underaged runaways and prostitutes is difficult. These are the most vulnerable people in our system to further abuse, even from the adults assigned to help them. In addition, anger at an unfair world sometimes spills over into antisocial acts, such as stealing or physical violence. Thus intervention beyond immediate needs must involve a network of services, therapy (including family therapy if the client returns home), and support (see Silbert & Pines, 1981; Weisberg, 1984). In spite of the depressing picture painted here, some victims survive. Kara, a runaway at age twelve and a heroin addict at age sixteen, is now happily married to a minister and is an effective, nonabusive mother and child care worker.

Alcohol and Other Drug Abuse

Many survivors have alcohol and drug dependency patterns modeled in their troubled families, and some have been encouraged to drink or take drugs by their abusers as a way of preventing effective protest.

Dan started hitting his father's "booze cabinet" when he was nine, replacing vodka with water so his father wouldn't notice. By his thirties, a career military man, he was "just like his father," drinking heavily and occasionally beating his wife. Eventually he received alcohol treatment and then entered counseling. Only then could he face his fear and pleasure at his father's violent treatment of his mother.

Alcohol and drug treatment often require a period of inpatient detoxification, followed by highly structured ongoing support through groups like Alchoholics Anonymous or Narcotics Anonymous, and counseling. Local resources, including treatment facilities, should be contacted on behalf of substance-troubled clients. Other helpful information and perspectives are found in Willoughby (1979) and Woititz (1983).

Suicidal Threats and Behaviors

Perhaps the most deadly mistake made with youth who talk about suicide is failing to take them seriously, attributing their talk to adolescent "hormones."

When anyone, particularly a teenager, attempts or discusses suicide, the possibility of sexual abuse should be explored with that person. The counselor-client relationship must be honest and direct. Many counselors insist on developing a strict contract with their client, which includes permission to call when suicidal feelings emerge, in exchange for a promise not to attempt suicide for a specified period of time.

Suicide threats and unsuccessful attempts sometimes become a way of reaching out for help. While each threat must be respected for its potentiality, the client needs strict contractual guidelines for what to expect from the counselor, even in an emergency—she must know that any threat will be taken seriously and that the proper intervention will be summoned (e.g., calling emergency medical services). Above all, therapists are advised not to allow suicidal clients to become dependent entirely on them, especially not for emergency interventions. Although initially it is emotionally gratifying to feel one is saving a client's life, the long-term drain of frequent threats is devastating even to the accomplished professional. Sometimes even the most caring efforts eventually fail.

Cecelia called a rape crisis center saying she had been raped and was considering suicide. Two volunteers were immediately dispatched, and after a few hours she said she had changed her mind. They gave her their phone numbers and referred her to a therapist, who also gave her his home phone number for emergency use. Soon she was calling all three people for an hour or more at least once a day. For the next two years, when they tried to cut down on the length or frequency of her calls she would talk about her desperate feelings of suicide or mutilate herself. They began to suspect her rape story, since the details changed several times, but felt there was a sexually abusive history. During a holiday weekend, she could not reach any of the three by phone and committed suicide by slitting her wrists. After her death, Cecelia's brother confessed to sexually abusing her repeatedly during her childhood and giving her drugs to keep her quiet.

Therapists, crisis workers, or friends caught up in this type of difficulty need to seek professional consultation to help them decide how and where to set limits and to help resolve feelings about the client's actions should a suicide attempt succeed.

NOTES

1. Clients looking for parental protectiveness may seek to fill their emotional void with a temporary dependence on their therapist. While offering support, the counselor must also set clear limits on roles.

2. We have observed male therapists who take on the task of providing a model of a ''healthy'' relationship for their own ego gratification. Thus, for example, the older man who behaves as a charming father figure (i.e., acts seductively) because he wants his incest client to ''trust him not to go all the way'' may do more harm than good, even in the absence of physical contact. The client is being asked to conform to his needs rather than her own, replicating the incest power dynamic.

3. Clinics specializing in agoraphobia and panic attacks have developed across the

United States, and support groups are available in many places. The agoraphobic client should be assisted in finding both. Helpful information is found in Brehony (1987) and from the Phobia Society of America, 133 Rollins Ave., Suite 4B, Rockville, MD 20852.

4. Based on the models developed by Brother to Brother (Providence, RI) and Emerge (Cambridge, Mass.), men's organizations that are dedicated to ending violence against women, which run therapy groups for battering husbands.

5. From interviews by Linda O'Malley, University of Rhode Island, 1985.

6. Local battered women's resources should be contacted for helping the client with shelter, legal advice, and support.

RECOMMENDED READINGS

Bass, E., & Davis, L. *The Courage to Heal: A Guide for Women Survivors of Child Sexual Abuse.* New York: Harper & Row, 1986.
Sanford, L. T., & Donovan, M. E. *Women and Self-Esteem.* New York: Penguin, 1984.
Sgroi, S. M. *Vulnerable Populations: Evaluation and Treatment of Sexually Abused Children, Adult Survivors, and Mentally Retarded Adults.* Vol. 1. Lexington, Mass.: Lexington Books, 1988.

CHAPTER APPENDIX 8A: DEALING WITH LOSS OF FAMILY

A flexible approach is essential in replacing or rebuilding the bonds normally found within a healthy family. The client may need to change the definition of family and the definition of her own role within a family dynamic. One helpful approach is to evaluate each relationship not in terms of how good the other person seems to be, but in terms of how good the client feels about herself when she is with that other person. Many women, particularly those from dysfunctional families, have never thought of themselves in these terms. Other options the client can explore are as follows:

1. The familial bonding can be spread out among different friends, so that no one person is over-whelmed by the client's dependency needs. This requires the client to join social activities and to reach out and become a friend first. For example, the client may give a party, inviting friends and coworkers, and form a network with those who respond.

2. A social group, such as a church or an organization like Parents without Partners, can become a consistent source of bonding, through regular meetings and identification with common goals. The individual must be strong enough, however, to maintain a sense of self within the group. Absolute obedience or overidentification with any group can be dangerous, especially for the low self-esteem client.

3. A new family group can be created. Adults from disrupted childhoods often devote special attention to providing a healthy environment for their own partner and children, replacing the family bonds they never had. Healthy alternatives to traditional family structure may also be considered; for example, a group of friends can deliberately decide to become a family and share a house.

4. Older relatives or friends can fill the abandoned roles. One woman, moving after a divorce, found that her new landlord and landlady were terrific substitute grandparents for her children; they in turn found the child and grandchildren they never had. Another woman, who had moved to another state after her divorce, began what continue to be treasured annual traditions by inviting other singles and people who couldn't be with their original families to holiday parties. The

parties are potluck and often involve work-share as well, as with a tree-trimming party at Christmastime.

These new relationships should be monitored by the client to ensure that they are mutually beneficial, helping, and trusting, with positive goals. If the client does not feel good about the relationship or does not feel good about herself within that relationship, she should end it and look to another source for her healthy new family.

CHAPTER APPENDIX 8B: HELPING FAMILY AND FRIENDS

The victim is not the only person who suffers from a sexual abuse; lovers and husbands, family members, and close friends experience a range of traumatic responses to the victimization, even years after the incident. People close to the victim react with shock, anger, confusion, disgust, and fear—as if they were themselves victims. Parents may feel guilty for failing to protect their child from abuse. Husbands, lovers, and fathers may personalize the abuse as a "win-lose" battle with another man, and seek revenge against the abuser. In even the most supportive social settings, the reactions of others may be influenced by cultural stereotypes, reactions of shame and embarrassment, and the need to deny their own vulnerability through mechanisms like blaming the victim.

Because the responses of other people in the victim's life are critical to recovery, it is important for them to get help for themselves. The victim does not need to "take care of others" while coping with her own needs. Family members or partners may need to arrange family or couples therapy or go to a rape crisis center, support group, or private counseling for their own help. Clear separation of the victim's and others' needs is essential.

Common mistakes by friends and family can be avoided. Consider these examples:

Cathy was raped in her first apartment, in another city. Her parents were very supportive and caring. Although she only came home for temporary recovery, her parents insisted that she withdraw from college and stay home, because living alone was "too dangerous." She was unable to see her boyfriend because of the distance separating them, and she lost her job. Believing they knew what was best, they screened her calls and told the rape crisis volunteer not to contact her again because they were taking good care of her.

Katie was an adult when she finally told her parents about her childhood sexual abuse by a relative. Through counseling, she was prepared to reassure her parents that it was not their fault and that she had not suffered serious harm other than her emotional pain. But she was not prepared for her mother's anger. Her mother accused her of "bringing shame to the family" and of being "weak" because she had needed counseling. To Katie, this was more evidence that she had failed her mother.

To avoid mistakes, family members, partners, and friends should follow these guidelines:

1. Never place your own needs over those of the victim. Ask her what she needs, and let her know she can inform you how and when you should respond differently.

2. Believe the victim's story. Signs of disbelief will only prevent the full story from emerging.

3. Avoid statements that appear to blame the victim—suggestions that the victim didn't respond in the best way or should have acted differently.

4. Do not add to the victim's shame. While discretion may be reasonable in some cases—for example,

not telling a frail grandmother about the abuse—efforts to silence a victim only create greater private shame. A more effective response is, "We're proud of you for being able to share your story; maybe it will help others."

5. Never demand information from the victim about the abuse. It is natural to try to find out details about the experience, but it may not be good for the victim, who may be exhausted from retelling her story to officials, or just not be ready to share her experience. She should be free to tell only what she is able to at the time.

6. Try to allow the victim to talk about the abuse when she wants to. Attempts to distract her or prevent her from talking about the experience interfere with validation for her feelings and may increase the negative consequences. Close supporters may at some point have to direct the victim to counseling.

7. Avoid overprotecting the victim. It is hard to keep from trying to prevent further harm, especially to a young person, but a balance between protection and independence must be found. Others can provide a secure base of support, from which the survivor is encouraged to move back out into the world in increasingly wide circles, but which is safe to return to in moments of fear or pain.

McEvoy and Brookings (1984) have written a helpful guide recommended for husbands, fathers, and male friends of sexual abuse survivors.

9

Counseling Models

In this chapter, model formats are offered for brief counseling interventions focused primarily on sexual abuse issues, designed to assist the counselor and the client in structuring the process toward resolution. These models are based on a blend of our own experience, the experience of other counselors, and the sexual abuse research literature. A range of options is provided, to be matched to the client's needs and the type of assault.

These models are presented without much consideration for diversity among the individual clients, because basic steps are being outlined. Individual differences and issues must not be ignored; they must be incorporated and dealt with in a manner appropriate to each client. Special issues around which these models should be adapted are discussed in Chapter 10. Long-term therapy for other problems is beyond the scope of this book. However, some of the specific tactics of Chapter 8 apply to a range of other problems and should be helpful.

The first model is designed to meet the immediate needs of a client in crisis shortly after an abusive incident. It is illustrated through two case studies: one of a student dealing with an ongoing situation of sexual harassment, which incorporates institutional as well as therapeutic intervention strategies, and one of a gang rape victim, for whom managing fear and making decisions are critical needs.

For clients in the resolution phases of recovery, five intervention models are offered. The first is an individual short-term counseling model focused on an incident of sexual abuse, again illustrated through two case studies: one of a young adult victim of a recent rape by a stranger, and one of an adult raped years earlier on a date. Adult survivors of childhood incest are the clients for the second model, an individual intervention, and the third model, an 18-week therapy group. The fourth model is an intensive short-term therapy group, demonstrated with young adults who had experienced child sexual abuse. In the fifth model, two types of support groups are described: a sexual abuse peer support group and a consciousness-raising group in which sexual abuse may be raised as one of the topics.

CRISIS INTERVENTION

Crisis intervention may be as brief as one or two sessions or may become longer-term as the client pursues a complaint or as she recognizes the myriad other issues raised by the incident. As discussed in Chapter 4, counseling immediately after a trauma is different from the more general counseling process, since the client is still in shock and has probably not had time to process emotional reactions. The best approach is to allow the client to determine her level of need for emotional counseling as issues arise and to focus initial intervention on the client's more immediate coping strategies.

One of the trauma survivor's most pressing needs is to recover a sense of normalcy and a feeling of being in control of her destiny. Thus, counseling may be viewed as a short-term, supportive, fairly intensive process focused on the effects of the traumatic incident. Meeting two times a week for two to three weeks provides a good starting framework for most crisis clients. In general, crisis counseling should focus on establishing the client's needs and helping her achieve them; evaluating the effectiveness with which others are addressing the client's needs; providing skills for coping with situations and other people; helping the client discuss the experience with parents or friends, and helping them deal with it; and assessing and handling the emotional responses. These target goals can be achieved in a set of six steps,[1] outlined in Table 9.1.

Table 9.1

Steps for Crisis Counseling

1. Establish trust.
2. Negotiate the relationship.
3. Validate experiences.
4. Process decisions:
   a. Assess situation.
   b. Review options.
   c. Develop action plan.
   d. Assess other resources.
   e. Pursue action plan.
5. Come to catharsis and temporary emotional resolution.
6. Develop future goals and plans.

Step 1: Establish Trust

This important step, discussed in detail in Chapter 3, must be compressed in a crisis situation. An important need in crisis situations is a feeling of safety, which depends in large part on the physical environment, so a first priority should be a quiet, well-protected area in which to talk. A second critical issue is personal trust. The client does not have time or energy to "shop" for the right helper. Thus it is essential that the crisis counselor be caring, skilled, and above all careful to avoid potentially damaging actions.

Step 2: Negotiate the Relationship

If the client's levels of shock and disorganization are high, or if medical and safety needs are pressing, protracted negotiations around the nature of the client-counselor relationship are not likely to be productive. However, the counselor should be clear about her role and her limits, and share them gently and firmly with the client as such issues arise. The client must also be informed of the potential roles various individuals may play in helping her, the rules and regulations that protect her, and the requirements that may be involved (e.g., other employees of a university may be required to report any incident of professor-student abuse coming to their attention).

In many crisis situations it is not necessary to engage the client in specific discussions of future sessions. The counselor can assure the client that the intervention is expected to be short-term, specifying an amount of time—perhaps six sessions—with an option to renegotiate after a few sessions. Because sexual abuse occurs as an abnormal event in a normal life, in which the clients has not anticipated needing "therapy," this process should include a discussion of the client's feelings about being in a help-seeking situation.

Step 3: Validate Experiences

During crisis, most clients are willing to talk about the traumatic experience. They should be encouraged to share every detail they can remember about the experience, the abuser, their reactions. This step helps both the counselor and the client. The counselor can obtain information about the incident(s), with which she can help assess the extent and type of intervention needed. At the same time, the counselor can also provide two types of feedback important to the client. First, events may be reported out of sequence, especially when multiple incidents are reported. The counselor can help the client sort out the details, to see the experience in a more coherent way. Second, the client's behavior and emotional reactions can be given validation, discussed in Chapter 3 as an essential component of helping.

Step 4: Process Decisions

Together, the client and counselor should assess the current situation realist-ically, particularly the potential for additional immediate abuse, and outline ways to prevent such abuse. After this assessment, the client and counselor should together review various needs, guided by the choice points in Chapter 4. For example, options for justice can be reviewed, along with the potential conse-quences of each option—considering both the worst and the best that could happen. They may then pursue the action together; if not, the client is referred to the appropriate resource person(s).

During this discussion, the counselor should assess the extent to which the client's needs are already being met by other helpers and institutions. Resources and additional referrals should be offered, such as medical assistance, court information, child care, and counseling for family or partner.

An important decision is whether to tell others about the experience. If the counselor is the only person to whom the client has revealed an incident, the reasons for her silence should be explored. If possible, the client should be encouraged to tell others who will be understanding, to provide a broader base of support during the crisis period. The counselor may work through role playing of parents' or friends' reactions or may consider being present when the client reveals an incident to significant others.

Since many sexual harassment and acquaintance-rape situations involve on-going contact with the offender, such clients will need techniques for handling subsequent interactions in a businesslike manner. This should begin with a clear acceptance that the client has a right to an abuse-free environment and that the offender is responsible for his own actions. This firm understanding is essential to enable the client to cope with any future approaches. The client may wish to consider how others will react to her situation when and if it becomes public. If the offender is particularly powerful or popular, she may have to be prepared to cope with negative responses from others in her social or work environment.

Step 5: Come to Catharsis and Temporary Emotional Resolution

During this process, emotional reactions are likely to occur, notably stress, fear, anger, and guilt. Descriptions of such feelings may be vague, but may signal deeper reactions. Vague expressions of self-blame such as "Why me?" may turn into more direct self-blame at a future time, so it is important that the counselor counteract them. In general, the counselor's role is to pro-vide empathic understanding and a safe place for the cathartic expression of all emotions.

The client may be encouraged to express any feelings that arise, no matter how bizarre they seem to her at the time, so that they can be interpreted and addressed. Often the client is harboring "secret" fears: something that makes her feel particularly bad, something she anticipates about others blaming her. For example, a client may have kept secret a childhood sexual abuse, which now is creating secondary guilt. Encouraging the client to reveal all of her feelings, including those that make her feel judgmental about herself, seems to result in some relief from fears and guilt reactions. Reassurances, such as pointing out that previous experiences have had nothing to do with this assault, are helpful. The sooner those secrets are brought forward and addressed, the better.

In the days following an incident, reactions of fear and anger should be expected. The client and counselor may choose to focus on these cathartic needs at that point. One or two sessions are probably the maximum needed for this aspect of crisis intervention, following guidelines in Chapter 4.

Step 6: Develop Future Goals and Plans

As the client begins to feel more in control of her emotions, she should review her options in terms of immediate and long-term needs, and the counselor should adopt a supportive (rather than directive) role in pursuing those options. For example, a college student who chooses to withdraw for a semester and live at home needs help in making the transition, including developing a new support system in her home town. A student making the opposite decision—to stay in school and complete the semester—may need help dealing with instructors over missed classes and handling her parents' insistence that she leave school and return to their home.

If appropriate, the counselor may help the client locate an ongoing support group for issues raised by the incident, especially a peer support group. If the process of pursuing the complaint will be lengthy, an ongoing counseling relationship may be negotiated to give the client a sense of continued support. Termination should include information about potential long-term effects and referrals for subsequent counseling, following the approaches outlined in Chapter 4.

Case Study 1: Sexual Harassment Crisis Counseling

Nan's professor made sexual advances during her first semester of graduate school. After her refusal, he gave her a low grade. A friend urged her to talk to a counselor in the campus counseling center who was well known for working in this area. Arriving for her first appointment late, Nan admitted that she was embarrassed and almost hadn't come. She had always strived to be independent, and felt that she should be able to handle this problem by herself.

The counselor assured Nan that her feelings were normal and offered to help by providing information and strategies for handling situations such as sexual harassment. They discussed what Nan would like to get out of the session and decided to proceed in a pragmatic vein, leaving any emotional issues until later.

Nan told her story in rather haphazard fashion, indicating a high level of stress. Reflecting back in the order in which incidents occurred helped Nan remember another aspect of the professor's approach—his reassurance that he always met with students after class and that they would probably be joined by a few others. This gave her perspective on why she hadn't anticipated the approach and helped ease her feelings that she had given him "special signals" by joining him voluntarily.

Nan had initially reported that the case was "closed," that she had ended it by refusing his advances. However, as she reviewed the past week, she realized that her professor had stopped by her office several times and that other graduate students seemed to think she liked him. When asked about his relations with other students, she remembered that another woman student, Janice, had expressed disgust about this particular professor a few weeks earlier. The counselor suggested he had probably done this to Janice and to other women, pointing out the typical pattern among harassers.

Nan was not sure she wanted to do anything about the grade, but she was aware that a low final grade would hurt her chances for a fellowship she wanted. She was also afraid that if word got out about this incident, her peers would accuse her of being responsible, of trying to use her sexuality to get a higher grade. There were only two women in her program, and she felt they were under constant scrutiny.

Nan decided that, with the counselor's help, she could write a letter, and she was given a copy of the guidelines for doing so. (See Chapter Appendix 6A.) She also decided to talk to Janice about her experience. The counselor considered the situation important enough to report it to the harassment officer, but assured Nan that her attempt to resolve it without a formal hearing would be respected. The counselor agreed to handle that process. Before the session ended, Nan was given suggestions for handling uncomfortable interactions with the professor in a firm, pleasant manner. An appointment was made for later that week, to review the letter.

Nan came into her next appointment on time, her letter in hand. The counselor suggested minor changes, to which Nan agreed. During the process of writing it, Nan had discovered some strong feelings of anger, guilt, and fear, which she was more than ready to talk about. They decided to spend two sessions discussing these feelings, focusing on positive ways to handle them.

By the third session, Nan had talked to Janice and discovered that the professor had approached her, too. They decided to file a joint complaint with the university after the semester ended. She and Janice had begun to take time out each day to talk over coffee about the status of women in their department, and had been joined by the only woman on their faculty. Together they had formed a solid base of mutual support. Nan was also encouraged to join an ongoing support group for first-year graduate students, to deal with the other pressures in her life.

Case Study 2: Rape Crisis Counseling

Norma is a 32-year-old recently divorced nurse, reliable and sensible in her approach to herself and her life. Three men stopped to ask her directions on the street, then abducted her at knifepoint. They took her to an unknown apartment where they took turns raping her, then dropped her off on a street corner at 4 A.M. She was able to get the license plate number and a description of the car as they drove off. She called the police after her assailants left, and the police transported her to the emergency room of the hospital where she worked. She called a friend, who helped her through the examination process. The next day, at her friend's insistence, she called a counselor at a local women's center. The counselor agreed to see her immediately.

Norma appeared to be calm and spent the first session telling the counselor as many of the details as she could remember. The ordeal of the night was still somewhat unreal to her, and she expressed no emotion except terror. The counselor reassured her that her confusion was normal and that in time other feelings would emerge. Norma expressed concern for her parents, who were older, but with the counselor's help in sorting out her reasons, she decided it was better to tell them as soon as she could. She and the counselor role-played how to talk to them, and how to handle any bad reactions on their part. She decided to call from the counselor's office, and arranged to meet her parents that afternoon. She also debated about contacting her ex-husband, but decided not to do so because she was not happy with other contacts they had had about less important issues.

Norma returned for her second session later that same week. The hour was spent reviewing her experience of the few days that had passed, what the police were doing about the rape, and how her family had reacted. She began to talk more about some of the feelings that were emerging. In particular, she had become obsessed with her own feelings of complicity. When the issue was pursued to its source, Norma mentioned that one of the men had asked her if she was okay and offered a glass of water, indicating some sensitivity to the fact that she was a human being. She felt appreciative of him for that action, and then noticed how odd it was to feel something positive for someone who had also raped her. In her effort to make sense out of the rape, she had decided it had happened because she was "too nice." The counselor targeted this interpretation as a mode of self-blame and shifted the responsibility to the three men, including the man who had helped her a little. The session ended with a discussion of Norma's strengths, which she was beginning to discover, in particular her ability to survive such a trauma and her new awareness of the support and comfort of her friends and family.

The third session brought the expression of anger as Norma realized the brutality of what had been done to her, her frustration that the offenders had not been caught and that her parents' lives were now deeply and daily affected by the rape. She was still sore from the bruises and scrapes she had received and was wondering how long she would have to continue to suffer. Since expressing feelings was still overwhelming, the counselor suggested that she move through her anger at her own pace, but reassured Norma that her anger was a sign that she was coping well.

Norma moved her fourth session up by one day, because the police had caught the men and she had been asked to come to the station and identify them that afternoon. She was feeling both relieved that they were in jail and frightened that she might have to see them again. The session was devoted to the potential outcomes, including the fact that they would likely be free on bail pending a trial. She called the local victim advocacy group and was reassured that she was probably safe, as the offenders did not know where she lived.

In the fifth session, Norma was feeling much better about the legal process, particularly since the detective at the line-up was so helpful. In discussing her feelings, she allowed her anger to emerge in full force and was encouraged by the counselor to continue, although the session lasted several extra minutes. She was able to cry about the harm the men had caused her and to express her fears for herself and for her parents, who were now showing the wear and tear of the stress. She decided to take a two-week extension of her leave from work and to enroll in a self-defense course right away to gain back a sense of control.

The sixth session was spent reviewing Norma's needs and her strategies for meeting those needs. She and the counselor talked at length about the legal process and what she could expect, her choices, and ways to protect herself emotionally as well as physically. The inner strengths she had shown in coping with this trauma were identified again for her, and her self-respect was reinforced. She was invited to return at any time and to call if she needed anything. She agreed to call the counselor and let her know what happened.

INDIVIDUAL RESOLUTION COUNSELING

The relatively structured brief intervention models in this section are somewhat therapist-directed and focus on specific reactions to a sexual assault troubling the client. For most sexual abuses, the general time frame is five to six weeks, depending on the client's readiness, her ability to recall the abusive incident and to identify its personal impact, and the extent of compounding factors. For adult survivors of incest, a special extended model developed by Paula Lundberg-Love (1987) is offered. Eight steps for the general model are outlined in Table 9.2, and the model is illustrated in a treatment plan for two women introduced as victims in Chapter 1. They represent common situations: Ann is a victim of stranger rape who enters counseling specifically to discuss the assault; Carol enters therapy for nonspecific problems, which therapy reveals may have resulted from a date rape.

Table 9.2

Steps for Individual Resolution Counseling

1. Establish rapport.
    a. Enhance trust.
    b. Relaxation techniques.
2. Negotiate the relationship.
3. Take general history.
4. Take specific sexual abuse history.
    a. Memory retrieval.
    b. Details of assault.
    c. Specific issues raised by assault.
5. Come to catharsis and resolution of emotional reactions.
6. Reconstruct self-concept and self-esteem.
7. Practice behavioral skills and strategies for change.
8. Develop future goals and plans.

When a client enters counseling for other problems, the sexual abuse issue should be considered as only one of several possible background factors. The progress of the counseling, of course, depends on the client's recall of the experience and her willingness to work on its effects. Steps 1 through 3 may take one or two sessions apiece, and the remaining steps may take one session each.

Step 1: Establish Rapport.

The initial interchange is usually fairly straightforward, as the counselor establishes rapport and begins the process of developing the client's trust.

Step 2: Negotiate the Relationship.

Issues such as limiting the intervention to a focus on sexual abuse, what to do if the therapy uncovers other issues, and the therapist's role in the process should be explicit. If the client has had problems with prior therapy, these should be discussed and new ground rules established to reduce her concerns about similar problems with this relationship.

Step 3: Take General History.

The counselor learns about the client by talking about her history, interests, activities, and family and friends. This discussion should help the counselor assess the client's emotional strengths, her areas of vulnerability, her need for external support, and her existing effective support systems.

Step 4: Take Specific Sexual Abuse History.

Memory Retrieval. This step is only necessary if the client does not report a sexual abuse, but it indicates problems around sexuality, relationships, trust, or guilt. The client may be asked directly about any sexual experience that was unwanted or negative, or a less direct process may be utilized, such as writing a relationship diary, which may help elicit well-hidden memories. Memory retrieval may take an additional session, as the client first comes to recognize the abuse experience, and then to acknowledge its harmful effects.

Details of Assault. When the client is fully aware of the reality of the experience, the counselor can elicit a detailed description of the sexual abuse, reflecting back the events in the sequence in which they occurred and offering nonjudgmental validation. This description—which may be the first time the client has ever told anyone about the experience—is likely to be interspersed with interpretations such as self-blame. Throughout, the counselor should focus on the actual events while defining the offender's responsibility for the abuse.

Step 5: Emotional Catharsis and Resolution

This step, usually taking at least one intensive session, is emotionally draining, because of its four goals: (1) cathartic reexperiencing of the assault in a supportive, safe environment; (2) learning more about specific emotional reactions and compounding factors; (3) utilizing the client's emotional strengths in preparing the most helpful recovery plan; and (4) identifying target issues and priorities for the remaining sessions.

Since cathartic needs are strong, the issues that should be addressed are those that arouse more intense emotions: anger/rage, trauma, fear, hurt, disgust, and the existential meaning of the experience. Coping techniques, such as relaxation exercises, are often helpful.

Step 6: Reconstruction of Self

As cathartic needs diminish, the client should become able to analyze cognitive constructions of the experience and to evaluate issues such as trust, self-esteem, and her own self-concept. The next step is to identify these problems and to develop strategies for overcoming them using tactics described in Chapter 8.

Step 7: Behavioral Skills and Strategies.

Specific techniques, such as behavioral skills that may be helpful in maintaining the client's new level of personal satisfaction or reducing the probability of future abuse, may be introduced. These may include assertiveness, effective communication skills, journaling, and techniques such as thought-stopping or positive imaging.

Step 8: Future Goals and Planning.

In a wrap-up session, any unfinished issues are addressed and future tasks are identified. Skills helpful to self-management and to accomplishing those tasks are reinforced, and other resources, including future counseling options, are identified. If possible, this session should allow identification of long-term goals with appropriate resources or referrals provided. As the session ends, closure should be achieved by reviewing the client's accomplishments and wishing her well.

Case Study 3: Stranger Rape Resolution Counseling

Ann, the first victim described in Chapter 1, was attacked and raped at knifepoint by a man who had just been released from prison. After the incident, the police had verbally abused her. A compounding problem existed for Ann: She was in counseling at the time of the assault, trying to cope with an unwanted divorce and with sexual approaches from several men she thought were friends, including a minister from whom she had sought help earlier. Her counselor had been working on "her problem" of giving off unwanted sexual signals. As a result of these earlier messages, she interpreted the rape as being her fault, the product of those sexual signals. She was unable to continue working with her regular counselor because of her own embarrassment. Two months later, she sought out a rape crisis center counselor.

Since two months had passed since the assault, long-term counseling seemed appropriate for Ann. She had moved quite rapidly through the acute phases, perhaps because her previous experiences in counseling had reduced any resistance to seeking help. At the same time, her negative experiences with counseling made the process of developing trust especially critical.

During the first session, Ann related the details of her rape freely, relieved that she could do so without fear of judgment, in contrast to her experiences with the police and with her previous counselor. She still had difficulty with self-blame, however, and the counselor had to directly counteract Ann's misinformation about "sexual signals," as well as directing blame to the offender.

The second session was a cathartic session for Ann, whose prior relationships with men and betrayal by male "helpers" clearly compounded her current reactions. She raged about being treated as if she were only good for sex. She demonstrated spunk and a willingness to work on these issues, and this was pointed out to her. Three major targets emerged for the next sessions: fear, trust, and sexual self-image.

At the beginning of the third session, Ann was taught how to apply relaxation techniques to herself, and she was reassured by the fact that she could control her anxiety. The men's roles and actions in Ann's past relationships and in her rape experience were compared in a way that allowed her to see that self-blame was not justified. The therapeutic role of educating clients was evident as Ann recognized the ways in which several men had betrayed her, along with her misconceptions about her responsibility. She also was able to develop a better appreciation of her own survival tactics and strengths in the face of those betrayals.

Ann's upcoming tasks included testifying at the assailant's upcoming trial, so concrete resources for court preparation were offered during the fifth week. She realized that talking to other women—something she had never done much—might be helpful and supportive, so a women's consciousness-raising group was located and a referral was arranged.

In the sixth session, Ann identified two long-term goals: future counseling, after the trial was over, focused on increased self-awareness, and a career change that would let her work daytime hours as well as increase her job satisfaction. She also decided to spend more time with her two nieces, because she could offer them a model of strength and survival and perhaps prevent similar traumas from happening to them.

Case Study 4: Date Rape Resolution Counseling

Carol, whom we met in Chapter 1, had been dating Jim for two years when he drugged her and raped her in his home. She never saw him again. She had not thought directly about the incident for years. She sought private counseling after she became convinced she was going crazy. She was having sexual problems in her relationship with her husband, feeling put off by his advances. Recently two other men had made suggestive approaches that terrified her, yet she thought she must have led them on. Her children were now in school, and she felt she should get out into the career world, but specific planning made her anxious. She had had several mild panic attacks, one on the way to a job interview, and now she was concerned about driving as well.

During the initial interview, Carol exhibited a general fear of authority, so an egalitarian relationship with the counselor was explicitly negotiated to help her feel at ease. Carol's panic attacks emerged as a clear concern, and a referral for a complete physical was made. Carol's feelings of being "crazy" were counteracted with the information that her feelings were normal stress symptoms, allowing a better sense that she could successfully go through this therapy. Upon learning of her sexual problems and concerns around men, she was asked if she had ever had any unpleasant sexual experiences. She couldn't recall any, but wasn't sure. Her memory of her teen years was particularly vague. She was asked to write a "relationship diary," exploring her feelings and experiences starting with her first date.

Carol's diary revealed the rape experience, to her surprise. The next session was thus devoted to remembering the details, validating her memories, defining the incident as rape, and establishing her boyfriend's responsibility for his actions. In the next session, the current problems she was experiencing were linked to her prior abuse, and the urgent nature of those problems was explained as the time bomb effect. Further information about stress responses to trauma helped assure Carol that her feelings were normal. Her medical information was also reviewed. Carol's examination had turned up a mild hypoglycemia, which helped account for her panic symptoms, which could be controlled through better diet. Specific coping strategies, such as deep breathing, were offered for anxiety symptoms.

At the beginning of the next session, Carol's ability to handle the stress of expressing her rage was assessed. The lack of any panic attacks for the past week helped her feel able to move forward. Carol found the therapist's inquiries about rage difficult, and initially insisted she was not angry. However, after the therapist asked how she would feel if the same thing happened to her daughter, the anger surfaced. The remainder of that session was exceptionally cathartic, leaving Carol drained but relieved.

Carol spent the next session looking ahead to her future. She decided her first priority should be to develop her self-esteem, which would include finding a good job. For Carol, self-help books like *Women and Self-Esteem* (Sanford & Donovan, 1984) were helpful. She also identified a desire to improve her relationship with her husband and chose a marriage enhancement program offered by her church, possibly as a prelude to marital therapy. By the last session she had sought out a job placement service, which both enhanced her resume (and consequently her self-esteem) and made the interview process seem less frightening.

The counselor agreed to see Carol for one more session after her job interviews to review her progress and help her feel confident about her decision. That session also allowed the counselor to evaluate her progress regarding the panic attacks. Although she had not experienced another full attack, Carol was still concerned about the possibility of recurrence, so she was referred to an agoraphobia support group in her neighborhood.

Individual Counseling Model for Incest Survivors

Lundberg-Love (1987) has developed a comprehensive treatment strategy for adult survivors of incest. This model is based on Lundberg-Love's successful work with 21 women and incorporates helpful exercises from Giarretto (1982) and Mayer (1983). It is intended to be brief, depending on the individual client's needs. Lundberg-Love's work reminds us that the counselor should routinely ask about various experiences, including negative childhood sexual encounters, whether or not the client presents with a sexually abusive history.

Steps 1 (establishing rapport), 2 (negotiating the relationship), 3 (general history), and 8 (future goals and plans) are the same as those in the general individual model, with one important additional warning. Trust can be so damaged by childhood sexual abuse that the client may resist initial efforts to encourage trusting behavior (Sgroi & Bunk, 1988). The therapist should recognize a client's reluctance to acknowledge trust and allow her to develop it at her own pace. The remaining steps represent Lundberg-Love's strategies adapted to the specific long-term issues raised by incest. Steps 4 through 7 are dealt with in the following sections.

Step 4: Sexual Abuse History. Inquiry forms the first step of Lundberg-Love's treatment strategy directed to the abusive experiences. Terms like "incest" or "rape" may elicit a negative response, often out of the client's fear, so more subtle questions like "were you ever touched in a way you didn't like?" may be more appropriate. If the client is able to recall specific sexually abusive experiences, the counseling process can move directly through the second and third steps. However, if the client suspects that incest may have occurred, because of vague uncomfortable feelings, but cannot recall specific experiences, an extra intervention (Step 4a) to retrieve lost memories will be needed.

Incest work is anxiety-producing, and most clients need skills with which to manage strong emotions. Relaxation techniques can provide some of these skills. Relaxation tapes, imagery, and meditation techniques are often particularly helpful.

4a: Memory Retrieval. Extra intervention to help the client remember the incident(s) is often necessary for incest clients. Most are unable to recall every specific abusive experience, and some cannot recall any specific act but know there was a problem. Helpful retrieval techniques include guided relaxation, of 20–40 minutes, during which questions about childhood are raised; age regression ("You are age 5; what is happening?"); dream or personal diaries; or viewing movies or reading self-help books like *Courage to Heal* (Bass & Davis, 1988). If appropriate, family interviews or "site visits" may provide additional memory cues. When specific memories have been recovered, the treatment moves to Step 6b. If memories cannot be recovered after a few sessions, the treatment process should move forward and focus instead on specific symptoms.

4b: Recount the Incident(s). The client's story needs to be told in her own words, with as much detail as possible. Exercises offered by Mayer (1983) and Sgroi and Bunk (1988) are good ways to elicit specifics, utilizing both direct questions and indirect methods, such as filling in a floor plan of the room in which the abuse occurred. Courtois (1988) provides a detailed questionnaire for eliciting the incest history. Sgroi and Bunk (1988) warn against encouraging too much information from a multiple-abuse victim during any single session; although the immediate reaction may be great relief, over subsequent days the client may be overwhelmed by the magnitude of the experiences described during a short period of time.

4c: Identify and Label Feelings and Salient Issues. As the recounting of specific incidents occurs, the focus moves into an area that is particularly difficult for many incest clients: identifying and labeling the feelings raised by childhood traumas. As the child distances herself from painful or frightening feelings, early emotions are likely to be denied; this protective mechanism then becomes a shell through which adult emotions are also denied. Allowing oneself to recognize feelings thus becomes a skill that may need to be taught as part of incest counseling.

At this point, the client and counselor work together to identify the major long-term reactions to the incest experience to be addressed in the therapeutic process. Books and movies identifying long-term reactions of other incest survivors, such as *Outgrowing the Pain* (Gil, 1988), *The Broken Taboo* (Justice & Justice, 1979), or *The Secret Trauma* (Russell, 1987), are also helpful guides to this process.

Step 5: Catharsis and Resolution of Emotional Reactions. The client is now ready to move into active processing of the incest experience. As with other treatment plans, catharsis is an important aspect. Since emotions are difficult to raise, and even more difficult to experience, exercises may again be helpful to the process. Lundberg-Love utilizes empty-chair role play; written letters to the perpetrator (and the nonprotector, if perceived), which are read aloud, taped, and replayed; a feelings diary or autobiography; symbolic or ritualistic activities to release emotions, such as bubble baths to eliminate "dirty" feelings, and physical exercise; and future-oriented protective responses such as security checks, self-protection classes, and specific protective measures that could not be applied as a child, such as sleeping with a light on or purchasing transparent shower curtains. A "safe" location and counselor relationship are essential to cathartic expression.

Step 6: Reconstructions of Self. As emotional responses are ventilated, the meaning of the experience to the client's own life becomes the focus of resolution. Clients may imagine interactions with their perpetrator and nonprotector via an interchange of letters (including the client's rebuttal) or use guided imagery to create the desired resolution outcome. Confronting the perpetrator and or the nonprotector may occur, with adequate preparation for the client, but should be undertaken only when and if the client wishes.

Step 7: Behavioral Issues. At this point, specific symptoms such as fears or phobias, depression, self-esteem, loss, sexual dysfunction, eating disorders, abusive behaviors toward others, or substance abuse are dealt with, according to the salient issues identified by client and counselor. Specific approaches are found in Chapter 8. Concurrent group therapy is also recommended for most survivors during this phase of the treatment program, which may extend after individual treatment is ended.

Since incest victims are particularly vulnerable to further victimization (e.g., Koss, 1987), therapy should include skills to reduce the likelihood of future abuse. Clients should be given safety tips to increase awareness, practice of assertive responses to threat, and if desired, referred to self-defense classes. In addition, many clients need help to recognize and change the attitudes that have led to their passive acceptance of adult abusive treatment, including learned helplessness and low self-esteem. An explicit gender role analysis (described as part of the feminist therapy approach, Chapter 7) is also appropriate for many clients, since gender roles underlie attitudes prevalent in abusive adult relationships.

GROUP COUNSELING MODELS

Two models developed by counselors working with victims of sexual abuse utilize structures that seem to be especially effective. Tsai and Wagner's (1978) 5-week model and Swink and Leveille's (1986) 18-week model represent reasonable minimum and maximum time frames for successful groups in the sexual abuse literature. While the principles developed for these groups have been applied here to adult victims of childhood sexual assault, they are applicable to groups formed around any type of sexual abuse.

These group models are structured around several principles.

1. The group members have been carefully screened in advance for appropriateness for group work. (See Chapter 7.)
2. Clients who are brought together in a group share common experiences, such as the same type of abuse (e.g., father-daughter incest), or at least two persons have experienced the same type of abuse.
3. The external structure of the group is clearly defined, and its members are expected to commit themselves in advance to participate fully. Expectations may include being drug-free, arriving on time, and paying fees (however small) on time.
4. Rules of behavior are established within the group to maximize support and effective communication. Exercises may be incorporated to teach these skills to group members.
5. Members of the group who cannot meet the expectations are not summarily dismissed, but their problems are discussed with some exploration of their underlying causes and, where possible, resolved within the group. For example, fear of continuing is cast as a group safety issue and ways of enhancing feelings of trust are defined by the group together.

While the group process is more difficult to identify as a series of steps, it is clear that the group progresses along similar lines to the individual process. Table 9.3 presents the steps of the individual therapy process adapted for group therapy models.

Table 9. 3

Steps in Group Therapy

1. Screen group members.
2. Establish group ground rules.
3. Develop skills for group process.

4. Share detailed sexual abuse histories.

5. Come to catharses and emotional reactions.

6. Reconstruct sense of self and trust in others.

7. Individualize future goals and plans.

Five-Week Therapy Group Model

Tsai and Wagner (1978) developed an excellent brief intervention for recognizing and coming to terms with childhood victimization. The five-to six-week group fits well with the grief process described in Chapter 8, with movement through the stages of grief resolution in the sessions. The goals of these groups are very focused: to identify and alleviate sexual guilt and shame and to recognize the psychological consequences of the sexual abuse.

Tsai and Wagner (1978) formed groups of four to six adult women from nineteen to fifty-three years old who shared the experience of sexual abuse during their childhood years. The severity of abuse ranged from fondling to repeated intercourse. The model reported by Tsai and Wagner was led by a male and a female cotherapist.[2] While their original groups met weekly or biweekly for a total of four sessions one and one-half hours long, Tsai and Wagner suggested that four sessions might not be sufficient. We recommend at least one additional session concerned with the psychological consequences of sexual abuse.

Session 1. The therapists introduce themselves, establish group guidelines, including confidentiality, and discuss the phenomenon of child sexual abuse. The members are then asked to describe their molestation experiences in detail. Specific questions are asked by the therapist whenever a member speaks in generalities, until an extremely detailed story is available. For many survivors this will be the first time they have told their story to anyone, so this session is particularly anxiety-laden and emotional. In telling their stories, they learn that they are not alone, and the group members form a special bond with one another. Another first for many women during such a session is learning to trust and support others.

Sessions 2–4. Following the first session, many clients become preoccupied with their sexually abusive experiences, and more depression is noted during the second and third sessions. The members are guided through discussions of their experience of the various psychological effects of their molestation. These include difficulty in relationships, sexual dysfunctioning, and emotional problems such as guilt, negative self-image, depression, feelings of isolation, low self-esteem, and displaced anger (especially toward the mother). The therapists respond to and clarify feelings and provide information about their reactions to the abuse. At the same time, group members listening to their peers learn that such responses as shame and feelings of isolation are common, undeserved, and unnecessary.

Session 5. The final session is designed to individualize the continuing resolution process, as each participant recognizes her progress and develops personal goals and future plans. A follow-up session is scheduled two or three months later, which eases termination anxiety. Pragmatic information is provided, including ways to help prevent children from being molested.

Eighteen-Week Therapy Group Model

An eighteen-week model was developed by Swink & Leveille (1986) for adult victims of incest, using a victim-to-survivor conceptual framework in a structured group design.[3] Six to eight incest survivors and two female facilitators work with each group. Groups are same-gender (Swink and Leveille have worked only with women). Group members may be in individual therapy concurrently with the group, and in fact this conjoint work is often recommended.

Swink and Leveille (1986) point out that incest families often suffer from confused boundaries and lack clear lines of responsibility, and it is important for the group to be able to offer a replacement model for the client's chaotic, undefined family experience. In their undefined roles and dependence on the "expert" therapist, traditional open-ended groups are too much like the incestuous family; in contrast, Swink and Leveille's groups are designed to prevent recurrence of the well-learned patterns of noncommitment, unrealistic goals, and inappropriate boundary behaviors with others. In addition, the group is committed to an environment of trust and safety, with each group member responsible for promoting trust and support so that all may benefit.

Group meetings are organized around specific topics (see Chapter Appendix 9A) and last two hours. While other issues may be discussed, self-examination is particularly important for incest victims, who may be unaware of their own behaviors and thoughts arising from the incest experience. Each group member is allowed to analyze her own experience in the topic area and to help others in her group resolve their experiences. Various methods, including psychodrama, behavioral training, reality therapy, and other methods consistent with the groups' eclectic approach are utilized within group sessions, depending on the specific issues and group member needs.

At the first group meeting the structure is explicitly laid out, and contracts are signed. Members are presented with a list of 26 proposed topics and vote on them at that time. The next sixteen meetings are structured around the topics generated at the first meeting. The eighteenth and last session is a wrap-up meeting with closure exercises. Clients have the option of attending a subsequent group, and about one-half recontract for one additional group. Clients will recontract over several years if given the opportunity, depending on the depth of the betrayal (Swink, personal communication, 1989). Leveille (personal communication, 1987) recommends follow-up contact, since she has observed different dependency behaviors—alcohol and other drugs, eating disorders—at about a year following the group experience. These may be prior issues surfacing as problems when the major crises of the incest experience are resolved.

Sprei (1987) also offers a ten-week incest therapy group model. The members move from a focus on the past (raising issues and sharing experiences), to a focus on the present effects of the incest, to a future-oriented termination process. Specific topics are oriented around Courtois' (1988) analysis of eight life areas affected by incest (Chapter Appendix 9B).

SUPPORT-GROUP MODELS

For some clients, long-term counseling is not necessary, but intervention is still appropriate. Many harassment survivors do not experience severe personal adjustment problems, but need support and new perspectives on their experiences. Some survivors of assault or incest who already have engaged in successful therapy feel a need for more insight into the gender and power issues experienced in their lives. Even individuals who have never experienced sexual abuse recognize their own fears and find that others with similar feelings can help them deal with those fears. For all of them, a support group is an important option.

Support groups, described in Chapter 7, are generally organized around a common theme. One approach brings together people sharing a particular experience (e.g., members have been targets of sexual assault, as in our first group). Another approach organizes the group members according to role (e.g., "women in science" defines our second group). Support groups vary widely in their level of intensity, in the range of topics discussed, and in their flexibility in membership and in joining or leaving the group. These details are not essential to the success of one group over another; however, it is important for ground rules to be established within each group and refreshed or reevaluated at regular intervals.

Sexual Abuse Survivor Group

The support group for survivors of sexual abuse brings together incest survivors who have worked out their more intensive difficulties with the incest prior to becoming members of a support group. Many move to a support group with other members of therapy groups that are structured or short-term, and they end up developing trust and openness with others that could not be developed previously. Recognition of a need may come from either the member of a therapy group or a therapist, or from a committed individual who has had no therapy but is able to spearhead the formation of a group through her own wishes or need.

The ideal support group size is eight to twelve persons; the group's size could be up to twenty, but increasing the size reduces the time allotted for each member to speak. An hour and a half is a good time frame; two hours is a maximum. The group may choose to begin or end each session with social interaction, over a pot-luck dinner or dessert. Social time, however, should be clearly distinguished from the time for group work.

Several cautions are important. First, as with the therapy group, agreements about the structure and boundaries of the group and member contact must be clear. Boundaries and privacy are violated in family incest, and the support group allows new learning to take place.

Second, a therapist may be present or not, but some knowledgeable person must be prepared to remind the group of agreements made, of limits being tested, and of privacy in danger of being violated should such incidents occur. A leader is usually needed for direction and limit-setting. When no one was prepared to intervene competently, naïveté has resulted in discomfort for group members and in dissolution of support groups.

Third, confidential information must never be relayed to others outside a support-group—trust violated is rarely rebuilt without a great deal of skilled leadership.

The setting for the support group may be a member's home or a meeting room that is private. Safety and security with other women survivors can help members develop a sense of secure self over an extended period of time. Each person, however, has the responsibility to take care of herself. Protection from others is not necessary and reduces the person's opportunity to assert herself and thus to grow. To enhance these feelings, the following ground rules may be followed:

1. Members agree to avoid judging and to focus on support and positive statements to each person, even when making a difficult point.

2. Time arrangements (beginning and end) are agreed upon and honored by all members.

3. Members agree to come every time.

4. If food is involved, each person contributes in some way, but the group does not revolve around eating.

5. One person acts as leader of each session, although the leadership may rotate.

6. Any confronting is clear, gentle, and nurturing.

Consciousness-Raising Support Group

Women in business, women administrators and executives, feminist men, and other relatively isolated individuals have recognized the value of coming together to share and discuss relevant issues. Successful support group models vary widely in structure and definitions of membership. Members may be invited by job type or special interest; an open invitation may be issued through newpaper ads; or several people may merely decide to meet regularly. Topics may be decided in advance and adhered to by all members, or the topics may change as external events or members' issues dictate. Attendance may be expected for all members at all meetings, or the group membership may be those who show up at any given meeting. In general, however, it is useful to have an external leader or to appoint one person to take on the leadership role at each meeting.

Groups may meet once a week or less frequently, but should have a regular meeting time established in advance. Because these groups often form at a workplace, the meeting time may be over a lunch hour. The food should not become the focus of the meeting, however.

The Women in Science group at the University of Rhode Island is an example of the unstructured format. Young women entering nontraditional fields such as science are vulnerable to a range of pressures that constitute barriers to success: perceived conflicts between the isolating demands of scientific laboratory work and a family or social life; negative and deprecating attitudes of other students towards "brainy" women; sex discrimination, in such forms as lowered grades and restricted opportunities for research; and sexual harassment (Quina, 1986).

Group membership is not structured or required; any woman in any scientific field is welcome to attend the meetings, and members may skip meetings without penalty. "Bag lunch" meetings are held on a regular basis in the same room on campus. At the beginning of the semester, the group lists topics of interest (which may change during the semester) and determines the meeting time and place. The coordinator lines up faculty members or other experts on campus to facilitate meetings on specific topics (e.g., a psychologist on the family-scientist dilemma, a successful woman chemist on professional opportunities, a communications specialist on job searches). Among these topics may be sexual harassment.[4]

An example of a more structured support group is a women's consciousness-raising group in a small community, formed by eight women who have met together weekly for several years. The topics are generally not determined in advance, although the group may read a book or article of interest and plan to discuss it at the next session. However, personal matters take precedence over any other topic. The group has shared joy and grief, provided feedback and encouragement on artistic and other achievements, and worked together on social issues to change the history of its small town. Over the years the membership has changed very little, and the level of sharing and trust is very deep, while the discussions of gender issues are very sophisticated.

In a support group such as one of these, a woman may have her first opportunity for sharing her fears and problems, as well as her joy, in being a woman (as well as a scientist, artist, or mother). A support group can break through the isolated, competitive individualism created by the social environment, whether the laboratory or the home, and enable its members to see their problems as social, not personal. If discussions of sexual harassment arise, the group members are provided with a label for their experience and a focus for their vague feelings of anxiety. Indeed, other cases of harassment involving the same offender are sometimes uncovered. Thus, for meetings on this topic, facilitators should be especially prepared to work with individual emotional consequences and group anger and frustration, and also to provide strategies for handling a formal case.

Regardless of the topic under discussion, the leader's role is to facilitate group awareness of the commonality of the themes in the members' lives. This can be done by encouraging sharing of experiences among group members and by maintaining a focus on external rather than internal causes. A positive future orientation can be created through the presence of successful, caring role models, or just through sharing hopes and dreams with one another.

Active planning to change problem areas is an effective empowerment strategy, keeping the group from getting bogged down with negative stories. Some examples of positive actions from support groups on university campuses include a petition to increase safety measures on the campus, a group letter to a department chair supporting a woman faculty member, a group complaint about a sexually harassing faculty member, and establishment of a child care center. Similar support groups in business have formed important professional networks, brought in educational workshops on topics from self-esteem to setting up a small business, and formed career advising systems to assist individuals in changing jobs. Smaller personal groups, such as the neighborhood group described here, have been credited with helping members undertake—and finish—major art works, books, and career changes. More importantly, they have helped their members cope with everyday life, from relatively common concerns such as good parenting and time management, to life choices about career, marriage, and motherhood and crises such as the deaths of loved ones.

NOTES

1. The term "steps" should not be interpreted as an absolute sequence or a rigid process guideline. The order and extent of overlap of the steps depends on the client's preferences, willingness to share emotions, and other internal and external demands.

2. Though others may question the presence of a male, in this particular situation the therapist provided the benefit of a nonabusive, supportive male, and also modeled a healthy egalitarian relationship with the female therapist.

3. Swink and Leveille (1986) reported that earlier groups lasting twelve weeks were less successful, because trust and bonding had only begun to form when the group was ending. Longer groups, on the other hand, tended to drag out and stagnate.

4. The Women in Science group was led by Grace Frenzel, a psychologist on the staff of the University of Rhode Island Counseling Center. Because the content of the discussions of this group, like other support groups, was confidential, the specific topics and outcomes examples are gathered from a variety of similar support groups.

RECOMMENDED READINGS

Brody, C. M., ed. *Women's Therapy Groups*. New York: Springer, 1987.
Courtois, C. A. *Healing the Incest Wound: Adult Survivors in Therapy*. New York: Norton, 1988.

CHAPTER APPENDIX 9A:

SAMPLE TOPICS FOR INCEST GROUPS

Accepting reality of abuse   Self-concept

Myths and facts   Isolation and withdrawal

Dreams, nightmares, and flashbacks   Fear and phobias

Family dynamics   Role reversals

Guilt and responsibility   Depression

Body image   Physical manifestations

Trust   Relationships

Role of men in our lives   Sexuality

Intimacy   Control

Anger   Power

Media images—film or book   Confrontation decision

Writing or artistic expression   Abusive relationships

Self-destructive behaviors: eating problems, substance abuse

Skills: decision making, communication, assertiveness, relaxation training, parenting, self-defense.

Source: Swink & Leveille (1986).

CHAPTER APPENDIX 9B:

LIFE AREAS AFFECTED BY SEXUAL ABUSE

Social: feeling isolated, different from others, unable to interact, mistrustful of others.

Psychological/emotional: over- or under-control; specific emotional reactions.

Physical: nausea, pain, soreness, headaches, and activities with which these symptoms are assoated, if any.

Sexual: confusion, fears, hyper- or hypo-sexuality, sexual preference.

Familial: estrangement, parents' relationship, closeness.

Sense of self: self-concept, shame, power.

Relation to men: intimacy, trust, hostility.

Relation to women: intimacy, trust, hostility.

Source: Courtois (1988), Appendix A.

10

Individual Considerations

The principles and models offered in the previous chapters are appropriate for any client. Intervention should always be adapted to the characteristics and concerns of the individual, however, especially those characteristics and concerns raised by gender, culture, and life circumstance. Suggestions for modifying intervention with special client populations are offered in this chapter.

Many helpers harbor fears about working with clients who are different from themselves. These include fear that these clients will be offended by a comment that seems insensitive, fear that the helper will be inadequate to work with them because of stereotypes or expectations, and even fear of the clients themselves. For that reason, the issues raised in this chapter are particularly important for white, heterosexual, nondisabled helpers. Reading a chapter, however, is not enough to counteract personal prejudices. Before entering counseling or other intensive intervention with a client, a helper must evaluate her or his own ability to be nonjudgmental and giving with that individual. Each must recognize her or his own racism, homophobia, and fear of disability and be willing to deal with it when it arises, especially when a client calls attention to it. Garcia et al. (1987) provide insight into the complexities, and the value, of learning how to cooperate and communicate across differences, something applicable to the client-helper relationship as well as to personal relationships.

With many of the clients who will be discussed in this chapter, preexisting stressors fanned by cultural attitudes and social experiences are important. For example, ethnic minorities, disabled clients, and the elderly are more likely to be living in poverty, with accompanying problems of poor health and lack of access to resources such as health care (Robbins & Siegel, 1983). Ethnic minorities, particularly recent immigrants, may be torn between two worlds, living a bicultural existence (e.g., Gibson, 1983; LeVine & Padilla, 1980). Daily experience with prejudice and social rejection may have already created low self-esteem and poor self-concept for the client prior to the abuse (Melville, 1980; White, 1985). Each of these factors may have created a preexisting level of stress, making recovery counseling a more complex rebuilding process.

Clients belonging to the groups we will discuss in this chapter may have been assaulted *because of* their sexual orientation, ethnicity, disability, or age. Bias violence has been on the increase in our culture, particularly against gays, lesbians, and racial minorities, and sexual assault appears to be one of the primary forms of expressing hatred for men and women who are "different" (Herek, 1989). Being targeted for victimization because of a personal feature such as skin color or same-sex companion strikes at the deepest levels of personal identity, compounding the issues discussed above. The recovery process for victims of bias violence may involve resolution of existential questions about human violence as well as becoming more comfortable with one's identity, and the client may benefit from a support group of similar men or women.

At the same time, the client who has dealt with negative life circumstances may have developed powerful internal strengths that can be validated and utilized in the process of recovery (Robinson, 1983).[1] An important caution should be noted, however. The helper should not assume that the client who has overcome other problems is a "superwoman" and does not need the intervention (Trotman & Gallagher, 1987). Rather, the client should be allowed to expose and explore weaknesses and needs, while incorporating successful past coping strategies into the rebuilding process.

MALE CLIENTS

The extent of sexual abuse of males is not well measured or understood in our culture, although it has been estimated that as many as one in four men has been molested during childhood. (See Chapter 1.) Even today, many male victims find that, unless there is serious injury, others will not readily label their experience as abuse (Krueger, 1985). Societal attitudes continue that "men cannot be raped." The situation is somewhat like the plight of female victims of the 1960s: few men dare to come forth to tell their stories, and their silence creates its own emotional aftermath.

Male victims are also subject to a cultural norm that men must not show emotions other than anger. While the ability to find and express anger is helpful to any survivor, there are other feelings that arise after abuse that may be difficult for men to recognize or cope with. Expressions of sadness and fear may also be blocked by friends and family who cannot deal with a man expressing emotional pain. The male survivor instead is asked to "tough it out."

When men do try to tell their stories of abuse, they are often met with a set of myths and assumptions that interfere with healthy resolution. These cultural attitudes are similar to the ones we have described for women, but with important twists.

- Men who are victims deviate from the expectations for the masculine role of strength and ability to defend themselves. Role-inconsistency is particularly strong when the abuser is female, since cultural myths insist that men are supposed to be dominant over women. Male victims are viewed as weak and "unmasculine," which people confuse with "feminine," a negative attribution for men in our culture.
- When the abuser is male, as in the majority of offenses (84 percent, according to Finkelhor, 1979), attributions about sexual orientation abound. Heterosexual men who are raped are suspected of having wanted the abuse (the "latent homosexual" or "masochist" accusation), while gay men are accused of secretly trying to attract male attention.
- Many people, including some victims themselves, believe that sexual contact with another man causes homosexuality. These attributions are particularly disturbing because they reveal misunderstanding and prejudice about homosexuality along with misunderstandings about sexual abuse. Even the term "homosexual rape," often applied to these assaults, misleads the listener into thinking of sexual orientation rather than of violation.

As with any victim, men often question their actions during the abuse. In the absence of social support, many accept the attributions of others. Heterosexual men may worry about latent homosexuality (which they fear will continue to "lead" them into similar experiences) causing sexual difficulties with subsequent women partners. Gay men abused as children or adolescents may question whether their homosexuality was caused by the abuse. Gay men assaulted as adults may place the blame for their victimization on their homosexuality, and they may hate themselves because of their sexual orientation.

The physical sexual responses of men, which are not well understood by most men or women, also can have an impact on their reactions to abuse. Physical sexual responses are considered synonymous with pleasure. Yet men can experience erections and ejaculations without pleasure, even in the face of terror or disgust. Groth (1979) reported that in about one-half of the male rape cases he worked with, the assailant made an attempt to force the victim to ejaculate. Men who have an erection or an orgasm may believe that their "bodies don't lie," reinforcing the myth that they secretly enjoyed or wanted the assault. Maltz and Holman (1987) discuss these issues further for male incest victims.

Reactions are compounded by treatment from authorities and institutions (Kaufman, 1984). While male child victims are receiving more caring attention than before, men who report sexual abuse to authorities are still subjected to rejection and mistreatment, particularly if they are gay or perceived as gay. Victim blame may be particularly harsh from policemen and other males working with male victims, who experience a strong need to distance themselves from their own vulnerability. Many men report that they would prefer to talk to a woman after sexual abuse because they would anticipate greater empathy and less judgment.

In general, male survivors experience the same range of emotions felt by females, compounded by issues of sexuality and gender role. Male survivors are often more readily able to express anger and fantasies about revenge, which can be utilized to hasten their recovery (Groth, 1979). Anger may be dangerous, however, to the client himself and to others. Unfortunately, in our culture, most men resist opening up to the vulnerability shown by their experiences, refusing to seek help unless they are in a crisis state. They may be more likely to numb their feelings with alcohol or other substance abuse. When they do open up to counseling, however, the resolution process offers an opportunity for tremendous personal growth not otherwise available to most men in our culture (Carlson, 1981).

In addition to the general models, the special interventions discussed in the following sections are especially helpful with male clients:

Support

Men need emotional support as much as women, especially after victimization, but they are less likely to receive it in their personal environment. Therefore a support group for male clients is highly recommended. Most therapists prefer not to mix male and female sexually abused clients. If a group for male survivors is not available, a nontraditional men's support group can be an excellent alternative. In these groups, violations of gender role expectations, emotional expression, and feelings of vulnerability are acceptable; the experience of victimization can be recognized and validated. The National Organization for Changing Men (Box 93, Charleston, IL 61920) can provide information about local men's organizations and resources. Lew (1988) offers information and help to men recovering from incest and childhood sexual abuse.

Gender Role Analysis

Exploration of the client's notions of gender roles can be used to help male clients see that vulnerability and victimization are *human* experiences, not relegated to one gender, and that being overpowered by an abuser is independent of gender or role. Since most male victims are young and smaller than average, this process requires us to distinguish between physical disadvantage and gender role: the victim may have been vulnerable because he was smaller, but that is unrelated to his personal masculinity. Gender role analysis can lead to important insights into the other negative effects of role stereotyping and of the quest for masculinity by males in our culture. For example, sexual orientation and gender role are often confused. Our culture stereotypes gay men as "feminine," and men who do not fit the cultural stereotype of "masculine" (especially those who are gentle, soft, or small) as gay. Homosexuals who blame their abuse on their "femininity" may experience self-hate and reject potentially healing relationships with other gay men. Heterosexual and gay clients need to understand the distinction between sexual orientation and gender role in order to overcome the harmful effects of their own and others' socially induced homophobia.

Sexuality

Sexual abuse and sexual orientation may also become confused. Gay men victimized as children, especially by their mother or father, may feel they were forced to become gay by their experience. Heterosexual victims of assault by men may fear that their trauma will cause homosexuality. In either case, clients experience self-doubt, and often self-hate. Since these feelings are not easy for clients to talk about, the helper can facilitate their expression by gently questioning the client about personal fears. The first step is to identify the relationship between the sexual abuse and the client's concerns about sexual orientation and to educate the client about the myths and stereotypes that have fostered those concerns. Then the client should be helped to clarify his own sexual orientation and his feelings about that orientation outside the context of the abuse. In any case, the helper must not attempt to determine for the client his sexual orientation through suggestive labels.

A common error, fostered by some psychological theories, is the notion that every person is either heterosexual or homosexual, and that sexual fantasies or experiences with other men necessarily indicate a repressed "homosexual identity." According to Kinsey Institute studies, a substantial number of men who comfortably identify themselves as heterosexual or bisexual have had voluntary sexual contact with another man, or have engaged in homoerotic fantasizing about men (Bell & Weinberg, 1978; Kinsey et al., 1948). Clients may need to be reassured that these thoughts or experiences are normal. For men wishing to pursue questions about sexual orientation, referral to a gay support group or center would be helpful.

Long-Term Goal Setting

An important aspect of counseling is the raising of new possibilities for future life choices and roles. Male survivors who open up to their emotions and fears often become less rigid, less bound by masculine stereotypes, more aware of the range of options in their own lives, and more tolerant of others' options, because their consciousness is raised by their experience. Carlson (1981, 1988) offers suggestions for counseling men toward a new consciousness, summarized in Chapter Appendix 10A.

LESBIAN CLIENTS

The richness and variety of sexual identity patterns and life-styles among women who identify themselves as lesbians, women who express primary emotional attachments to women, and bisexual women, is described by Golden (1987) and Shuster (1987). The first implication for lesbian and bisexual clients, then, is to avoid any assumptions about their life-styles or relationship patterns—a caution appropriate for any client, but particularly important in relationships imbued with stereotypes such as "butch-femme." It is as dangerous to attempt to force a client to conform to a stereotype of "lesbian" behavior as it is to work towards a stereotype of "femininity."

Some of the questions raised by lesbian survivors are similar to those raised by gay males (Maltz & Holman, 1987). If the sexual abuse occurred early in life, the client may ask whether her lesbian identity was "caused" by the abuse, or whether she is lesbian only because she experiences physical revulsion toward, or is afraid of, men. Some studies have reported a relatively high incidence of incest histories among lesbians (Meiselman, 1981), but the connection may not be direct (i.e., lesbians may be more willing to seek treatment). It is important to deal with these questions in a way that views being lesbian as a positive orientation rather than as a lack or loss of heterosexuality. Loulan (1989) offers self-help exercises and valuable information for lesbian incest survivors.

Sexuality Counseling

The approach recommended for clients concerned about their lesbian sexual orientation is similar to that for gay men. A review of the client's current satisfaction with her roles, life-style, and current relationships can be used to help her separate personal adjustment issues—which may need to be addressed as part of the counseling process—from questions about her sexual orientation and her personal identity. Rather than searching for causes or "what might have been," the focus should be on whether these questions signal deeper frustrations or fears, such as parental or societal rejection in a world hostile to homosexuality (Margolies et al., 1987), and ways to resolve or cope with those issues. A nonjudgmental acceptance of the client's orientation, and an emphasis on her own self-esteem in the face of external pressure, can give her strength for coping with the abuse issues. Specific problems such as unhappy relationships should be treated as any other normal adjustment concern. A client who is exploring lesbian issues, or who identifies herself as lesbian but has not found a way to express her feelings, should be assisted in finding a support system. Nichols (1987) offers specific suggestions for sex therapy.

For a woman abused after she had identified herself as a lesbian, self-doubts and others' questions often take another form: was she assaulted because of her identity? In *The Women of Brewster Place*, a lesbian is brutally gang-raped with the apparent cooperation of heterosexual women neighbors, becoming the victim of homophobia and fear as well as personal violence (Naylor, 1983). It is important to long-term recovery to see such hostile acts as beyond the victim's control, and to understand that sexual identity—or the way in which a lesbian identity was assumed or identified (e.g., dress, walking arm in arm with another woman)—does not ever justify abuse.

Parental Issues

Starzecpyzel (1987) has identified five core parental issues she sees frequently in the lesbian incest survivors she counsels. These issues are overidentification with the father (80 percent); protectiveness toward the mother, not as a desired role but as a sacrifice for her; strong, conscious rejection of the mother and her role (80–90 percent); intense longing for the nurturing and gentle physical contact of a mother; and conscious feelings of abandonment by the mother (50–60 percent). As a result, the broken mother-bond caused by incest is particularly important to address with lesbian incest survivors. Starzecpyzel identifies unresolved feelings for the mother as an important therapeutic issue because of the confusion it can cause in current relationships. In resolving feelings about the mother, the emphasis should be on achieving healthy, egalitarian relationships with other women and on replacing the mother bond with healthy substitutes. (See Chapter Appendix 8A.)

Support

Most large towns and cities have a lesbian community, at least with social activities. The lesbian community can help clients regain a secure base, providing a rich and consistent source of support and self-esteem (Rand et al., 1982; Pearlman, 1987). Care must be taken to avoid the same overprotection that can occur in close-knit family groups. The tight structure of some communities may delay or prevent the client's utilization of outside resources for help. For an emerging lesbian client, it is especially important to help her find a supportive community, and to clarify community values and politics, while she develops her own individual identity, hopefully in the context of community support (Rainone, 1987).

In addition, one must be aware that abuse does take place within lesbian couples and that the emotional effects are similar to those after heterosexual abuse. Since relationships with women in general are expected to be "safe" from physical violence and sexual abuse, lesbian clients experiencing abuse by other women may have special problems with issues of trust, self-blame, and their general safety. Furthermore, the abusive partner is likely to remain a participant in the same lesbian community and to abuse other women. The fear of losing the support of the lesbian community is threatening to many abuse survivors, so counselor and client must be prepared to develop an alternative support system as well as cope with grief over the abuse.

RACIAL AND CULTURAL MINORITY CLIENTS

Intervention of all types is done primarily by white, middle-class individuals, who predominate among crisis workers, legal and medical professionals, and counselors (Carrow, 1980). As a result, the cultural style and value systems of the white middle class also dominate most helping efforts, which may not be appropriate to the culturally different client (Holmes, 1980). Formal training rarely considers culturally sensitive intervention or special issues that may arise for minority clients (Bronstein & Quina, 1988). To a certain extent, this is based on the correct assumption that victimization and abuse cause universal experiences of pain and suffering. There are additional factors for many racial and cultural minority clients, however, that should be considered.

In the United States, a disproportionate number of minority group members suffer from lower economic and social status, and thus greater vulnerability to victimization. In the workplace, the minority woman is more likely to be underpaid and socially isolated than her nonminority peers, and unsupported when concerns are raised—making her a vulnerable target for the harasser (MacKinnon, 1979). Crisis centers receive many reports from minority women of rape and harassment by white authorities such as police.

After abuse occurs, minority women are less likely to receive helpful intervention, often because of the personal prejudices of the interveners, and they are less likely to be able to afford private treatment. Many minority victims choose not to seek intervention because they do not expect any helpful outcome (Feldman-Summers & Ashworth, 1981), or because a lack of minority personnel at various agencies makes them uncomfortable or mistrustful.

Working with culturally different clients depends most on openness and honesty. However, there are important reminders even for the most sensitive helper. First, within every cultural or racial group there is greater diversity among members of the group than between groups (Bronstein & Quina, 1988). The intervener must never allow cultural or racial patterns, real or stereotypic, to dominate assumptions about an individual client.

Second, assumptions like "I can never understand her because she is from another country" are not helpful, and only exaggerate differences. There are important commonalities among all people that can be shared by an empathic helper, regardless of race or culture. The intervener and client need to place their commitment to working on a helping relationship first, and to resolve differences as part of that commitment.

Third, intervention will probably require active countering of cultural barriers: the helper's incorrect assumptions about the client, the client's own internalized negative images, and mistrust of the helper by the client.

The issues arising for minority clients vary according to the phase of intervention. Crisis reactions may be subject to culturally different patterns of emotional expressiveness. The crisis intervener must be prepared to appreciate a wide range of reactions, from stoic to emotionally expressive (Williams & Holmes, 1981). However, expectations about "normal" crisis reactions, whether based on experience within one's own culture or on general patterns of emotional expressiveness for a different culture, may not hold for an individual client.

Advocacy for a minority client takes place in a system likely to harbor racial or cultural prejudices, especially stereotypes about sexuality and emotionality.

E. C. White (1985) points out that speaking up about racism can be an empowering act to a survivor—but if she is not emotionally ready for confrontation, it may be a negative, draining experience. The advocate may help the client sort out these feelings and decide when and how to address inappropriate treatment and provide support during any confrontation. Depending on the client's wishes, others may take on the confrontational role while the client is allowed to heal in relative peace. For example, Black men and women students at a small college joined together in a widely publicized protest against a pattern of campus sexual harassment targeting minority women, after the rape of a fellow student. As a result, important protective and educational programs were instituted. Such an experience of combining voices can empower the group, as well as lending important support to the individual survivor.

Because of historical patterns ranging from insensitivity to abuse, many minorities have an aversion to utilizing services from White or culturally different professionals (White, 1985). Advocacy may have to be present for both parties, sensitizing the agency to the needs of the client while giving the client reason to trust the agency. It may be beneficial to lay the groundwork for that mutual trust by inviting minority women to review and assess services on a regular basis and by encouraging minority women to become involved personally as volunteers or staff members.

Counseling requires intensity and absolute trust, and therefore it will be even more important to recognize and deal with cultural and racial differences. A number of excellent resources are available on cross-cultural counseling (Pederson, 1985; D. W. Sue, 1981), and S. Sue and N. Zane (1987) provide a valuable list of references on counseling for specific minority groups. But one must appreciate that "cross-cultural" counseling goes beyond merely learning about another's cultural history and experience and using that perspective in treatment when appropriate (S. Sue & Zane, 1987; Vazquez-Nuttall et al., 1987); the counseling process itself must be open to examination and feedback by the client. The counselor must be willing to address a client's concerns about racism and to discuss comments or actions the client perceives as racist when they arise, even if they were unintentional.

Different communication styles and expectations about information the client should share may require the counselor to adapt to the client's style. Julia, a Hispanic woman, described these differences: "White women come and they say, 'We're open, let's talk about it, let's get it together, we have an hour.' . . . Our cultural stuff says we sit down, we have coffee, we eat, we sit down, we talk, we move . . . and American culture says . . . we have a time limit" (Garcia et al., 1987, p. 149).

In spite of the demands of intercultural or interracial counseling, the potential rewards are enormous. Again borrowing Julia's words describing her interracial relationship, "we are getting the goodies of learning there are different ways to do different things, learning not to be judgmental, learning to try to pay attention to differences" (Garcia et al., 1987, p. 159).

Black Americans

Black American women are stereotyped in a number of ways, sometimes conflicting with each other, usually negative (White, 1985): as highly sexual and promiscuous, as not capable of loving relationships or long-term bonds, as tough and unemotional, as superwomen who can overcome any obstacle, as long-suffering victims, and as quick-tempered and aggressive. These stereotypes have led to damaging and incorrect assumptions about Black sexual abuse victims: that they are not as affected by trauma as whites, that they don't need counseling or emotional help, that they are more difficult to help.[2] The helper may need to work with other interveners to counteract stereotypes that may interfere with appropriate treatment. The helper may also need to counteract her own stereotypes—for example, one should never assume that a quiet Black client is not emotional, that an angry Black client is violent "by nature," or that a Black client's intelligence or achievement is due to "street smarts" rather than giftedness (Trotman, 1984). H. Landrine (1988) warns us of damaging labeling of, and clinical assumptions about, Black clients.

More difficult to counteract may be overt racial discrimination or racism by others who are supposed to help the victim. For example, when the victim is Black and the offender is White, police (who are likely to be White as well) may accuse her of being seductive or they may refuse to intervene.

Laura, a professional who is a Black woman, was walking down her street when a White man pulled up in an expensive car and began making sexual threats. She ran to a policeman and asked for help. Instead of intervening, he suggested the driver merely thought she was available. Then he commented that he might be interested himself.

Physical delineation of "neighborhoods" may create a double standard: White men can sometimes move freely in so-called "Black neighborhoods," but a Black person who goes into a predominantly White neighborhood may be chastised—or arrested. A few years ago a Black woman who had been kidnapped and taken into an upper-class White neighborhood and raped was escorted by police to the border and told not to come back into that part of the city. A predominantly White jury might have responded the same way. This kind of treatment makes the "passive" reactions of many Black survivors reasonable under the circumstances. It is not surprising that, as Quina and coworkers found, only one of 32 minority women raped by a White man had reported the assault to the police.[3]

When the offender is Black, another set of problems arises. The victim may find it difficult to report the abuse out of "race loyalty" (White, 1985). Non-minority opinions about Black men are strongly negative, and filing a complaint against another Black person will reinforce those stereotypes. There is also intracultural pressure to tolerate violence by Black men. Black women are urged to understand their men's needs and frustrations and to view the violence as a normal outcome of racism. Brownmiller (1975) and White (1985) discuss this problem and effectively counter it as a misapplication of blame. Finally, there is a real chance that excessive force and punishment will be applied to a Black offender (Brownmiller, 1975). Many Black victims stay silent to avoid causing further violence.

Support from other Black women is an important aspect of recovery. Trotman and Gallagher (1987) describe a therapy group for Black women in which support is an important element. Two support structures in the Black community are also important to consider: the extended family, where Black women in particular enjoy close bonds, and the church, which serves as the moral and social center for the Black community. Frequently, these strong supports enable Black survivors to cope with the emotional aftermath of sexual assault without external intervention. However, if family members attempt to keep the abuse silent, or the pastor or church elders are not sympathetic (White, 1985), their influence may be damaging. Because they are such powerful forces in the client's life, it is especially important to ensure that family members and the church are being helpful. If not, intervention with those others may help them to understand her situation, or the client may need to link up with a new support group to overcome their negative influences. White (1985) suggests that women should organize to help educate their church elders and members before any abuse issues arise, to prepare them to assist survivor members. This can be done through guest speakers or self-study programs, ideally with the goal of linking the church to related community agencies such as a women's shelter or rape crisis center.

Hispanic Americans

A number of different minorities are included under the rubric "Hispanic," having very different cultural histories and patterns, and different levels of integration into the majority culture. Variables such as education, income, and family structure may differ dramatically across different Hispanic cultures and among individuals within each culture (Amaro & Russo, 1987). It is important to recognize each client's individuality and, if a long-term relationship is to take place, to learn more about her cultural perspective.

As with other minorities, Hispanic women are subjected to extensive stereotyping—for example, that they are very sexual and overtly seductive. The stereotyped image of *machismo* among Hispanic men (critiqued by Vazquez-Nuttall et al., 1987) is often extended by implication to Hispanic women, who are assumed to like rough treatment by dominant men. As with Black American clients, the helper may need to counteract her own stereotypes and also the mistreatment created by these stereotypes from others involved in the case.

For some Hispanic clients, particularly recent immigrants, the language barrier is a significant problem (Espin, 1987a; Gibson, 1983). If the client and helper must work through an interpreter, an extra layer of potential mistrust and miscommunication arises. Therefore, for clients for whom English is difficult, it is important to try to find a Spanish-speaking helper as early as possible in the intervention process. Many community agencies have bilingual staff members who can assist in emergencies as well as carry out long-term counseling. The role of advocate, helping the client obtain appropriate services and ensuring that other service providers understand sexual abuse issues and needs, is thus very important. For any person planning to work in an area with a Spanish-speaking population, it is a good idea to take courses in conversational Spanish and appropriate Hispanic history or culture.

As a culture, Hispanics tend to be more open about their feelings, allowing greater emotional expressiveness, particularly from women (Williams & Holmes, 1981). For clients who follow this cultural pattern, it may be easier to determine the nature of their problem, to elicit information about the abuse, and to determine needs. Emotionally expressive clients may also need more time to express their feelings before taking any concrete actions. It is especially important to avoid stereotyping such emotional states as pathological or hysterical, as a crisis intervener accustomed to a less expressive culture might tend to do (Holmes, 1980).

La familia (the extended family) and the community are strong forces in the lives of Hispanics (Baron, 1981; Espin, 1987b); and family and community supports should be utilized wherever possible. However, a strong family may also prevent obtaining help for a victim, especially when a family member is the offender.[4] The general community mistrust of external authorities is compounded by intrafamilial protectiveness. These constraints must be appreciated, and reactions such as guilt over family disloyalty must be considered as potentially serious problems in any incest case.

Amaro and Russo (1987) have edited a helpful volume on Hispanic women's mental health, which includes information on specific groups and a bibliography of helpful resources.

Asian-Pacific Americans

As with Hispanics, a number of subpopulations are lumped under this general term, with tremendous individual, subcultural, and generational variations. However, all persons with "oriental" features tend to be treated with a singular stereotype; and for women, that image is especially problematic. Asian-Pacific women are viewed as extremely passive, servile, and sexually exotic, like the geisha. Asian bride catalogs advertise their female offerings as submissive servants, ready to meet every whim. Tragically, the women who come to the United States under these arrangements often become battered wives, victims of men who bought them to satisfy their dominance needs.

During the Korean and Vietnamese conflicts, a large number of American men engaged in or witnessed a violent dehumanizing of the citizens of those countries, especially the women. (Brownmiller, 1975, documents the systematic raping and murdering of women during those wars.) Having dehumanized these men and women as "enemies," and blaming them for two terrible wars, already violent American men may target Asian-Pacific women for sexual and other violence.

Strong cultural norms interfere with help-seeking by many Asian-Pacific Americans, for whom stoicism and saving face are important. Public emotional displays are forbidden, and seeking help for personal problems is imbued with personal shame. Help may only be sought when emotional distress is extremely serious, often of crisis proportions (Tsai & Uemura, 1988). The helper must appreciate the difficulty, and shame, the client has experienced just reaching the decision to seek help and must assist the client in coping with those feelings early in the helping process.

Recent immigrants from Southeast Asia are a special population of concern for any kind of intervention, but especially sexual abuse. Their language problems are often severe, because few Americans understand or speak the various Southeast Asian languages, and most immigrants have not had time to learn English. Furthermore, some of their customs are very different, and little cultural assimilation has had time to occur. The Southeast Asian interpreter may not understand or sympathize with an American view of sexuality or American ideas about what constitutes help; the community may close so tightly around a victim to protect her that well-intentioned helpers cannot get through. Some cultural responses are particularly upsetting. For example, one 16-year-old rape victim was forced to marry her assailant, because to do otherwise would be shameful from her parents' cultural perspective. As with other newly introduced cultures, greater assimilation may be expected to occur as second-generation immigrants come of age, and among them such problems should become less severe. Before the need arises, helpers living in areas with new immigrant populations would do well to identify resources such as translators and empathic counselors fluent in their native languages.

The recent Southeast Asian immigrant who makes it to the United States has often done so under extraordinary life-and-death circumstances and has lost or left many loved ones behind (Tsai & Uemura, 1988). The fact that the United States is perceived as "safe" may enhance the trauma of a sexual abuse that occurs here. Expression of the enormous accumulation of grief and fear over all these life traumas may be elicited by a sexual abuse, sometimes for the first time. On the other hand, survival may have depended in the past on a stoic, pragmatic approach to trauma, so that sexual abuse, while traumatic, does not elicit focused emotional energy. Those who intervene must consider all of these issues, including the client's past experiences, her expressed needs, and her personal strengths and coping strategies.

DISABLED CLIENTS

Most individuals with disabilities have worked hard to overcome physical and social barriers to achieve acceptance and full participation in society. Sexual abuse is often experienced as a negation of all that effort. Feelings of power-lessness are especially strong when the victim was unable to prevent abuse because of physical or mental disability. People with disabilities may also be targeted for abuse; Browning and Boatman (1977) suggest that disabled children are particularly at risk for incest. The reality of this helplessness may initiate or heighten self-directed anger at a body that doesn't "work right," feelings of lack of control over personal destiny, and fear of future victimization.

Several attitudinal errors are important to avoid when working with a disabled client. First, a disability is commonly seen as the defining characteristic of the person, which restricts the helper's perspective on the client (Asch, 1984).

Second, disabled individuals are often viewed as dependent, as help seekers and not as help givers (Fine & Asch, 1988). Counselors and other helpers should include help-giving options in the client's recovery plan whenever possible (such as volunteering for a rape hotline, as described in Chapter 8).

Third, stereotypes of retardation, asexuality, neuroticism, and psychopathol-ogy resulting from disability abound in society and have been promoted by the clinical literature, especially by psychoanalytic writings (Asch & Rousso, 1985). Every helper should be aware of these restrictive stereotypes and their potential impact on the intervention process. When any client, especially a disabled client, is experiencing emotional distress, it is important to look to external situational causes such as social rejection rather than to assume internal psychopathology.

The counselor should find out as much as possible about any neurological or emotional implications of the disabling condition or of medication taken to treat the condition, and take these into account at all times. Mentally handicapped clients may need a special therapist who is familiar with the process of interpreting and communicating in the client's own language and level of comprehension. However, accommodations in the counseling process should never diminish the client's dignity or be allowed to reduce her potential for resolution.

The problems that may be encountered with disabled clients depend on the nature and extent of their disabilities and their past experiences coping with them. Some potential areas of concern are the following:

1. The disabled client who has always been treated—and has seen herself—as different from others may need help seeing that much of her experience of sexual abuse is the same as others' experience (Center for Women Policy Studies, 1984). Support net-works that include nondisabled survivors can help in dispelling myths for disabled and nondisabled clients.

2. The disabled survivor who already had a tendency to separate mental from physical functioning in daily life may need to work toward integrating mind and body on a more fundamental level. The client's level of emotional comfort with her body and adaptation to her physical condition may be considered as part of the overall resolution.

3. Disabled persons, particularly women, may not have had any sexual experience prior to the abuse, and in some cases they may lack any self-perception as a sexual person (A. Asch & Fine, 1988). Sexual abuse may create a belief that one's only sexual

value is as an object of abuse. Differentiating abuse from sexuality, and helping the client define her own sexuality independent of a relationship, are important considerations.

4. A physical or mental disability, often already the object of hate or anger, may provide a concrete target for the rage that arises after abuse. Assisting the disabled client to direct anger appropriately must take this additional potential for self-hate into account.

5. For a person who must live with at least some level of reliance on others, the loss of trust after abuse takes on broader implications. When the offender had played a helping role in the client's life, daily existence becomes unsafe. In addition to dealing with the need to redevelop trust, more direct and immediate care may be required. The helper may need to assist the client in arranging for new service providers who can be trusted and offer options for protection and reporting if future abuse occurs.

OLDER CLIENTS

Women over the age of sixty tend to be frightened about their vulnerability to crime in general because of their reduced physical ability to avoid or escape it (Law Enforcement Assistance Administration, 1980). However, many still think of rape as a sexual act that only happens to young women, not to them, and are shocked that it is even a possibility. Sexual victimization of an older woman is an especially difficult experience to comprehend and cope with, for the victim and for her friends and family.

Rape is the most commonly reported sexual abuse of older women. It most often occurs within or in the immediate area of the victim's home and is perpetrated by a stranger or someone not well known (Groth, 1979). It tends to be opportunistic, that is, part of another crime such as burglary. Sexual assaults on the elderly also seem to be more violent; 21 percent involve multiple offenders (Hicks & Moon, 1980), and humiliating acts are also performed during the assault. Furthermore, the physical status of many older persons—more brittle bones, thinner and less lubricated vaginal walls—leaves them seriously injured more often. Hicks and Moon (1980) reported that 63 percent of sexual assault victims over age fifty experience body trauma, and 38 percent experience vaginal trauma; for younger victims these figures are 19 percent and 5 percent, respectively.

Many sexual abuses of older men and women may go unreported. Increasingly, however, elderly survivors are finding a voice to tell of physical abuse at the hands of caretakers and family members (Filinson & Ingman, in press; Hotaling et al., 1988). These facts are emerging slowly; many of the victims are afraid, and many are unable to report the abuse because the abuser is the sole source of care or support, because they are not allowed outside contact, because others respond to their claims as "senility," or because they are suffering from disabling physical or mental conditions that prevent communication.

Because of these situations and for other reasons, the older survivor is likely to suffer a high level of trauma after sexual abuse (Burt & Katz, 1985). In spite of claims that the elderly deserve respect, the elderly survivor is likely to be treated with little concern. One tendency is to assume that older people are less capable and to "take over" for them. Those who intervene must maintain a strong respect for the individual client's needs, while including special assistance in the treatment plan for physical concerns, emotional reactions, and independence (Russo, 1985, pp. 24–27). For example, hearing and speed of processing information decline with age, so with some clients the helper will have to speak louder and more slowly, and repeat information. Not all older clients have these difficulties, however, and many are insulted when a younger person shouts at them.

Physical Needs

The physical damage from sexual abuse of an elderly client is likely to require more extensive treatment and may not ever heal. Advocacy may require searching for appropriate and sensitive medical care and accompanying the client to the physical examinations and treatment. Some older clients must have an advocate who will take careful written notes on treatments and medications that they can refer to later. It may be helpful to assist the older client in filling out forms for reimbursement from Medicare or other insurance policies, to negotiate payment plans for remaining bills, and to locate alternate forms of assistance, such as victim assistance funds.

Fear

Extreme fear is common for the older survivor (Davis, 1980). For someone who is retired, or living alone, this fear may be paralyzing—reducing activities outside the home and dominating thoughts while inside. Fear of repeated abuse may generalize and become a feeling that the client has lost control over her whole life, which may increase vulnerability to depression and physical illness (Davis, 1980; Langer & Rodin, 1976).

The first step in assisting the client is to encourage her to exert some control over her life. Specific prevention tactics are offered by Davis (1980) and Davis and Brody (1979). The client should be helped to obtain and install reasonable protective devices, such as window and door locks or alarms. These devices should be easy to operate, so that she does not feel like a "prisoner in her own home," bolted and locked in so heavily that she cannot easily receive guests or leave.

Humiliation

The older women of the 1980s grew up during a period when sex was associated with silence and shame, and more older than younger women have never experienced sex with anyone except their husbands. A sexual assault may be interpreted in the context of these beliefs and this sexual fidelity. Talking about details, whether to strangers such as policemen or to other family members, is particularly difficult for women who may seldom have discussed anything about sex with anyone. Some victims are not familiar with acts like anal or oral sex, or associate those acts only with extreme moral degradation. Humiliating to any victim, such acts may carry additional moral connotations for an older woman. Furthermore, the majority of assaults on older victims, as with younger victims, are carried out by young men (Groth, 1979). The assailant may be the same age as the son or grandson of the older woman, and in cases of "con" assaults, may remind her of a loved young family member. This psychological association is particularly traumatic.

The husband of an older victim is likely to hold similar beliefs about sex and may see his wife as unfaithful or defiled, or be unable to touch her or express feelings for her after "sex with another man." The client may choose not to tell her husband, fearing his rejection. The spouse or affected family members of older victims often need intervention in resolving their feelings.

The older client may occupy a social role as the strong family member, the person who takes care of others. With an outside helper she doesn't have to be the "strong one" and can receive the care she needs. Many older survivors have felt that no matter how supportive their families have been, they appreciated having a person in whom they could confide their deepest feelings without burdening their children or subjecting themselves to the humiliation of revealing sexual information to them.

Depression and Coping

Older Americans are particularly vulnerable to depression, because they are not so likely to be participating in structured activities and because the deaths of life partners and age peers may leave them sad and lonely. The grief and loss associated with sexual abuse increase the likelihood of serious depression, particularly if the client lives alone or has few social activities. In addition to the standard interventions for depression, the older client often needs to have daily contact with some support system. In-home options include the Visiting Nurses Association, Meals on Wheels, or a local eldercare group. Since physical and social activity counteract depression, the best option may be a senior citizens' activity center that may be visited on a daily basis. While the depressed older client is likely to be resistant (as with any other depressed client), a few visits to such a center are likely to change her view dramatically.

Independence

Living independently ranks high among the needs of older citizens, and the home is psychologically very important to the older woman, especially a widow (O'Bryant & Nocera, 1985). One-third of elder female victims are living alone at the time of the assault, directly threatening that independence and compounding the trauma of sexual abuse. In some cases there is no option but to move into a facility where physical therapy or care is available. If so, assisting the client to find an appropriate facility and supporting her in her move becomes an important intervention function. In other cases, adjustments should be made to the client's existing home or routine in order to help her feel independent. Social networks should be developed in conjunction with physical security systems. If neighborhood protective groups exist, she should be connected with them; in some instances an attack on an elderly neighbor mobilizes the formation of such a group.

Well-meaning family members may attempt to move the older survivor into a nursing home or senior citizens' facility against her will, feeling it is safer and more sheltered. An important advocacy role is to help the family members review their reasons for these efforts, to try to get them to hear and respect the client's feelings, and to place her needs first in the decision-making process.

CLIENTS ABUSED BY A PRIOR THERAPIST

Pope and Bouhoutsos (1986) have documented and described what is unfortunately a common experience for clients of a substantial minority of therapists: a sexual relationship taking place within the context of (or in place of) therapy. In studies of the effects of sexual contact with a therapist, the outcomes for the client are overwhelmingly negative, even when the client feels she or he agreed to the relationship willingly. The adverse effects include decreased social and personal functioning, including problems with sexual and intimate relationships; increased drug and alcohol abuse; and severe problems with trust of men (who are the vast majority of the abusive therapists) and of therapists in general. In spite of the difficulty in trusting therapists, an estimated 90 percent seek subsequent therapy to cope with the abuse (Stone, 1980, discussed in Pope & Bohoutsos, 1986).

Many who study therapist-client sex compare the relationship to incestuous abuse: an older, paternal man socializes a younger, inexperienced woman into the "ways of the world" with a combination of assurances that his actions are helpful to her and threats. The incest survivor may be particularly vulnerable to sexual abuse on the part of a therapist, partly because her confusion of love and sex prevents her from seeing the abusive nature of the therapist's behavior, partly because of her learned helplessness, and partly because her existing pattern of self-blame will apply to the therapist's actions as well. In one well-publicized case, an abusive therapist had specifically advertised for clients who had been incest victims.

The relationship between therapist and client is always complex and likely to involve transference and countertransference (discussed in incest counseling by Courtois, 1988). The abusive therapist uses the transference to invoke her submission, seeming to meet the client's need for a caring person. In return, the client often feels a strong emotional commitment and a desire to help the therapist, in spite of the sexual betrayal. The problems that brought the client to therapy in the first place, including sexual abuse, are not likely to be treated (Bouhoutsos et al., 1983), leaving her with a combination of unresolved prior issues, plus new problems created by this sexual abuse. Furthermore, the abusive therapist is likely to link the client's mental health or "chance to get well" to the sexual relationship, creating a new terror.

The "second therapist," the person called upon to help the client recover from abuse by a former counselor (or any other trusted professional), has an important set of tasks.

- Trust must be built from scratch, often with concrete assurances such as "no physical contact," and the level to which the client has put up her guard or is suspicious of each therapy activity must be appreciated and worked through.

- Intervention must help the client recognize the prior sexual relationship (whether perceived as voluntary or not) as an abuse of power and a violation of ethical codes. The responsibility for the sexual relationship must be placed squarely on the shoulders of the prior therapist. Even if the client invited contact, the therapist was required by professional ethics to refuse the request.

- Therapy must deal with the emotional aftereffects of the sexual abuse, including anger, betrayal of trust, depression, emotional numbness, guilt, and shame. (See Pope & Bouhoutsos, 1986, for specific suggestions.)

- Feelings toward the abusive therapist, which may be mixed, must be resolved in much the same way as for a client with an abusive parent. The client's attachment to, or love for, the therapist may be as strong as the rage and hurt associated with his betrayal of power and trust. Such apparently conflicting emotions are often confusing and frightening to the client. Helping her separate feelings about the person from feelings about his abusive acts, and validating both sets of feelings, are often helpful.

- The client may be informed of her option to file complaints or seek reparation for the damage done by the prior therapist and offered support if any of these options are pursued. Sometimes, for the second therapist angered by the irresponsibility of a colleague, a client's unwillingness to report an incident is frustrating but the counselor's primary responsibility is to the client, and the client's confidence must be inviolate.

- The therapist must never attempt to serve as legal advisor for the client; a carefully selected lawyer is best suited to determine the appropriate steps to take and cautions to consider (Pope & Bouhoutsos, 1986, p. 87).

NOTES

1. Helpers should not limit their thinking about their client's strengths to their own experience. Some strengths may not be familiar—for example, the Black woman's willingness to protect herself in the presence of a weapon (Bart & O'Brien, 1985) is not typical for White women. The helper who listens may model new strengths from her client as well.

2. Appreciation is due to Karen Green and Gwendolyn Jones, who assisted us with resources and reactions to the issues of client stereotyping.

3. This research project was carried out in 1975–1976 and was led by Judith Jasper, Willa Lunsford, and Kathryn Quina, assisted by other members of the University of Wisconsin–Milwaukee Rape Action Team.

4. Carmen Tovez (personal communication, 1985) identified the issue of protectiveness in Hispanic families for us and provided other valuable input.

RECOMMENDED READINGS

Boston Lesbian Psychologies Collective. *Lesbian Psychologies*. Chicago, Ill.: University of Illinois Press, 1987.

Bronstein, P., and Quina, K. *Teaching a Psychology of People: Resources for Gender and Sociocultural Awareness*. Washington, D.C.: American Psychological Association, 1988.

Scher, M.; Stevens, M.; Good, G.; & Eichenfield, G.A. *Handbook of Counseling and Psychotherapy with Men*. Newbury Park Calif.: Sage, 1988.

Stuart, I.R., and Greer, J.G., eds. *Victims of Sexual Aggression: Treatment of Children, Women and Men*. New York: Van Nostrand Reinhold, 1984.

CHAPTER APPENDIX 10A: COUNSELING MEN

1. Most men have been raised to believe the desired male role is that of an independent, aggressive, and unemotional person (Broverman et al., 1970). A healthy role is more complex and not so limiting. Growth issues in working with male clients revolve around developing intimacy, emotional expression, and relating to others.

2. Dominance, control, and power are issues that prevent intimacy for men. They should be addressed as barriers to emotional growth. Fears about losing control must be dealt with and overcome.

3. Vulnerability is often viewed as "feminine" and therefore "bad." Men need to come to terms with their own vulnerability, first coming to value it as a strength (Miller, 1986) and then integrating it into their personalities.

4. Exploring emotional needs can be frightening for men, and that terror can block the counseling process. The counselor may have to move slowly and carefully in assisting the client with recognizing and accepting feelings and needs, coping with issues such as insecurity and lack of worth, and understanding emotions and finding safe and productive ways to express them.

5. Men often prefer a woman counselor because they feel "safe." However, some men expect her to take on a role of caretaker, as other women in their lives have done. The female counselor must watch for signs of her client's expectations that she will help him avoid facing his fears, and see that he confronts them whenever necessary.

6. Many men, especially victimized men, have a low sense of self-worth, even though they may cover it with a "tough" exterior. Easy assurances of the client's worth will only shore up rigid defenses and delay growth. Rather, the therapeutic environment should foster the client's self-discovery of his own worth, and assurances should come

later in the process when the client is ready to assimilate the counselor's recognition of his worth.

7. Reactions of pain to issues raised in counseling may be expressed as aggressiveness toward the therapist or as a refusal to accept anything the counselor offers. It is easy to respond to such attacks with defensiveness, but instead the counselor should counter the aggression with a nondefensive effort to clarify the issues of pain and fear, in order to create greater trust.

8. Sex and intimacy are often fused for men, and in therapy they must be kept clearly differentiated.

9. Homosexuality is often associated with "feminine" qualities, and both are feared by many men. Sexual orientation and gender role must be clearly differentiated and the client's fears about each addressed and resolved.

Source: Carlson (1981, 1988).

Epilogue: Empowerment

Throughout this volume, the concept of power has been used in a negative context, as we worked with the consequences of abuses of power. However, some forms of personal power are essential to the recovery process, as well as to healthy intervention work. In this epilogue, we offer some concrete ways to help ourselves and our clients gain personal power.

Miller (1986) has pointed out that gentle people, and women in particular, tend to react to the term ''power'' negatively because it has traditionally been defined in a hierarchical fashion of who dominates whom. In the traditional framework, in order for one to gain power, another must lose power. Miller offers a new framework for understanding and regaining power, and that framework is adopted here for both internal growth and external action.

Miller has redefined power in terms of making things happen, collectively as well as individually. Power is obtained through accomplishment, through achieving goals, and is enhanced when others become more powerful (or accomplished) as well. This kind of power is already inside each of us, but must be recognized and nurtured through *empowerment*. Empowerment, a process consistent with the therapeutic approach adopted in this volume, helps the individual appreciate her own strengths and find a voice for their expression for the common good rather than for external control or power over others.

This epilogue offers the ideas of the women, men, and children who have shared their visions with us. It is easy to feel powerless, to give up because it seems that, working alone or even in a small group, one individual cannot have an impact. However, the success of the rape crisis movement has shown that the whole of social change is greater than the individual acts and that every person can have a positive influence. Thus we conclude this volume with some concrete steps people take toward the goal of ending sexual exploitation, of others and of themselves.

STEPS TOWARD PERSONAL EMPOWERMENT

Taking Charge of the Past

Empowerment must begin with the belief that each person has the ability to have some power over her own life. This is one of the core beliefs destroyed by sexual abuse; yet some personal power over the past must be reestablished in order to take charge of the future.

In the face of past victimization, and knowledge of the possibility of future abuse, this belief cannot be accomplished with simple reassurances. In fact, we must be careful not to encourage a false belief in control over the external events of the future. What should be nurtured is a *belief in one's ability to direct her own outcomes—emotionally and socially—including the ability to overcome the effects of sexual abuse*. A person may not be able to prevent an abusive act, but she can find the internal strength and the external support to cope. As an incest survivor told us, "I had to learn that the incest was not going to rule me; I was going to decide how and whether it was going to dominate the rest of my life." This choice, which often takes the form of an active decision, can be the turning point in the shift from victim to survivor.

Developing Awareness and Wariness

Specific situations and cues have been identified as particularly dangerous for sexual abuse, and some behaviors have been identified as making the individual particularly vulnerable to assault. This information must be handled carefully, however. First, vulnerability must never be associated with blame of the person who is victimized in one of these situations or after engaging in a more vulnerable behavior. No person is ever free of risk, and certainly being vulnerable does not invite or condone sexual abuse. Second, the helper must not give a false sense that avoiding certain situations or behaviors will prevent sexual abuse; at best, a person can only reduce her chances for certain types of abuse.

The major approach taken in prevention advice may be characterized as "assertive wariness." Recognizing risky situations or behaviors is combined with developing alternative escape or avoidance strategies. A good general analogy is found in strategies for avoiding purse-snatching. Most women have developed protective ways of holding their purses, or use alternatives for carrying their money and other belongings. It is easy to demonstrate the issue of vulnerability by showing two ways of carrying a purse (tucked under the arm with a shoulder strap versus a light grip at the end of a small handle), but noting that the latter person neither invites nor deserves to have her money stolen. Conroy and Ritvo

(1977) offer specific defense strategies and Levine-MacCombie and Koss (1986) offer strategies for avoiding acquaintance rape.

Explicit in these strategies is permission for the individual to take preventive steps. Ironically, some of the most effective strategies have been discouraged because they seem "unfeminine" or "impolite." Many women, on hearing these strategies, become frightened of seeming paranoid. It is important to believe for oneself that it is better to risk seeming overly careful than to risk assault.

Developing Confidence in Physical Strength

The work of Bart and O'Brien (1985) and others shows clearly that in many situations the best way to cope with a potential sexual abuse is an immediate response, including physical actions such as screaming and running. Part of the problem is that women have been told they are too weak to fight back and should submit; in addition there is the belief that physical resistance means the victim must overcome any assailant. The new approach developing within the feminist movement is twofold: helping women develop the confidence to attempt some action, and recognizing that the best physical reaction may be an active escape strategy, not a battle with the assailant. "Common sense" self-defense strategies are based on this approach (e.g., Smith, 1978).

Until recently, women were discouraged from any physical activity or exercise, much less active self-defense. With the new positive image of sports for women, it is much more acceptable for women to work toward personal physical enhancement. Classes in aerobics, dance, and weight training are widely available; partners for sports such as tennis and racquetball are easy to find; and one can jog or exercise with only basic training. Those who are physically unable to participate in sports or active exercise can still find ways to work with individual strengths to enhance physical coping strategies. While the individual's goal for this physical exercise may be health, flexibility, or strength, the most important outcome is likely to be body awareness and confidence.

Self-defense classes are also valuable for building self-confidence. The classes should be evaluated in advance for the approach taken by the instructor (e.g., defense v. attack strategies, weapons v. physical action) and the level of commitment required (some courses require two or more nights per week over several months). Women who have been able to study self-defense have reported extraordinary gains, not just in strength but in their confidence in their own power to react in emergency situations. *Fear into Anger* (Bateman, 1978) is a good starting point for someone wanting to undertake a self-defense course.

An important caution, however, must be placed throughout any discussion on physical action. In the event of an attack, physical action—including the most practiced self-defense tactic—may not be the reaction of choice, or it may be unsuccessful. Unfortunately, being victimized in spite of physical preparation often leads to anger at oneself, for not being prepared enough, not hitting in the right place, being too frightened to react. The individual must balance confidence in her physical strength with the understanding that if it does not help her avoid a sexual assault, the assault is not her fault for "not doing enough." There are times when the best action is no action, and there are times when we are outmaneuvered or physically overpowered.

Educating Ourselves and Others

Those interested in reducing victimization on a larger scale will want to understand more about the sources of external power imposed on women, power that starts with the socialization of masculinity and femininity. A women's studies course at a local college or university is the best resource for the most recent literature on socialization, victimization, and the other relevant issues raised in Chapter 2. Such courses also attract other aware, concerned individuals, who can form a supportive environment for personal empowerment. Some courses, formal and informal, are specifically geared toward awareness and empowerment (Quina & Paxson, 1987). If no course is available, an individual or small group can read texts such as Lott's (1987) *Women's Lives: Themes and Variations in Gender Learning*, which provides an excellent review of the literature as well as perspective on the processes of learning—and unlearning—gender roles.

EXTERNAL EMPOWERMENT

In the face of rising rates of sexual violence against women, it is hard to maintain a sense of hope for a brighter future. However, there are ways to link together with others to promote positive change by reducing sociocultural tolerance of sexual exploitation, establishing mechanisms to deal with abuse when it occurs, and helping survivors recover by assisting sexual victims. Some specific suggestions are offered here.

Sociocultural Change: The Case of Media Violence

Malamuth and Donnerstein (1984) have suggested that the media are an important starting point, because the increasingly violent television and movie images, which are also increasingly associated with sex and degradation of women, have been demonstrated to affect tolerance for a more violent reality. The extent to which the actual flow of images can be censored is hotly debated as a First Amendment civil rights issue. Some individual actions, however, are clearly possible. For example, the reactions engendered in the individuals viewing these violent and degrading images can be altered with educational interventions (Eron, 1986).

Many images pass by without awareness of their sexually exploitive message, including common advertisements. The awareness films *Killing Us Softly* (Kilbourne, 1979) and *Still Killing Us Softly* (Kilbourne, 1987) come with information about organizations and actions to address the advertising industry and other offenders.

As few as two letters can have an enormous impact on advertisers and corporations. One individual letter to a corporation that has an offensive advertisement, or with a product that is being advertised during an offensive show, often calls the offensive message to their attention. A second letter sent to a magazine such as *Ms.* encouraging others to join in the protest lets the corporation feel the force of an entire movement. The effect of consumer power has forced even huge conglomerates, such as Nestle, to change offensive practices.

Parents can take time to discuss with their children—and their teenagers—the feelings the victims of violence or of stereotyping might experience and the reasons the violence and stereotyping are disempowering. Alternative ways to handle situations can be offered, in concrete terms. Concerned individuals can talk to their family members, friends, and coworkers about experiences such as feeling degraded by a particular movie or ad. More often than not, their reaction is surprise ("I never thought of it that way") and appreciation for increasing their awareness.

Institutional Pressure

Increasingly, schools, hospitals, government agencies, and corporations are recognizing that sexual harassment and internal abuse are more costly than they are worth, both in terms of publicity and in losses in court settlements. More employees and students are demanding formal policies and action on individual cases. Steps toward developing such policies, as well as model cases, are found in Clarke (1982) and Paludi (in press).

The most influential force shaping the work or learning environment, however, is upper management. Convincing the people at the top to feel concerned and to express their concerns openly can create the most dramatic change toward fairness and equity in the workplace or classroom (Meyer et al., 1981). Approach the management with a group of other concerned individuals, bringing proposals for working together to end all forms of sex discrimination, offering positive solutions and alternatives.

Taking Back the Night

In cities and towns across the nation, one night each year a special march is held—a march of women to "take back the night." The feeling that is aroused by walking together with hundreds of other women, safe even on streets a woman would avoid during the daytime, is an extraordinary sense of empowerment. Each woman reading this volume is encouraged to join the march the next time it is held nearby; call the local National Organization for Women (NOW) chapter or rape crisis center for details.

That feeling of empowerment in a group can extend throughout the year.

Literally dozens of groups need help and provide ways to bring individual voices into collective power. Although some of the actions described are controversial, *Fight Back* (Delacoste & Newman, 1981) allows a glimpse of some of the ways women have worked together on specific empowerment issues, notably projects to end violence against women, many with great success. Some women have formed living communities around such projects and have found personally fulfilling life-styles emerging alongside social change.

Raising Nonviolent Children

As stressed throughout this volume, our culture's gender roles of masculinity and femininity are consistent with the sexually abusive roles of victimizer and victim. The way in which girls and boys are taught to ''fit'' their prescribed roles may also incorporate violence; for example, women and men who ''step out of line'' or don't fit the role are regarded as fair targets for hostility.

Children model their parents and other adults, and concerned adults can provide models of nonsexist, nonviolent behavior. Other social forces are at work on children everywhere—in nursery schools, where boys and girls are more or less subtly guided to active and passive toys, respectively; in toy stores, where the pictures on the boxes clearly tell children where to look; in children's stories, where boys act and girls look on. Parents must be alert and express their concerns, providing their children with a range of toys and activities that counteract these stereotypes.

At the same time, one must not forget that it is difficult for a child to be ''different,'' particularly when the child is a male learning to be nonviolent. Some children may be subject to hostility, even from other children. Thus a special requirement is that the child be taught specific ways to handle her or his differences and to rely on herself or himself to judge right and wrong behavior. The *Free to be* . . . books are good places to start discussions of being different (Thomas, 1987; Thomas et al., 1987).

A number of rape crisis centers and other agencies have developed programs for educating children in sexual abuse prevention, using the ''good touch, bad touch'' model. The Rhode Island Rape Crisis Center (1660 Broad Street, Cranston, RI 02905) offers such a program in school, church, camp, and other settings, adapted for children as young as three through older adolescents. The national Child Abuse Prevention Project offers model programs and helpful information for establishing a local program (National Assault Prevention Center, P.O. Box 02005, Columbus, OH 43202).

Growing in Relationships

In adulthood it is not too late to change, even after years of stereotypical living. Men and women in relationships can learn how to love and live with each other in egalitarian, respectful ways (Miller, 1986). Helping a partner appreciate and adopt nonstereotyped patterns may be the most important change one can make towards ending violence. Men and women who are living under the negative effects of stereotypical gender roles are encouraged to explore their options, notably, emotional expression for men and self-confidence for women. The resulting enrichment of their lives and their relationships will make the effort well worthwhile.

THE PROMISE OF A BRIGHTER FUTURE

Reviewing the stories of the women and men of this volume, we are often deeply impressed by the models they offer of successful resolution, even after the most terrible experiences. We will end with one survivor's story, to remind the reader that there is a brighter future possible for every victim—not just to survive, but to thrive.

Lee's early years were happy, with a loving father. When she was eight her father died, and her mother, claiming she "needed a man," remarried right away. When Lee was twelve, her stepfather took her on a trip to a nearby city. There, he began fondling her and talking about sex. She pushed him away but he pressed on, saying that both her sisters took trips with him and there had been "no problems with them." When she still refused, he raped her.

Lee informed her mother, who refused to believe her. Her sisters sided with their stepfather as well. Still frightened and angry, she sought help from the police, who prosecuted him and moved her into an orphanage in another town. Her stepfather was eventually acquitted in court on the basis of testimony from her mother and his friends. Rather than return home, Lee stayed at the orphanage and was ultimately taken in by members of her extended family.

Over time, Lee struggled with her feelings of anger, grief over the death of her father and her betrayal by her stepfather, mother, and sisters. Drawing upon the brief but important model her father had provided and the love and caring from others after she left home, she resolved to become a good partner, parent, and friend. Now in her forties, she views the experience as a reality in her life that she has overcome. She has memories that sadden her for short periods, but she handles them by talking to her husband, who is supportive and loving. She has made a special effort to teach her children about sexual abuse and to develop their skills for handling bad experiences. She maintains a high level of personal control, sometimes seeming tense, but her relationships with others are warm, loving, perceptive, and wise.

Appendix I: Types of Professional Counselors

Professionals who can offer effective therapeutic assistance in dealing with the long-term effects of sexual abuse may be trained in various settings. As discussed in Chapter 3, good counseling depends on the level of training and experience of the professional, particularly with respect to sexual abuse issues. In this appendix we will describe the types of counselors a victim might see, with an emphasis on the special reasons for seeking out each type. For some types of therapists, the state has designated a board to certify and to oversee the professional's work, including grievances. For any counselor working under the auspices of an agency, the agency itself is also liable for its employee's work and should be notified in case of a problem or grievance.

Before entering counseling with any professional, the client should know her or his training, experience, and licensing status. If the professional is licensed, the client can contact the appropriate state licensing board to confirm that she or he is in good standing. If the professional is not licensed, the client should seek more information, perhaps from the local rape crisis center, about that professional's qualifications and helpfulness.

Many rape crisis centers offer short-term counseling at reduced or no cost to sexual abuse victims and their families. These options should be explored for clients, including the use of this counseling as an adjunct to ongoing counseling for more general problems.

Psychiatrists are physicians, trained in medical school, with a specialization in emotional disorders. In order to work with clients privately, psychiatrists must have completed a specialized residency and be licensed by the state in which they practice. They are the only professionals allowed to prescribe medications such as tranquilizers or antidepressants. The medical model underlying their training makes psychiatrists especially appropriate when physical symptoms are predominant or when hospitalization is appropriate. Caution must be adopted, however, when the prescription of medication is used in place of therapy.

Psychologists have received graduate training in diagnosing and treating a range of mental disorders. Their specialties include counseling, clinical, community, and school psychology. As a group, psychologists are well trained for therapeutic intervention and are especially appropriate when other emotional or familial problems are compounded with sexual abuse. Psychologists engaged in private practice must in most states have earned a doctorate or equivalent, have one to two years' supervised experience, and be licensed according to regulations of the state.

Psychiatric social workers should have earned at least a master's degree in a graduate program emphasizing mental health and counseling. In general, social workers are oriented toward helping people within institutional systems, and they may be employed as staff members to assist clients in hospitals or state agencies. Social workers usually have special knowledge of legal and institutional issues and may be assigned to a case when child protective agencies or state funding are involved. Many states regulate private practice by licensing social workers.

Psychiatric nurses have been trained within a school of nursing, usually at the master's level, and have considerable medical knowledge. Although unable to prescribe medication or perform many medical treatment procedures, the combination of medical with psychological training especially qualifies psychiatric nurses for work with victims in hospitals or health centers. Registered nurses are licensed by the state in which they practice.

Ministers, priests, rabbis, or other religious agents, including *pastoral counselors*, vary widely in training for counseling or therapeutic intervention. Some have little or no formal education in psychology and rely solely on religious writings or beliefs to guide treatment. Others are highly trained, including doctoral-level course work and supervision, and are able to blend religious commitment and emotional healing effectively. Since religious organizations are not regulated by state or federal agencies, affiliated counselors must be evaluated on an individual basis, preferably with checks on background and references. The client's commitment to the religious belief system used is a key factor in appropriateness.

The terms *counselor, psychotherapist*, and *therapist* are usually not governed by state agencies and can be used in many states by people without any special training or regulation. Therefore one must exercise caution in selecting a helper from one of these categories. Many counselors are well qualified, holding a master's degree from a program in counseling, plus specialized training or experience in an issue such as sexual abuse. In fact, many women enter the field of counseling because of their extraordinary sensitivity to human issues. However, a few have abused the title by setting up a psychotherapy business without the appropriate training or credentials. Always ask for the counselor's training and references prior to treatment. In those states regulating master's-level counselors, certification should be expected.

Appendix II: The Victim Booklet

Several groups have developed helpful guides for victims of sexual abuse and their families and friends. The University of Rhode Island has distributed *Sexual Harassment and Assault: Myths and Realities* (Quina, Carlson, & Temple, 1982) to all students, staff, and faculty every few years. The book contains myths and facts about harassment and rape, the laws and policies concerning each, sections with information for victims, preventive tips, and resources on campus as well as in the community. It is available from Kathryn Quina at the Department of Psychology, The University of Rhode Island, Kingston, RI 02881.

The Philadelphia-based rape crisis center, Women Organized Against Rape (WOAR), has an exemplary booklet for sexual abuse victims in crisis, called *We Can Help*. The contents include questions and answers about the crisis center, the hospital, the police, the courtroom, and emotional reactions. The information is specific (e.g., why the hospital is chosen, details of the examination, information about sexually transmitted diseases, medications and side effects, and follow-up medical advice). WOAR is located at 1220 Sansom Street, Philadelphia, PA 19107.

The Rhode Island Rape Crisis Center gives its clients a small, easy-to-follow booklet in which to record pertinent information. In addition to guiding the victim through the process she is likely to experience post-abuse, the booklet has blanks for such data as the names of the advocate, police, and detectives involved in the case, and the physician, the forms signed, and when to expect the advocate's next contact. The volunteer advocate from the center usually takes responsibility for filling out the booklet during the medical examination and police interviews. A copy may be obtained from the Center at 1660 Broad Street, Cranston, RI 02905.

Bibliography

Abarbanel, G. (1980). The roles of the clinical social worker: Hospital-based management. In C.G. Warner, *Rape and sexual assault: Management and intervention*. Germantown, MD: Aspen Systems Corp.

Abel, G.G., Blanchard, E.B., & Becker, J.V. (1976). Psychological treatment of rapists. In M. Walker & S. Brodsky (Eds.), *Sexual assault: The victim and the rapist*. Lexington, MA: Lexington Books.

Abrahamsen, D. (1952). *Who are the guilty? A study of education and crime*. New York: Grove.

Abrams, R.D., & Finesinger, J.E. (1953). Guilt reactions in patients with cancer. *Cancer*, 6, 474–82.

Abramson, L.Y., Seligman, M.E. & Teasdale, J.D. (1978). Learned helplessness in humans: Critique and reformulation. *Journal of Abnormal Psychology*, 87(1), 49–74.

Adams, H.J., & Durham, L. (1977). A dialectical base for an activist approach to counseling. In E.I. Rawlings & D.K. Carter, *Psychotherapy for women: Treatment toward equality* (pp. 111–28). Springfield, IL: C.C. Thomas.

Adams, P.R. & Adams, G.R. (1984). Mount Saint Helens's ash fall: Evidence for a disaster stress reaction. *American Psychologist*, 39, 252–60.

Adler, A. (1929). *Problems of neurosis*. London: Kegan Paul.

Aftel, M., & Lakoff, R.T. (1985). *When talk is not cheap, or how to find the right therapist when you don't know where to begin*. New York: Warner.

Alliance Against Sexual Coercion. (1981). *Fighting sexual harassment: An advocacy handbook*. Boston: Alyson.

Alpert, J.L. (Ed.). (1986). *Psychoanalysis and women: Contemporary reappraisals*. Hillsdale, NJ: Analytic Press.

Amaro, H., & Russo, N.F. (Eds.). (1987). Hispanic women and mental health: Contemporary issues in research and practice. *Psychology of Women Quarterly*[Special Issue],11(4).

American Psychiatric Association. (1987). *Diagnostic and statistical manual of mental disorders* (3rd. ed.,Rev.). Washington, DC: American Psychiatric Association.

American Psychological Association. (1981). Ethical principles of psychologists. *American Psychologist*, 36, 633–38.

American Psychological Association. (1988). Ethics update[Statement of the APA Ethics Committee]. *APA Monitor*, 19 (12), 36.

Annas, G. (1975). *The rights of hospital patients*. New York: Avon [American Civil Liberties Union Handbook].

APA Task Force on Victims of Crime and Violence. (1984). *Final report*. Washington, D.C.: American Psychological Association.

Armsworth, M.W. (1987, August). *Abuse and support of adult incest survivors by helping professionals*. Paper presented at the American Psychological Association, New York, N.Y.

Asch, A. (1984). The experience of disability: A challenge for psychology. *American Psychologist*, 39, 529–36.

Asch, A., & Fine, M. (Eds.). (1988). Moving disability beyond stigma [Special Issue]. *Journal of Social Issues*, 44(1).

Asch, A., & Rousso, H. (1985). Therapists with disabilities: Theoretical and clinical issues. *Psychiatry*, 48, 1–12.

Asch, S. (1946). Forming impressions of personality. *Journal of Abnormal and Social Psychology*, 41, 258–90.

Baisden, M.J., Jr. (1971). *The world of rosaphrenia: The sexual psychology of the female*. Rancho Cordova, CA: Allied Research Society.

Bard, M., & Sangrey, D. (1986). *The crime victim's book* [2nd ed.]. New York: Brunner/Mazel.

Barnard, C.P., & Hirsch, C. (1985). Borderline personality and victims of incest. *Psychological Reports*, 57(3), 715–18.

Baron, A., Jr. (Ed.). (1981). *Explorations in Chicano psychology*. New York: Praeger.

Baron, L., & Straus, M.A. (1986). *Four theories of rape: A macrosociological analysis*. Paper presented at the International Congress on Rape, Jerusalem, Israel.

Bart, P., & O'Brien, P.H. (1985). *Stopping rape: Successful survival strategies*. Elmsford, NY: Pergamon.

Bass, E., & Davis, L. (1988). *The courage to heal: A guide for women survivors of child sexual abuse*. New York: Harper & Row.

Bassuk, E.L. (1980). A crisis theory perspective on rape. In S.L. McCombie (Ed.), *The rape crisis intervention handbook: A guide for victim care* (pp. 121–30). New York: Plenum.

Bateman, P. (1978). *Fear into anger: A manual of self-defense for women*. Chicago: Nelson-Hall.

Baum, A., Fleming, R., & Singer, J.E. (1983). Coping with victimization by technological disaster. *Journal of Social Issues*, 39(2), 119–140.

Beck, A.T. (1972). *Depression: Causes and treatments*. Philadelphia: University of Pennsylvania Press.

Beck, A.T., & Greenberg, R.L. (1974). Cognitive therapy with depressed women. In V. Franks & V. Burtle (Eds.), *Women and therapy: New psychotherapies for a changing society* (pp. 113–31). New York: Brunner/Mazel.

Beck, J. (Ed.) (1985). *The potentially violent patient and the Tarasoff decision in psychiatric practice.* Washington, D.C.: American Psychiatric Press.

Becker, J.V., & Skinner, L.J. (1984). Behavioral treatment of sexual dysfunctions in sexual assault. In I.R. Stuart & J.G. Greer (Eds.), *Victims of sexual aggression: Treatment of children, women and men* (pp. 211–33). New York: Van Nostrand Reinhold.

Becker, J.V., Skinner, L.J., Abel, G.G., & Treacy, E.C. (1982). Incidence and types of sexual dysfunctions in rape and incest victims. *Journal of Sex and Marital Therapy*,1, 65–74.

Bell, A.P., & Weinberg, M.S. (1978). *Homosexualities: A study of diversity among men and women.* New York: Simon & Schuster.

Bellak, L.B., & Small, L. (1978). *Emergency psychotherapies and brief psychotherapies* (2nd ed.) New York: Grune.

Bender, L., & Blau, A. (1937). The reaction of children to sexual relations with adults. *American Journal of Orthopsychiatry*, 7, 500–506.

Beneke, T. (1982). *Men on rape.* New York: St. Martin's.

Berne, E. (1978). *Games people play.* New York: Ballantine.

Bianco, D. (1984). Adolescent female drug abusers and their families: Some variables associated with successful treatment outcome. *Dissertation Abstracts International*, 45B 1005 (University Microfilms No. 03).

Biller, H.B., & Solomon, R.S. (1986). *Child maltreatment and paternal deprivation: A manifesto for research, prevention and treatment.* Lexington, MA: Heath.

Binder, R.L. (1981). Difficulties in follow-up with rape victims. *American Journal of Psychotherapy*, 35(4), 534–541.

Blazevic, D.J. (1987). Judges sensitized to gender bias in the courts. *Litigation News*, 12(4), 1, 20–21.

Borgida, E. (1981). Legal reform of rape laws. In L. Bickman (Ed.), *Applied social psychology annual*, vol.2 (pp. 211–41). Beverly Hills, CA: Sage.

Boskind-Lodahl, M. (1976). Cinderella's stepsisters: A feminist perspective on anorexia nervosa and bulimia. *Signs: Journal of Women in Culture and Society*, 2, 341–56.

Bouhoutsos, J. et al. (1983). Sexual intimacy between psychotherapists and patients. *Professional Psychology*, 14, 185–96.

Braen, G.R. (1980). Physical assessment and emergency medical management for adult victims of sexual assault. In C.G. Warner, *Rape and sexual assault: Management and intervention* (pp. 47–66). Germantown, MD: Aspen Systems Corp.

Braun, B.G. (Ed.). (1986). *Treatment of multiple personality disorder.* Washington, DC: American Psychiatric Press.

Brehony, K.A. (1987). Self-help groups with agoraphobic women. In C.M. Brody (Ed.), *Women's therapy groups* (pp. 82–94). New York: Springer.

Briscoe, M.E., Woodyard, H.O., & Shaw, N.E. (1967). Personality impression change as a function of the favorableness of first impressions. *Journal of Personality*, 35, 343–57.

Brodsky, A.M., & Hare-Mustin, R.T. (Eds.). (1980). *Women and psychotherapy: An assessment of research and practice.* New York: Guilford.

Brody, C.M. (1987). Woman therapist as group model in homogeneous and mixed cultural groups. In C.M. Brody (Ed.), *Women's therapy groups* (pp. 97–117). New York: Springer.

Bronstein, P., & Quina, K. (Eds.). (1988). *Teaching a psychology of people: Resources for gender and sociocultural awareness*. Washington, DC: American Psychological Association.

Broverman, I.K., Broverman, D.M., Clarkson, F.E., Rosenkrantz, P.S., & Vogel, S. (1970). Sex-role stereotypes and clinical judgments of mental health. *Journal of Consulting and Clinical Psychology*, 34 1–7.

Brown, L. (1987). Lesbians' weight and eating: New analyses and perspectives. In Boston Lesbian Psychologies Collective, *Lesbian psychologies: Explorations and challenges* (pp. 294–310). Chicago: University of Illinois Press.

Browning, D., & Boatman, B. (1977). Incest: Children at risk. *American Journal of Psychiatry*, 134(1), 69–72.

Brownmiller, S. (1975). *Against our will: Men, women and rape*. New York: Simon & Schuster.

Bruckner-Gordon, F., Gangi, B.K., & Wallman, G.U. (1988). *Making therapy work: Your guide to choosing, using, and ending therapy*. New York: Harper & Row.

Bullmer, K. (1975). *The art of empathy: A manual for improving accuracy of interpersonal perception*. New York: Human Sciences.

Burden, D.S., & Gottlieb, N. (1987). Womens' socialization and feminist groups. In C.M. Brody (Ed.), *Women's therapy groups* (pp. 24–39). New York: Springer.

Burgess, A.W., & Holmstrom, L.L. (1974). *Rape: Victims of crisis*. Bowie, MD: Brady.

Burgess, A.W., & Holmstrom, L.L. (1979). Rape: Sexual disruption and recovery. *American Journal of Orthopsychiatry*, 49(4), 648.

Burt, M.R., (1980). Cultural myths and supports for rape. *Journal of Personality and Social Psychology*, 38, 217–30.

Burt, M.R., & Katz, B. (1985). Rape, robbery, and burglary: Responses to actual and feared criminal victimization, with special emphasis on women and the elderly. *Victimology*, 10, 325–58.

Butcher, J.N., & Koss, M.P. (1978). Research on brief and crisis-oriented therapies. In S.L. Garfield & A.E. Bergen (Eds.), *Handbook of psychotherapy and behavior change* (2nd ed.). New York: Wiley.

Caldwell, D. (1989). *Factors differentiating teenage mothers from successful contraceptors*. Paper presented to the Association for Women in Psychology, Newport, RI.

Cantrell, L. (1986). *Into the light*. Edmonds, WA: Charles Franklin.

Caplan, P.J. (1984). The myth of women's masochism. *American Psychologist*, 39, 130–39.

Cappon, D., & Banks, R. (1960). Studies in perceptual distortion: Opportunistic observations on sleep deprivation during a talkathon. *Archives of General Psychiatry*, 2, 346–49.

Carlsen, M.B. (1988). *Meaning-making: Therapeutic processes in adult development*. New York: Norton.

Carlson, N. (1981). Male client-female therapist. *Personnel and Guidance Journal*, 12, 228–31.

Carlson, N. (1988). Woman therapist: Male client. In M. Scher, M. Stevens, G. Good, & G.A. Eichenfield, *Handbook of counseling and psychotherapy with men* (pp. 39–50). Newbury Park, CA: Sage.

Carlson, N., & Courtois, C. (1972). *Choice points for victim advocacy*. Unpublished paper, College Park, University of Maryland.

Carrow, D.M. (1980). *Rape: Guidelines for a community response*. Washington, DC: Department of Justice.

Carson, E.G. (1986, fall). Rape victims strike back: Use of civil law suits for relief. *NCASA News*, 10–11.

CBS. (1984, August). *Child molesters* [Televison documentary]. New York: Columbia Broadcasting System.

Center for Women in Government. (n.d.). *Sexual harassment: A digest of landmark and other significant cases*. Albany, NY: Center for Women in Government, State University of New York.

Center for Women Policy Studies. (1984, March/April). Sexual exploitation and abuse of people with disabilities. *Response*.

Chambless, D.L., & Goldstein, A.J. (1982). *Agoraphobia: Multiple perspectives on theory and treatment*. New York: Wiley.

Chance, P. (1986, September). The divided self [Report of research of Rosalyn Schultz]. *Psychology Today*, 72.

Cherniss, G. (1980). *Professional burnout in human service organizations*. New York: Praeger.

Chodorow, N. (1978). *The reproduction of motherhood*. Berkeley: University of California Press.

Clarke, E. (1982). *Stopping sexual harassment: A handbook* (2nd. ed.). Detroit: Labor Education and Research Project.

Cleary, C. (1984, December). Incest victim sues father. *Ms.*,25.

Conroy, M., & Ritvo, E.R. (1977). *Common self-defense*. St. Louis: Mosby.

Cooke, C.W., & Dworkin, S. (1981). *The Ms. Guide to a woman's health*. New York: Berkeley.

Courtois, C.A. (1988). *Healing the incest wound: Adult survivors in therapy*. New York: Norton.

Coy, J.A. v. Iowa. (1988, June 28). *United States Law Week*, 56 LW 4931, 108 Sct 2798.

Crites, L.L., & Hepperle, W.L. (1987). *Women, the courts, and equality*. New York: Sage.

Davis, L.J. (1980). Rape and older women. In C.G. Warner (Ed.), *Rape and sexual assault: Management and intervention* (pp. 93–119). Germantown, MD: Aspen Systems Corp.

Davis, L.J., & Brody, E. (1979). *Rape and the older woman: A guide to prevention and protection* [Publication no. ADM 78–734]. Washington, DC: Department of Health, Education and Welfare.

Delacoste, F., & Newman, F. (1981). *Fight back: Feminist resistance to male violence*. Minneapolis: Cleis.

Deutsch, H. (1944–45). *The psychology of women*, vols. 1–2 New York: Grune and Stratton.

Dlugokinski, E. (1985). Victims of auto accidents: The quiet victims. *American Psychologist*, 40(1), 116–17.

Douty, H.I., Moore, J.B., & Hartford, D. (1974). Body characteristics in relation to life adjustment, body image and attitudes of college females. *Perceptual and Motor Skills*, 39, 499–521.

Dzeich, B.W., & Warner, L. (1984). *The lecherous professor: Sexual harassment on campus*. Boston: Beacon.

Eberle, P., & Eberle, S. (1986). *The politics of child abuse*. Secaucus, NJ: Lyle Stuart.

Egan, G. (1985). *The skilled helper: Model skills and methods for effective helping* (3rd ed.). Monterey, CA: Brooks-Cole.

Ellis, A. (1973). *Humanistic psychotherapy: The rational emotive approach.* New York: McGraw-Hill.

Ellis, A., & Bernard, M. (1985). What is rational-emotive therapy? In A. Ellis & M. Bernard (Eds.), *Clinical applications of rational-emotive therapy.* New York: Plenum.

Ellis, E., Atkeson, B., & Calhoun, K. (1981). An assessment of long-term reaction to rape. *Journal of Abnormal Psychology*, 90, 263–66.

Eron, L.D. (1986). Intervention to mitigate the psychological effects of media violence on aggressive behavior. *Journal of Social Issues*, 42(3), 155–69.

Espin, O.M. (1987a). Psychological impact of migration on Latinas: Implications for psychotherapeutic practice. *Psychology of Women Quarterly*, 11(4), 489–504.

Espin, O.M. (1987b). Issues of identity in the psychology of Latina lesbians. In Boston Lesbian Psychologies Collective, *Lesbian psychologies: Explorations and challenges* (pp. 35–55). Chicago: University of Illinois Press.

Factor, M. (1954). A woman's psychological reaction to attempted rape. *Psychoanalytic Quarterly*, 23, 243–44.

Farley, L. (1978). *Sexual shakedown: The sexual harassment of women on the job.* New York: McGraw-Hill.

Farmer, F. (1972). *Will there really be a morning? Autobiography by Frances Farmer.* New York: Putnam.

Feldman-Summers, S., & Ashworth, C.D. (1981). Factors associated with intentions to report a rape. *Journal of Social Issues*, 37(4), 53–7.

Field, H.H. (1978). Attitudes toward rape: A comparative analysis of police, rapists, crisis counselors, and citizens. *Journal of Personality and Social Psychology*, 36, 156–79.

Figley, C.R. (Ed.). (1985). *Trauma and its wake.* New York: Brunner/Mazel.

Filinson, R., & Ingman, S.R. (in press). *Elder abuse: Practice and policy.* New York: Human Science.

Fine, M., & Asch, A. (Eds.). (1988). *Women with disabilities: Essays in psychology, culture and politics.* Philadelphia: Temple University Press.

Finkelhor, D. (1979). *Sexually victimized children.* New York: Free Press.

Finkelhor, D. (1984). *Child sexual abuse: New theory and research.* New York: Free Press.

Finkelhor, D., & Yllo, K. (1985). *License to rape: Sexual abuse of wives.* New York: Holt, Rinehart & Winston.

Fitzgerald, L. (1987, May). *The lecherous professor: Portrait of the artist.* Paper presented at the Midwestern Society for Feminist Studies, Akron, OH.

Fitzgerald, L.F., Weitzman, L.M., Gold, Y., & Ormerod, M. (1988). Academic harassment: Sex and denial in scholarly garb. *Psychology of Women Quarterly*, 12(3), 329–40.

Fodor, I.G. (1974). The phobic syndrome in women. In V. Franks & V. Burtle (Eds.), *Women and therapy: New psychotherapies for a changing society.* New York: Brunner/Mazel.

Frankl, V.E. (1963). *Man's search for meaning: An introduction to logotherapy.* New York: Washington Square Press.

Frazier, P. & Borgida, E. (1985). Rape trauma syndrome evidence in court. *American Psychologist*, 40(9), 984–93.

Freeman-Longo, R.E., & Wall, R.V. (1986, March). Changing a lifetime of sexual crime. *Psychology Today*, 58–64.

Freud, S. (1933). Lecture 33: Psychology of women. *New introductory lectures on psychoanalysis*. New York: Norton.

Freudenberger, H.J. (1980). *Burn out: The high cost of high achievement*. Garden City, NY: Anchor.

Frieze, I.H. (1983). Investigating the causes and consequences of marital rape. *Signs*, 8, 532–53.

Fuhriman, A., Paul, S.C., & Burlingame, G.M. (1986). Eclectic time-limited therapy. In J. Norcross (Ed.), *Handbook of eclectic psychotherapy* (pp. 226–59). New York: Brunner/Mazel.

Gager, N. & Schurr, C. (1976). *Sexual assault: Confronting rape in America*. New York: Grosset and Dunlap.

Garcia, N., Kennedy, C., Pearlman, S.F., & Perez, J. (1987). The impact of race and culture differences: Challenges to intimacy in lesbian relationships. In Boston Lesbian Psychologies Collective, *Lesbian psychologies: Explorations and challenges* (pp. 142–60). Chicago: University of Illinois Press.

Gebhard, P.H., Pomeroy, W.B., & Christenson, C.V. (1965). *Sex offenders: An analysis of types*. New York: Harper & Row.

Gelles, R.J., & Cornell, C.P. (1985). *Intimate violence in families*. Beverly Hills, CA: Sage.

Giarretto, H. (1982). A comprehensive child sexual abuse treatment program. *Child Abuse & Neglect*, 6, 263–78.

Gibson, G. (1983). Hispanic women: Stress and mental health issues. In J.H. Robbins & R.J. Siegel (Eds.), *Women changing therapy* (pp. 113–33). New York: Haworth.

Gil, E. (1988). *Outgrowing the pain*. New York: Dell.

Gilbert, L.A. (1980). Feminist therapy. In A.M. Brodsky & R.T. Hare-Mustin (Eds.), *Women and psychotherapy: An assessment of research and practice* (pp. 245–66). New York: Guilford.

Gilligan, C. (1982). *In a different voice*. Cambridge, MA: Harvard University Press.

Gilmore, B.S., & Evans, J.W. (1980). The nursing care of rape victims. In S.L. McCombie (Ed.), *The rape crisis intervention handbook: A guide for victim care* (pp. 43–58). New York: Plenum.

Glasser, R.D., & Thorpe, J.S. (1986). Unethical intimacy: A survey of sexual contact and advances between psychology educators and female graduate students. *American Psychologist*, 41, 43–51.

Golan, N. (1978). *Treatment in crisis situations*. New York: Free Press.

Golden, C. (1987). Diversity and variability in women's sexual identities. In Boston Lesbian Psychologies Collective, *Lesbian psychologies: Explorations and challenges* (pp. 18–34). Chicago: University of Illinois Press.

Goldfried, M., & Davison, G. (1976). *Clinical behavior therapy*. New York: Holt, Rinehart & Winston.

Greenspan, M. (1983). *A new approach to women and therapy*. New York: McGraw-Hill.

Groth, A.N. (1979). *Men who rape: The psychology of the offender*. New York: Plenum.

Groth, A.N., & Burgess, A.W. (1980). Male rape: Offenders and their victims. *American Journal of Psychiatry*, 137, 806–10.

Hall, R.M., & Sandler, B.R. (1982). *The classroom climate: A chilly one for women?* Washington, DC: Association of American Colleges.

Hall, R.M., & Sandler, B.R. (1984). *Out of the classroom: A chilly campus climate for women?* Washington, DC: Association of American Colleges.

Harris, T.A. (1969). *I'm ok—You're ok*. New York: Harper & Row.

Hartman, S. (1987). Therapeutic self-help group: A process of empowerment for women in abusive relationships. In C.M. Brody (Ed.), *Women's therapy groups* (pp. 67–81). New York: Springer.

Harvey, R. (1984, August 22). Rampant child sex abuse calls for swift crackdown, study says. *Toronto Star*, p. 1

Henderson, P. (Producer). (1984, April). *Rape* [Television Documentary]. Providence, RI: Knight-Ridder.

Henn, F.A. (1978). The aggressive sexual offender. In I.L. Kutash, S.B. Kutash, & L.B. Schlesinger (Eds.), *Violence: Perspectives on murder and aggression*. San Francisco: Jossey-Bass.

Herek, G.M. (1989). Hate crimes against lesbians and gay men: Issues for research and policy. *American Psychologist*, 44, 948–955.

Herman, J.L. (1981). *Father-daughter incest*. Cambridge, MA: Harvard University Press.

Hicks, D.J., & Moon, D.M. (1980). Sexual assault of the older woman. In I.R. Stuart & J.G. Greer (Eds.), *Victims of sexual aggression: Treatment of children, women and men* (pp. 180–96). New York: Van Nostrand Reinhold.

Holmes, K.A. (1980). Working for and with rape victims: Crisis intervention and advocacy. In I.R. Stuart & J.G. Greer (Eds.), *Victims of sexual aggression: Treatment of children, women and men* (pp. 18–35). New York: Van Nostrand Reinhold.

Holmstrom, L.L., & Burgess, A.W. (1978). *The victim of rape: Institutional reactions*. New York: Wiley-Interscience.

Holroyd, J.C., & Brodsky, A.M. (1977). Psychologists' attitudes and practices regarding erotic and nonerotic physical contact with patients. *American Psychologist*, 32, 843–49.

Horos, C.U. (1975). *Vaginal health*. New Canaan, CT: Tobey.

Horowitz, M.J. (1976). *Stress response syndromes*. New York: Jason Aronson.

Hotaling, G.T., Finkelhor, D., Kirkpatrick, J.T., & Straus, M.A. (1988). *Family abuse and its consequences*. Newbury Park, CA: Sage.

Huckel, L. (1985). Personality correlates of parental maltreatment. *Dissertation Abstracts International*, 46(3).

Hursch, C.J. (1977). *The trouble with rape: A psychologist's report on the legal, medical, social and psychological problems*. Chicago, IL: Nelson-Hall.

Jackins, H. (1987). *The rest of our lives*. Seattle, WA: Rational Island Press.

Jackson, J. (1980). *The whole nurse catalog*. Philadelphia: Saunders.

James, J., & Meyerding, J. (1977). Early sexual experiences as a factor in prostitution. *Archives of Sexual Behavior*, 7(1), 31–42.

Janoff-Bulman, R. & Frieze, I. (1983). A theoretical perspective for understanding reactions to victimization. *Journal of Social Issues*, 39(2), 1–18.

Jones, C., & Aronson, E. (1973). Attribution of fault to a rape victim as a function of respectability of the victim. *Journal of Personality and Social Psychology*, 26, 415–419.

Justice, B., & Justice, R. (1979). *The broken taboo: Sex in the family*. New York: Human Sciences Press.

Kahn, A. (1984). The power war: Male response to power loss under equality. *Psychology of Women Quarterly*, 8, 234–47.

Kanarian, M., & Quina, K. (1981, April). *Attributions about rape: Effects of situational determinants across dependent measures, sex of subject, and attitudes toward women*. Paper presented at the Eastern Psychological Association Annual Meeting, New York, NY.

Kanin, E.J. (1985). Date rapists: Differential sexual socialization and relative deprivation. *Archives of Sexual Behavior*, 14(3), 218–32.

Kaplan, H.S. (1974). *The new sex therapy*. New York: Brunner/Mazel.

Kaplan, H.S. (1979). *Disorders of sexual desire and other new concepts and techniques in sex therapy*. New York: Brunner/Mazel.

Katz, B. (1987). *Prerape victim-rapist familiarity and recovery from rape: Psychological consequences*. Unpublished manuscript, Boston University.

Katz, B., & Burt, M. (1988). Self-blame in recovery from rape: Help or hindrance? In A. Burgess (Ed.), *Rape and sexual assault*, vol 2. New York: Garland.

Katz, S., & Mazur, M.A. (1979). *Understanding the rape victim: A synthesis of research findings*. New York: Wiley.

Kaufman, A. (1984). Rape of men in the community. In I.R. Stuart & J.G.Greer (Eds.), *Victims of sexual aggression: Treatment of children, women and men* (pp. 156–79). New York: Van Nostrand Reinhold.

Kegan, R. (1982). *The evolving self: Problem and process in human development*. Cambridge, MA: Harvard University Press.

Kempe, S., & Kempe, C.H. (1984). *Sexual abuse of children and adolescents*. New York: W.H. Freeman.

Kerns, D. (1981). Medical assessment of child sexual abuse. In P.B. Mrazek & C.H. Kempe (Eds.), *Sexually abused children and their families* (pp. 129–141). New York: Pergamon.

Keuls, E.C. (1985). *The reign of the phallus: Sexual politics in ancient Athens*. New York: Harper & Row.

Kidder, L.H., Boell, J.L., & Moyer, M.M. (1983). Rights consciousness and victimization prevention: Personal defense and assertiveness training. *Journal of Social Issues*, 39(2), 155–70.

Kikuchi, J.J., & Marceau, M. (1989). *Adolescents' attitudes on sexual abuse and violence*. Paper presented at the Association for Women in Psychology, Newport, RI.

Kilbourne, J. (1979). *Killing us softly*. Cambridge, MA: Cambridge Documentary Films.

Kilbourne, J. (1987). *Still killing us softly*. Cambridge, MA: Cambridge Documentary Films.

Kilpatrick, D.G., Resnick, P.A., & Veronen, L.J (1981). Effects of a rape experience: A longitudinal study. *Journal of Social Issues*, 37(4), 105–22.

Kilpatrick, D.G., Veronen, L., & Resnick, P. (1979). The aftermath of rape: Recent empirical findings. *American Journal of Orthopsychiatry*, 49, 658–69.

Kinsey, A.C., Pomeroy, W.B., & Martin, C.G. (1948). *Sexual behavior in the human male*. Philadelphia: Saunders.

Kinsey, A.C., Pomeroy, W.B., Martin, C.G., & Gebhard, P.H. (1953). *Sexual behavior in the human female*. Philadelphia: Saunders.

Klapholz, H. (1980). The medical examination: Treatment and evidence collection. In S.L. McCombie (Ed.), *The rape crisis intervention handbook: A guide for victim care* (pp. 59–68). New York: Plenum.

Knightley, P., & Simpson, C. (1970). *The secret lives of Lawrence of Arabia*. New York: McGraw-Hill.

Koss, M.P (1985). The hidden rape victim: Personality, attitudinal, and situational characteristics. *Psychology of Women Quarterly*,9(2), 193–212.

Koss, M.P. (1987, May). *Are there risk factors for rape*? Paper presented at the Midwestern Society for Feminist Studies, Akron, OH.

Koss, M.P., Dinero, T.E., Seibel, C.A., & Cox, S.L. (1988). Stranger and acquaintance rape: Are there differences in the victim's experience? *Psychology of Women Quarterly*, 12(1), 1–24.

Koss, M.P., & Leonard, K.E. (1984). Sexually aggressive men: Empirical findings and theoretical implications. In N.M. Malamuth & E. Donnerstein (Eds.), *Pornography and sexual aggression* (pp. 213–32). New York: Academic Press.

Krafft-Ebing, R. von. (1886/1965). *Psychopathia sexualis* (trans. by H.E. Wedeck). New York: Putnam.

Kravetz, D. (1980). Consciousness-raising and self-help. In A.M. Brodsky & R.T. Hare-Mustin (Eds.), *Women and psychotherapy: An assessment of research and practice* (pp. 267–80). New York: Guilford.

Kroll, J. (1988). *The challenge of the borderline patient: Competency in diagnosis and treatment*. New York: Norton.

Krueger, F. (1985). Violated. *Boston*, 77(5), 138–43.

Kubler-Ross, E. (1970). *On death and dying*. New York: Macmillan.

Kushner, H.S. (1981). *When bad things happen to good people*. New York: Schocken.

Landis, J.T., Jr. (1956). Experience of 500 children with adult's sexual relations. *Psychiatric Quarterly*, 30, 91–109.

Landrine, H. (1988). Revising the framework of abnormal psychology. In P. Bronstein & K. Quina (Eds.), *Teaching a psychology of people: Gender and cultural diversity in the curriculum* (pp. 37–44). Washington DC: American Psychological Association.

Langer, E.J., & Rodin, J. (1976). The effects of choice and enhanced personal responsibility for the aged: A field experiment in an institutional setting. *Journal of Personality and Social Psychology*, 34, 191–98.

Larson, D. (1980). Therapeutic schools, styles, and schoolism: A national survey. *Journal of Humanistic Psychology*, 20, 3–20.

Law Enforcement Assistance Administration. (1977). *Sourcebook of criminal justice statistics*. Washington, DC: National Criminal Justice Information and Statistics Services.

Law Enforcement Assistance Administration. (1980). *Florida's plan to reduce crime against the elderly*. Washington, DC: National Criminal Justice Information and Statistics Services.

Law Enforcement Assistance Administration. (1985). *Sourcebook of criminal justice statistics*. Washington, DC: National Criminal Justice Information and Statistics Services.

Lazarus, A.A. (1986). Multimodal therapy. In J. Norcross (Ed), *Handbook of eclectic psychotherapy* (pp. 65–93). New York: Brunner/Mazel.

Lemkau, J.P. (1988). *How should the research on abortion affect what psychologists do?* Paper presented at the Association for Women in Psychology, Bethesda, MD.

Lerner, M.J. (1980). *The belief in a just world*. New York: Plenum.

Lerner, M., & Simmons, C. (1966). Observers' reactions to the innocent victim: Comparison or rejection? *Journal of Personality and Social Psychology*, 4, 203–10.

LeVine, E.S., & Padilla, A. (1980). *Crossing cultures in therapy: Pluralistic counseling for Hispanics*. Monterey, CA: Brooks/Cole.

Levine-MacCombie, J., & Koss, M.P. (1986). Acquaintance rape: Effective avoidance strategies. *Psychology of Women Quarterly*,10(4), 311–20.

Lew, M. (1988). *Victims no longer: Men recovering from incest and other sexual child abuse*. New York: Nevraumont Publishing Co.

Lifton, J. (1982). Psychological effects of the atomic bombings. In E. Chivian, S. Chivian, & J.E. Mack (Eds.), *Last aid: The medical dimensions of nuclear war* (pp. 48–68). New York: Freeman.

Lindemann, E. (1944). Symptomatology and management of acute grief. *American Journal of Psychiatry*, 101, 141–46.

Linehan, M.M. (1987). Dialectical behavior therapy in groups: Treating borderline personality disorders and suicidal behavior. In C. Brody (Ed.), *Women's Therapy Groups* (pp. 145–162). New York: Springer.

Linehan, M.M., & Egan. K.J. (1979). Assertion training for women. In A.S. Bellack & M. Hersen (Eds.), *Research and practice in social skills*. New York: Plenum.

Liss-Levinson, N., Clamar, A., Ehrenberg, M., Ehrenberg, O., Fidell, L., Maffeo, P., Redstone, J., Russo, N.F., Solomons, H., & Tennor, D. (1985). *Women and psychotherapy: A consumer handbook*. Tempe, AZ: National Coalition for Women's Mental Health.

Lott, B. (1987). *Women's lives:Themes and variations in gender learning*. Monterey, CA: Wadsworth.

Lott, B., Reilly, M.E., & Howard, D.R. (1982). Sexual assault and harassment: A campus community case study. *Signs*, 8(2), 296–319.

Loulan, J. (1989) *Lesbian Passion*. San Francisco: Spinsters/Aunt Lute.

Lumiere, R., & Cook, S. (1983). *Healthy sex and keeping it that way*. New York: Simon & Schuster.

Lundberg-Love, P. (1987, May). *Treatment issues for incest survivors*. Paper presented at the Midwestern Society for Feminist Studies, Akron, OH.

Lundberg-Love, P., Geffner, R.A., & Crawford, C.M. (1987). Personality characteristics of adult incest survivors. Unpublished manuscript, University of Texas–Tyler.

MacDonald, J.M. (1971). *Rape: Offenders and their victims*. Springfield, IL: Thomas.

MacFarlane, K. (1978). Sexual abuse of children. In J.R. Chapman & M. Gates (Eds.), *The victimization of women* (pp. 81–110). Beverly Hills, CA: Sage.

MacFarlane, K., & Waterman, J. (Eds.). (1986). *Sexual abuse of young children: Evaluation and treatment*. New York: Guilford.

MacKinnon, C.A. (1979). *Sexual harassment of working women*. New Haven: Yale University Press.

Malamuth, N.M. (1981). Rape proclivity among males. *Journal of Social Issues*, 37(4), 138–57.

Malamuth, N.M., & Donnerstein, E. (Eds.). (1984). *Pornography and sexual aggression*. Orlando, FL: Academic Press.

Maltz, W., & Holman, B. (1987). *Incest and sexuality: A guide to understanding and healing*. Lexington, MA: Lexington Books.

Mann, J. (1981). The core of time-limited psychotherapy: Time and the central issue. In S.H. Budman (Ed.), *Forms of brief psychotherapy* (pp. 25–43). New York: Guilford.

Margolies, L., Becker, M., & Jackson-Brewer, K. (1987). Internalized homophobia: Identifying and treating the oppressor within. In Boston Lesbian Psychologies Collective, *Lesbian psychologies: Explorations and challenges* (pp. 229–41). Chicago: University of Illinois Press.

Masson, J.M. (1984). *The assault on truth: Freud's suppression of the seduction theory*. New York: Penguin.

May, R., Angel, E., & Ellenberger, H. (Eds.). (1958). *Existence*. New York: Basic Books.

Mayer, A. (1983). *Incest: A treatment manual for therapy with victims, spouses and offenders*. Holmes Beach, FL: Learning Publications, Inc.

McCahill, T.W., Meyer, L.C., & Fischman, A. (1979). *The aftermath of rape*. Lexington, MA: Lexington Books.

McCombie, S.L. (Ed.). (1980). *The rape crisis intervention handbook: A guide for victim care*. New York: Plenum.

McEvoy, A.W., & Brookings, J.B. (1984). *If she is raped: A book for husbands, fathers, and male friends*. Holmes Beach, FL: Learning Publications, Inc.

McNaron, T.A.H., & Morgan, Y. (1982). *Voices in the night: Women speaking about incest*. Minneapolis: Cleis.

Meiselman, K.C. (1981). *Incest*. San Francisco: Jossey-Bass.

Melville, M.B. (Ed.). (1980). *Twice a minority: Mexican American women*. St. Louis: Mosby.

Merit Systems Protection Board. (1981). *Sexual harassment in the workplace: Is it a problem?* Washington, DC: Government Printing Office.

Meyer, M.C. et al. (1981). *Sexual harassment at work*. Princeton, NJ: Petrocelli.

Miller, D.T., & Porter, C.A. (1983). Self-blame in victims of violence. *Journal of Social Issues*, 32(2), 141–54.

Miller, J.B. (1986). *Toward a new psychology of women* (2nd ed.) Boston: Beacon.

Miller, W.R., & Williams, A.M. (1984). Marital and sexual dysfunction following rape: Identification and treatment. In I.R. Stuart & J.G. Greer (Eds.), *Victims of sexual aggression: Treatment of children, women and men* (pp. 197–210). New York: Van Nostrand Reinhold.

Miller, W.R., Williams, A.M., & Bernstein, M.H. (1982). The effects of rape on marital and sexual adjustment. *American Journal of Family Therapy*,10, 51–58.

Mills, P. (Ed.). (1977). *Rape intervention resource manual*. Springfield, IL: C.C. Thomas.

Morokoff, P.J. (1983). Toward the elimination of rape: A conceptualization of sexual aggression against women. In A.P. Goldstein (Ed.), *Prevention and control of aggression* (pp. 101–44). New York: Pergamon.

Morris, G.O., & Singer, M.T. (1961). Sleep deprivation: Transactional and subjective observations. *Archives of General Psychiatry*, 5, 453–61.

Muehlenhard, C.L., Friedman, D.E., & Thomas, C.M. (1985). Is date rape justifiable?

The effects of dating activity, who initiated, who paid, and men's attitudes toward women. *Psychology of Women Quarterly*, 9, 297–310.

Nadelson, C.C. (1982). Incest and rape: Repercussions in sexual behavior. In L. Greenspoon (Ed.), *The Annual Review of Psychiatry*. Washington, DC: American Psychiatric Association.

Nadelson, C.C., Notman, M.T., Jackson, H., & Gornick, J. (1982). A follow-up study of rape victims. *American Journal of Psychiatry*, 139, 1266–70.

National Geographic Society. (1982). *The sharks*. Washington, D.C.: National Geographic Educational Services.

Naylor, G. (1983). *The women of Brewster Place*. New York: Penguin.

NiCarthy, G. (1982). *Getting free: A handbook for women in abusive relationships*. Seattle: Seal Press.

Nichols, M. (1987). Doing sex therapy with lesbians: Bending a heterosexual paradigm to fit a gay life-style. In Boston Lesbian Psychologies Collective, *Lesbian psychologies: Explorations and challenges* (pp. 242–60). Chicago: University of Illinois Press.

Norcross, J. (1986). Eclectic psychotherapy: An introduction and overview. In J. Norcross (Ed.), *Handbook of eclectic psychotherapy* (pp. 3–24). New York: Brunner/Mazel.

Norvell, M.K., Benrubi, G.I., & Thompson, R.J. (1984). Investigation of microtrauma after sexual intercourse. *Journal of Reproductive Medicine*, 29(4), 269–71.

Notman, M.T., & Nadelson, C.C. (1983). Psychodynamic and life-stage considerations in the response to rape. In S.L. McCombie (Ed.), *The rape crisis intervention handbook: A guide for victim care* (pp. 131–44). New York: Plenum.

O'Brien, S. (1983). *Child pornography*. Dubuque, IA: Kendall/Hunt.

O'Bryant, S.L., & Nocera, D. (1985). The psychological significance of "home" to older widows. *Psychology of Women Quarterly*, 9(3), 403–412.

Orbach, S. (1978). *Fat is a feminist issue*. New York: Berkeley.

Paludi, M. (Ed.). (In press). *Ivory power: Sexual and gender harassment in the academy*. Albany: State University of New York Press.

Parker, D.A., Parker, E.S., Harford, T., & Farmer G.C. (1987). Alcohol use and depression symptoms among employed men and women. *American Journal of Public Health*, 77, 704–7.

Pearlman, S. (1987). The saga of continuing clash in lesbian community, or Will an army of ex-lovers fall? In Boston Lesbian Psychologies Collective, *Lesbian psychologies: Explorations and challenges* (pp. 313–26). Chicago: University of Illinois Press.

Pederson, P. (Ed.). (1985). *Handbook of cross-cultural counseling and psychotherapy*. Westport, CT: Greenwood Press.

Perloff, L.S. (1983). Perceptions of vulnerability to victimization. *Journal of Social Issues*, 39(2), 41–61.

Peterson, C., & Seligman, M.E.P. (1984). Causal explanations as a risk factor for depression: Theory and evidence. *Psychological Review*, 91, 347–74.

Petrovich, M., & Templer, D.I. (1984). Heterosexual molestation of children who later became rapists. *Psychological Reports*, 54(3), 810.

Pines, A.M., Aronson, E., & Kafry, D. (1981). *Burnout: From tedium to personal growth*. Riverside, NJ: Free Press.

Pope, K.S., & Bouhoutsos, J.C. (1986). *Sexual intimacy between therapists and patients* New York: Praeger.

Poston, C., & Lison, K. (1989). *Reclaiming our lives: Hope for adult survivors of incest.* Boston: Little, Brown.

Powell, T.J. (1987). *Self-help organizations and professional practice.* Silver Spring, MD: National Association of Social Workers.

President's Task Force on Victims of Crime. (1982). *Final report.* Washington, DC: Government Printing Office.

"Presumptive treatment recommended for Chlamydia." (1988). *Brown University STD Update*, 3, 4.

Prochaska, J.O. (1979). *Systems of psychotherapy: A transtheoretical analysis.* Homewood, IL: Dorsey.

Prochaska, J.O. (1984). *Systems of psychotherapy* (2nd ed.). Homewood, IL: Dorsey.

Prochaska, J.O., & DiClemente, C.C. (1984). *The transtheoretical approach: Crossing traditional boundaries in therapy.* Homewood, IL: Dorsey.

Quina, K. (1986). *Feminist transformations in the research methods course: A multidimensional action plan* [Working Paper]. Wellesley, MA: Wellesley College Center for Research on Women.

Quina, K. (in press). The victimizations of women. In M. Paludi (Ed.), *Ivory Power: Sexual and gender harassment in the academy.* Albany, NY: State University of New York Press.

Quina, K., Carlson, N., & Temple, H. (1982). *Sexual harassment and assault: Myths and Realities.* Kingston, RI: The University of Rhode Island.

Quina, K., Lott, B., & Lemkau, J. (1987, March). *Post-abortion issues.* Symposium presented to the Association for Women in Psychology, Denver, CO.

Quina, K., & Paxson, M.A. (1987, March). *The Women's Studies Summer Institute.* Paper presented to the Association for Women in Psychology, Denver, CO.

Quina, K., & Tyre, T. (1975). *Sexual assault at the University of Wisconsin-Milwaukee.* Unpublished report.

Quina-Holland, K. (1979, March). *Long-term psychological effects of sexual assault.* Paper presented to the Association for Women in Psychology, Dallas, TX.

Quina-Holland, K., Angeli, M.J., & Smiegelski, T.S. (1977, May). *Attitudes toward rape and other crimes.* Paper presented to the Midwestern Psychological Association, Chicago, IL.

Rada, R.T. (Ed.). (1978). *Clinical aspects of the rapist.* New York: Grune & Stratton.

Rado, S. (1942). Pathodynamics and treatment of traumatic war neurosis (traumatophobia). *Psychosomatic Medicine*, 4, 362–69.

Rainone, F.L. (1987). Beyond community: Politics and spirituality. In Boston Lesbian Psychologies Collective, *Lesbian psychologies: Explorations and challenges* (pp. 344–54). Chicago: University of Illinois Press.

Rand, C., Graham, D., & Rawlings, E. (1982). Psychological health and factors the court seeks to control in lesbian mother custody trials. *Journal of Homosexuality*, 8, 27–39.

Rando, T.A. (1986). *Loss and anticipatory grief.* Lexington, MA: Lexington Books.

Rapaport, K., & Burkhart, B.R. (1984). Personality and attitudinal characteristics of sexually coercive college males. *Journal of Abnormal Psychology*, 93(2), 216–21.

Rawlings, E.I., & Carter, D.K. (1977). *Psychotherapy for women: Treatment toward equality.* Springfield, IL: Thomas.

Reik, T. (1948). *Listening with the third ear*. New York: Farrar, Straus.

Riger, S., & Gordon, M.T. (1981). The fear of rape: A study in social control. *Journal of Social Issues*, 37(4), 71–92.

Rimm, D., & Masters, J. (1974). *Behavior therapy*. New York: Academic Press.

Rimsza, M.E., & Niggemann, E.H. (1984). Medical evaluation of sexually abused children: Review of 311 cases. *Pediatrics*, 69, 8–14.

Rivers, C., Barnett, R., & Baruch, G. (1979). *Beyond sugar and spice: How women grow, learn and thrive*. New York: Putnam.

Robbins, J.H., & Siegel, R.J. (1983). *Women changing therapy*. New York: Haworth.

Robinson, C.R. (1983). Black women: A tradition of self-reliant strength. In J.H. Robbins & R.J. Siegel (Eds.), *Women changing therapy* (pp. 135–44). New York: Haworth.

Rogers, C. (1951). *Client-centered therapy*. Boston: Houghton-Mifflin.

Rosen, G.M. (1987). Self-help treatment books and the commercialization of psychotherapy. *American Psychologist*, 42, 46–51.

Rosenfeld, A.H. (1985, April). Discovering and dealing with deviant sex. *Psychology Today*, 8–10.

Ross, S.D., & Barcher, A. (1983). *The rights of women*. New York: Bantam.

Rowan, E.L., & Rowan, J.B. (1984). Rape and the college student: Multiple crises in late adolescence. In I.R. Stuart & J.G. Greer (Eds.), *Victims of sexual aggression: Treatment of children, women and men* (pp. 234–50). New York: Van Nostrand Reinhold.

Rowe, M. (1981, May–June). Dealing with sexual harassment. *Harvard Business Review*, 43.

Rowland, J. (1985). *The ultimate violation: Rape trauma syndrome—An answer for victims, justice in the courtroom*. New York: Doubleday.

Rush, F. (1980). *The best kept secret: Sexual abuse of children*. Englewood Cliffs, N.J: Prentice-Hall.

Russell, D.E.H. (1975). *The politics of rape*. New York: Stein & Day.

Russell, D.E.H. (1984). *Sexual exploitation*. Beverly Hills, CA: Sage.

Russell, D.E.H. (1987). *The secret trauma: Incest in the lives of girls and women*. New York: Basic.

Russo, N.F. (1985). Older women. In N.F. Russo (Ed.), *A women's mental health agenda* (pp. 24–27). Washington, DC: American Psychological Association.

Sales, B.D., Rich, R.F., & Reich, J. (1984). Victims of crime and violence: Legal and public policy issues. In APA Task Force on Victims of Crime and Violence, *Final report* (pp. 113–47). Washington, DC: American Psychological Association.

Sales, E., Baum, M., & Shore, B. (1984). Victim readjustment following assault. *Journal of Social Issues*, 40(1), 117–36.

Sandler, B. (1983). *Writing a letter to the sexual harasser: Another way of dealing with the problem*. Washington, DC: Project on the Status and Education of Women, Association of American Colleges.

Sanford, L.T., & Donovan, M.E. (1984). *Women and self-esteem*. New York: Penguin.

Sargent, N.M. (in press). Spirituality and the adult survivor of child sexual abuse: Some treatment issues. Excerpted from S.M. Sgroi (Ed.), *Vulnerable populations: Treatment of sexual abuse of children, adult survivors, and mentally retarded adults*, vol. 2. Lexington, MA: Lexington Books.

Sarrell, P.M., & Masters, W.H. (1982). Sexual molestation of men by women. *Archives of Sexual Behavior*, 11(2), 117–31.

Sartre, J.P. (1956). *Being and nothingness*. New York: Philosophical Library.

Sasko, H., & Sesek, D. (1975). Rape reform legislation: Is it the solution? *Cleveland State Law Review*, 24, 463–503.

Schaef, A.W. (1984). *Women's reality: An emerging female system in the white male society*. Minneapolis, MN: Winston Press.

Scheffler, L.W. (1984). *Help thy neighbor*. New York: Grove.

Schwendinger, J.R., & Schwendinger, H. (1983). *Rape and inequality*. Beverly Hills, CA: Sage.

Scully, D., & Marolla, J. (1983). *Incarcerated rapists: Exploring a sociological model*. Final Report. Bethesda, MD: Department of Health and Human Services, NIMH.

Seligman, M.E.P. (1975). *Helplessness: On depression, development, and death*. San Francisco: Freeman.

Selye, H. (1975). *The stress of life* (2nd ed.). New York: McGraw-Hill.

Sgroi, S.M. (1981). *Handbook of clinical intervention in child sexual abuse*. Lexington, MA: Lexington Books.

Sgroi, S.M. (Ed.). (1988). *Vulnerable populations: Evaluation and treatment of sexually abused children, adult survivors, and mentally retarded adults*, vol. 1. Lexington, MA: Lexington Books.

Sgroi, S.M., & Bunk, B.S. (1988). A clinical approach to adult survivors of child sexual abuse. In S.M. Sgroi (Ed.), *Vulnerable populations: Evaluation and treatment of sexually abused children, adult survivors, and mentally retarded adults*, vol. 1. Lexington, MA: Lexington Books.

Shaver, K. (1970). Defensive attribution: Effects of severity and relevance on the responsibility assigned for an accident. *Journal of Personality and Social Psychology*, 14, 101–13.

Sheehan, D.V. (1983). *The anxiety disease*. New York: Scribner.

Shuster, R. (1987). Sexuality as a continuum: The bisexual identity. In Boston Lesbian Psychologies Collective, *Lesbian psychologies: Explorations and challenges* (pp. 56–71). Chicago: University of Illinois Press.

Siegel, M. (1983). Crime and violence in America: The victims. *American Psychologist*, 38, 1267–73.

Silbert, M.H., & Pines, A.M. (1981). Sexual abuse as an antecedent to prostitution. *Child Abuse and Neglect*, 5, 407–11.

Silverman, D. (1977). First do no more harm: Female rape victims and the male counselor. *American Journal of Orthopsychiatry*, 47, 91–96.

Silverman, P.R. (1980). *Mutual help groups: Organization and development*. Beverly Hills, CA: Sage.

Smith, J.A. (1978). *Rapists beware: A practical guide to self-defense for women*. New York: Collier.

Small, L. (1971). *The briefer psychotherapies*. New York: Brunner/Mazel.

Sprei, J. (1987). Group treatment of adult incest survivors. In C.M. Brody (Ed.), *Women's therapy groups* (pp. 198–216). New York: Springer.

Sprei, J., & Courtois, C. (1988). The treatment of women's sexual dysfunctions arising from sexual assault. In J.R. Field & R.A. Brown (Eds.), *Advances in the understanding and treatment of sexual problems: Compendium for the individual and marital therapist*. New York: Spectrum.

Sproles, E.T., III. (1985). *The evaluation and management of rape and sexual abuse: A physician's guide*. Rockville, MD: National Center for Prevention and Control of Rape, National Institutes of Mental Health.

Stanko, E.A. (1985). *Intimate intrusions: Women's experience of male violence*. Boston: Routledge & Kegan Paul.

Stark, E. (1985). Views of child molesters [Review of B. Berleffi, "Men who molest," PBS Documentary]. *Psychology Today*, 19, 8.

Stark, J., & Goldstein, H.W. (1985). *The rights of crime victims*. New York: Bantam.

Starker, S. (1988). Self-help treatment books: The rest of the story. *American Psychologist*, 43, 599–600.

Starzecpyzel, E. (1987). The Persephone complex. In Boston Lesbian Psychologies Collective, *Lesbian psychologies: Explorations and challenges* (pp. 261–82). Chicago: University of Illinois Press.

Steinem, G. (1983). *Outrageous acts and everyday rebellions*. New York: New American Library.

Steiner, C. (1974). *Scripts people live*. New York: Grove.

Stern, E.M. (Ed.). (1985). *Psychotherapy and the terrorized patient*. New York: Haworth.

Stern, V.S., & Stern, E.M. (1985). Keeping faith with the terrorized patient: A dialogue. In E.M. Stern (Ed.), *Psychotherapy and the terrorized patient* (pp. 3–10). New York: Haworth.

Sue, D.W. (Ed.). (1981). *Counseling the culturally different: Theory and practice*. New York: Wiley.

Sue, S., & Zane, N. (1987). The role of culture and cultural techniques in psychotherapy: A critique and reformulation. *American Psychologist*, 42(1), 37–45.

Sutherland, S., & Scherl, D.J. (1970). Patterns of response among victims of rape. *American Journal of Orthopsychiatry*, 40, 503–11.

Swink, K.K., & Leveille, A.E. (1986). From victim to survivor: A new look at the issues and recovery process for adult incest survivors. *Women & Therapy* Special Issue: The dynamics of feminist therapy, 5, 119–41.

Symonds, M. (1975). Victims of violence: Psychological effects and aftereffects. *American Journal of Psychoanalysis*, 35, 19–26.

Symonds, M. (1980). The "second injury" to victims. In L. Kivens (Ed.), *Evaluation and change: Services for survivors* (pp. 36–38). Minneapolis: Minneapolis Medical Research Foundation.

Tatel, D.S. (1986). Supreme Court decision broadens definition of employment-related harassment. *Public Management*, 68, 21.

Thomas, M. (1987). *Free to be . . . you and me*. New York: McGraw.

Thomas, M., et al. (1987). *Free to be . . . a family*. New York: Bántam.

Tillich, P. (1952). *Courage to be*. New Haven, CT: Yale University Press.

Titchener, J.L., Kapp, F.T., & Wingett, C. (1976). The Buffalo Creek syndrome: Symptoms and character change after a major disaster. In H.J. Parad, H.P. Resnik, & L.G. Parad (Eds.), *Emergency and disaster management*. Bowie, MD: Charles.

Trotman, F.K. (1984). Psychotherapy with Black women and the dual effects of racism and sexism. In C.M. Brody (Ed.), *Women therapists working with women: New theory and process of feminist therapy*. New York: Springer.

Trotman, F.K., & Gallagher, A.H. (1987). Group therapy with Black women. In C.M. Brody (Ed.), *Women's therapy groups* (pp. 118–31). New York: Springer.

Tsai, M., Feldman-Summers, S., & Edgar, M. (1979). Childhood molestation: Variables related to differential impacts on psychosexual functioning in adult women. *Journal of Abnormal Psychology*, 88(4), 407–17.

Tsai, M., & Uemura, A. (1988). Asian Americans: The struggles, the conflicts, and the successes. In P. Bronstein & K. Quina (Eds.), *Teaching a psychology of people: Gender and cultural diversity in the curriculum* (pp. 125–33). Washington, DC: American Psychological Association.

Tsai, M., & Wagner, N.N. (1978). Therapy groups for women sexually molested as children. *Archives of Sexual Behavior*, 7(5), 417–27.

U.S. Department of Justice, Bureau of Justice Statistics. (1982). *National Crime Survey*. Rockville; MD: National Criminal Justice Reference Service.

U.S. Department of Justice, Bureau of Justice Statistics. (1983). *Report to the nation on crime and justice: The data*. Washington, DC: Government Printing Office.

Vazquez-Nuttall, E., Romero-Garcia, I., & DeLeon, B. (1987). Sex roles and perceptions of femininity and masculinity in Hispanic women: A review of the literature. *Psychology of Women Quarterly*, 11(4), 409–26.

Walker, L.E. (1979). *The battered woman*. New York: Harper & Row.

Walker, L.E. (1984). *The battered woman syndrome*. New York: Springer.

Walker, L.E. (Ed.). (1988). *Handbook on sexual abuse of children: Assessment and treatment issues*. New York: Springer.

Warner, C.G. (Ed.). (1980). *Rape and sexual assault: Management and intervention*. Germantown, MD: Aspen Systems Corp.

Weber, E. (1977, April). Sexual abuse begins at home. *Ms.*, 64–67.

Weiner, K. (1989). Multiple boundaries: A theory of development for female survivors of abuse. Paper presented at Association for Women in Psychology, Newport, RI.

Weisberg, D.K. (1984). *Children of the night: A study of adolescent prostitution*. Lexington, MA: Lexington Books.

Weiss, C.L., & Friar, D. (1974). *Terror in the prisons: Homosexual rape and why society condones it*. Indianapolis, IN: Bobbs-Merrill.

Weissman, M.M. (1980). Depression. In A.M. Brodsky & R.T. Hare-Mustin (Eds.), *Women and psychotherapy: An assessment of research and practice* (pp. 97–112). New York: Guilford.

Westerlund, E. (1986). Freud on sexual trauma: An historical review of seduction and betrayal. *Psychology of Women Quarterly*, 10(4), 297–310.

White, E.C. (1985). *Chain chain change: For Black women dealing with physical and emotional abuse*. Seattle: Seal Press.

Williams, J.E., & Holmes, K.A. (1981). *The second assault: Rape and public attitudes*. Westport, CT: Greenwood.

Willoughby, A. (1979). *The alcohol-troubled person*. Chicago: Nelson-Hall.

Wilson, J.P., Smith, W.K., & Johnson, S.K. (1985). A comparative analysis of PTSD [post traumatic stress disorder] among various survivor groups. In C.R. Figley, (Ed.), *Trauma and its wake* (pp. 142–72). New York: Brunner/Mazel.

Woititz, J.G. (1983). *Adult children of alcoholics*. Pompano Beach, FL: Health Communications, Inc.

Wolberg, L.R. (1965). *Short term psychotherapy*. New York: Grune & Stratton.

Wolfe, J.L. (1985). Women. In A. Ellis & M. Bernard (Eds.), *Clinical applications of rational-emotive therapy*. New York: Plenum.

Wolfe, J.L. (1987). Cognitive behavioral group therapy for women. In C.M. Brody (Ed.), *Women's therapy groups* (pp. 163–73). New York: Springer.

Wolpe, J., & Lazarus, A. (1966). *Behavior therapy techniques: A guide to the treatment of neuroses*. New York: Pergamon.

Women Organized Against Rape. (1981). *Family/juvenile court: What you need to know*. Philadelphia: Women Organized Against Rape.

Wooden, W.S., & Parker, J. (1982). *Men behind bars: Sexual exploitation in prison*. New York: Plenum.

Wooley, S.C., & Wooley, O.W. (1980). Eating disorders: Obesity and anorexia. In A.M. Brodsky & R.T. Hare-Mustin (Eds.), *Women and psychotherapy: An assessment of research and practice* (pp. 135–58). New York: Guilford.

Yalom, I.D. (1970). *The theory and practice of group psychotherapy*. New York: Basic Books.

Yunker, C.E. (1986, April 7). Stepfather must pay $500,000 to abused child. *National Law Journal*. 8, 27.

Name Index

Abarbanel, G., 56
Abel, G. G., 19, 23, 162
Abrahamsen, D., 36
Abrams, R. D., 76
Abramson, L. Y., 158
Adams, G. R., 76
Adams, H. J., 141
Adams, P. R., 76
Adler, A., 139
Aftel, M., 59
Alliance Against Sexual Coercion, 7–8,
  17, 24, 105
Alpert, J. L., 137
Amaro, H., 209–10
American Psychiatric Association, 37,
  71, 80, 126, 160
American Psychological Association, 9
Annas, G., 96
APA Task Force on Victims of Crime
  and Violence, 12
Armsworth, M. W., 10, 48
Aronson, E., 32
Asch, A., 115, 212–13
Asch, S., 47
Ashworth, C. D., 206

Baisden, M. J., Jr., 166
Banks, R., 75
Barcher, A., 105, 110, 116, 120–21
Bard, M., 26–29
Barnard, C. P., 157, 160
Baron, A., Jr., 210
Baron, L., 34
Bart, P., 217, 223
Bass, E., 140 172, 188
Bassuk, E. L., 127, 134
Bateman, P., 223
Baum, A., 76
Beck, A. T., 137, 146
Beck, J., 162
Becker, J. V., 19, 125, 137, 167
Bell, A. P., 203
Bellak, L. B., 129
Bender, L., 36
Beneke, T., 11, 20, 22–23, 34–35
Bernard, M., 157
Berne, E., 139
Bianco, D., 7, 169
Biller, H. B., 16
Binder, R. L., 74
Blanchard, E. B., 19

Blau, A., 36
Blazevic, D. J., 117
Boatman, B., 212
Borgida, E., 102, 118
Boskind-Lodahl, M., 163
Boston Lesbian Psychologies Collective, 218
Bouhoutsos, J., 9–10, 20, 23, 105, 216–17
Braen, G. R., 83, 86, 88–91, 93, 99
Braun, B. G., 161
Brehony, K. A., 154, 172
Briscoe, M. E., 47
Brodsky, A. M., 21, 135, 141
Brody, C. M., 132–33, 135, 141, 196
Brody, E., 214
Bronstein, P., 206, 218
Brookings, J. B., 174
Broverman, I. K., 218
Brown, L., 47, 163
Browning, D., 212
Brownmiller, S., 5, 11, 20, 24, 35, 39, 102–3, 120, 209–10
Bruckner-Gordon, F., 59
Bullmer, K., 51
Bunk, B. S., 188
Burden, D. S., 132
Burgess, A. W., 6, 13, 22, 31, 43, 72, 74, 79, 83, 86, 89, 94, 102, 125, 161, 167
Burkhart, B. R., 20
Burt, M. R., 22, 32, 34–35, 76, 147, 213
Butcher, J. N., 130

Caldwell, D., 7
Cantrell, L., 23
Caplan, P. J., 37
Cappon, D., 75
Carlsen, M. B., 140
Carlson, N., 67, 165, 202–3, 219, 231
Carrow, D. M., 41, 46, 55, 205
Carson, E. G., 106
Carter, D. K., 135, 141
CBS, 25
Center for Women in Government, 105
Center for Women Policy Studies, 212
Chambless, D. L., 154

Chance, P., 157
Cherniss, G., 58
Chodorow, N., 54, 136
Clarke, E., 225
Cleary, C., 107
Conroy, M., 222
Cook, S., 92
Cooke, C. W., 94, 96–97
Cornell, C. P., 5
Courtois, C. A., 67, 125, 131, 160–61, 167, 188, 193, 196–97, 216
Coy v. Iowa, 115
Crites, L. L., 117

Davis, L., 140, 172, 188
Davis, L. J., 214
Davison, G., 138
Delacoste, F., 226
Deutsch, H., 36, 136
DiClemente, C. C., 138
Dlugokinski, E., 26
Donnerstein, E., 224
Donovan, M. E., 30, 156, 172, 187
Douty, H. I., 163
Durham, L., 141
Dworkin, S., 94–97
Dzeich, B. W., 23

Eberle, P., 52
Eberle, S., 52
Egan, G., 55
Egan, K. J., 137, 160
Eichenfield, G. A., 218
Ellis, A., 137–38
Ellis, E., 125
Eron, L. D., 224
Espin, O. M., 209–10
Evans, J. W., 43, 56, 87, 95

Factor, M., 136
Farley, L., 35, 104
Farmer, F., 25
Feldman-Summers, S., 206
Field, H. H., 34
Figley, C. R., 39
Filinson, R., 213
Fine, M., 212
Finesinger, J. E., 76

Finkelhor, D., 5, 7, 12, 14, 16–17, 24, 201
Fitzgerald, L., 8, 19, 20, 104
Fleming, R., 76
Fodor, I. G., 154
Frankl, V. E., 76
Frazier, P., 118
Freeman-Longo, R. E., 21, 23
Freudenberger, H. J., 49, 58
Friar, D., 12, 35
Frieze, I. H., 5, 28
Fuhriman, A., 130, 138

Gager, N., 84
Gallagher, A. H., 200, 209
Garcia, N., 199, 207
Gebhard, P. H., 20, 23
Gelles, R. J., 5
Giarretto, H., 187
Gibson, G., 200, 209
Gil, E., 189
Gilbert, L. A., 141, 151
Gilligan, C., 54, 134
Gilmore, B. S., 43, 56, 87, 95
Glasser, R. D., 20
Golan, N., 43
Golden, C., 203
Goldfried, M., 138
Goldstein, A. J., 154
Goldstein, H. W., 27, 85, 103, 106, 112, 113, 115, 120–21
Good, G., 218
Gordon, M. T., 26
Gottlieb, N., 132
Greenberg, R. L., 137, 146
Greenspan, M., 134–35, 140–41
Greer, J. G., 218
Groth, A. N., 6, 11, 22–23, 39, 161–62, 201–2, 213, 215

Hall, R. M., 8, 35
Hare-Mustin, R. T., 135, 141
Harris, T. A., 139
Hartman, S., 128, 134, 140
Harvey, R., 6
Henderson, P., 102
Henn, F. A., 20
Hepperle, W. L., 117

Herek, G. M., 200
Herman, J. L., 7, 19, 156
Hicks, D. J., 213
Hirsch, C., 157, 160
Holman, B., 201, 204
Holmes, K. A., 206, 210
Holmstrom, L. L., 6, 13, 22, 31, 43, 72, 74, 79, 83, 86, 88, 94, 102, 125, 167
Holroyd, J. C., 21
Horos, C. U., 91
Horowitz, M. J., 14
Hotaling, G. T., 213
Huckel, L., 125
Hursch, C. J., 35

Ingman, S. R., 213

Jackins, H., 58
Jackson, J., 96
James, J., 169
Janoff-Bulman, R., 28
Jones, C., 32
Justice, B., 189
Justice, R., 189

Kahn, A., 34
Kanarian, M., 32
Kanin, E. J., 20, 23
Kaplan, H. S., 167
Kapp, F. T., 76
Katz, B., 22, 76, 147, 213
Katz, S., 4
Kaufman, A., 201
Kegan, R., 76, 128
Kempe, C. H., 52, 83, 86, 95–96
Kempe, S., 52, 83, 86, 95–96
Kerns, D., 83, 86, 91, 95–96
Keuls, E. C., 102
Kidder, L. H., 34
Kikuchi, J. J., 32
Kilbourne, J., 224
Kilpatrick, D. G., 74, 125
Kinsey, A. C., 6, 203
Klapholz, H., 83, 88, 93, 99
Knightley, P., 30
Koss, M. P., 19, 20, 22–23, 25, 125, 130, 189, 223
Kraft-Ebing, R. von, 20

Kravetz, D., 154
Kroll, J., 160
Krueger, F., 35, 200
Kubler-Ross, E., 144, 154
Kushner, H. S., 169

Lakoff, R. T., 59
Landis, J. T., Jr., 6
Landrine, H., 208
Langer, E. J., 214
Larson, D., 138
Law Enforcement Administration Assis-
  tance, 4, 213
Lazarus, A., 137, 153
Lazarus, A. A., 134, 139
Lemkau, J. P., 93
Leonard, K. E., 19, 20, 23
Lerner, M. J., 28
Leveille, A. E., 140, 162–63, 190–92,
  196–97
Levine, E. S., 200
Levine-MacCombie, J., 223
Lew, M., 202
Lifton, J., 27
Lindemann, E., 14, 63, 86
Linehan, M. M., 137, 160
Lison, K., 140
Liss-Levinson, N., 59
Lott, B., 8, 34, 224
Loulan, J., 167, 204
Lumiere, R., 92
Lundberg-Love, P., 76, 125, 154, 163,
  182, 187–89

MacDonald, J. M., 35
MacFarlane, K., 16, 23–24, 37
MacKinnon, C. A., 13, 24, 206
Malamuth, N. M., 21, 23, 37, 224
Maltz, W., 201, 204
Mann, J., 129
Marceau, M., 32
Margolies, L., 204
Marolla, J., 23
Masson, J. M., 37, 140
Masters, J., 138
Masters, W. H., 5
May, R., 139
Mayer, A., 187–88

Mazur, M. A., 4
McCahill, T. W., 48
McCombie, S. L., 79, 95–97, 99
McEvoy, A. W., 174
McNaron, T. A. H., 133
Meiselman, K. C., 204
Melville, M. B., 200
Merit System Protection Board, 8
Meyer, M. C., 36, 225
Meyerding, J., 169
Miller, D. T., 76, 147
Miller, J. B., 136, 141, 218, 221, 226
Miller, W. R., 125, 165
Mills, P., 51–52, 53, 55, 83, 85, 90
Moon, D. M., 213
Morgan, Y., 133
Morokoff, P. J., 35
Morris, G. O., 75
Muehlenhard, C. L., 32

Nadelson, C. C., 47, 52, 125, 167
National Geographic Society, 28
Naylor, G., 204
Newman, F., 226
NiCarthy, G., 158
Nichols, M., 167, 204
Niggemann, E. H., 89
Nocera, D., 215
Norcross, J., 135–36, 138
Norvell, M. K., 89
Notman, M. T., 47, 52

O'Brien, P. H., 217, 223
O'Brien, S., 23, 25
O'Bryant, S. L., 215
Orbach, S., 163

Padilla, A., 200
Paludi, M., 23, 225
Parker, D. A., 81
Parker, J., 35
Paxson, M. A., 224
Pearlman, S., 205
Pederson, P., 207
Perloff, L. S., 29
Peterson, C., 157–58
Petrovich, M., 161
Pines, A. M., 58, 169–70

Pope, K. S., 9–10, 20, 23, 105, 216–17
Porter, C. A., 76, 147
Poston, C., 140
Powell, T. J., 141
President's Task Force on Victims of
    Crime, 13
Prochaska, J. O., 135–36, 138–39, 141

Quina, K., 5, 30, 32, 38, 76, 93, 195,
    206, 208, 218, 224, 231
Quina-Holland, K., 26, 38, 76, 125, 149

Rada, R. T., 23
Rado, S., 72
Rainone, F. L., 205
Rand, C., 205
Rando, T. A., 143, 144
Rapaport, K., 20
Rawlings, E. I., 135, 141
Reich, J., 13, 102, 112, 114
Reik, T., 53
Rich, R. F., 13, 102, 112, 114
Riger, S., 26
Rimm, D., 138
Rimsza, M. E., 89
Ritvo, E. R., 222–23
Rivers, C., 156
Robbins, J. H., 135, 199
Robinson, C. R., 200
Rodin, J., 214
Rogers, C., 52
Rosen, G. M., 140
Rosenfeld, A. H., 21
Ross, S. D., 105, 110, 116, 120–21
Rousso, H., 212
Rowan, E. L., 162, 164, 167
Rowan, J. B., 162, 164, 167
Rowe, M., 120
Rowland, J., 101, 106
Rush, F., 6–7
Russell, D. E. H., 3–5, 7, 11–12, 17,
    19, 23, 189
Russo, N. F., 209–10, 214

Sales, B. D., 13, 102, 112, 114
Sandler, B. R., 8, 35, 120
Sanford, L. T., 30, 156, 172, 187
Sangrey, D., 26–29

Sargent, N. M., 168–69
Sarrell, P. M., 5
Sartre, J. P., 139
Sasko, H., 102
Schaef, A. W., 149
Scheffler, L. W., 141
Scher, M., 218
Scherl, D. J., 14, 126
Schurr, C., 83
Schwendinger, H., 11
Schwendinger, J. R., 11
Scully, D., 23
Seligman, M. E. P., 157–58
Selye, H., 86
Sesek, D., 102
Sgroi, S. M., 16, 172, 188
Shaver, K., 32
Sheehan, D. V., 154
Shuster, R., 204
Siegel, M., 26
Siegel, R. J., 135, 199
Silbert, M. H., 169–70
Silverman, D., 46
Silverman, P. R., 133
Simmons, C., 28
Simpson, C., 30
Singer, J. E., 76
Singer, M. T., 75
Skinner, L. J., 137, 167
Small, L., 129, 130
Smith, J. A., 223
Solomon, R. S., 16
Sprei, J., 167, 193
Sproles, E. T., III, 83, 89, 90, 96–97
Stanko, E. A., 8, 35, 39
Stark, E., 39
Stark, J., 27, 85, 103, 106, 112, 113,
    115, 120–21
Starker, S., 140
Starzecpyzel, E., 23, 205
Steinem, G., 36
Steiner, C., 139
Stern, E. M., 73, 154–55
Stern, V. S., 73, 154–55
Stevens, M., 218
Straus, M. A., 34
Stuart, I. R., 218
Sue, D. W., 207

Sue, S., 207
Sutherland, S., 14, 126
Swink, K. K., 140, 162–63, 190–92, 196–97
Symonds, M., 35, 38, 76

Tatel, D. S., 105
Teasdale, J. D., 158
Temple, H., 17, 231
Templer, D. I., 161
Thomas, M., 226
Thorpe, J. S., 20
Tillich, P., 139
Titchener, J. L., 76
Trotman, F. K., 200, 208–9
Tsai, M., 14, 125–26, 148, 190–91, 211
Tyre, T., 5

Uemura, A., 211
U.S. Department of Justice, Bureau of Justice Statistics, 3, 24

Vazquez-Nuttall, E., 207, 209

Wagner, N. N., 14, 125, 148, 190–91
Walker, L. E., 16, 138, 156–57
Wall, R. V., 21, 23
Warner, C. G., 43, 71, 86, 96–97, 99, 163

Warner, L., 23
Waterman, J., 16, 37
Weber, E., 169
Weinberg, M. S., 203
Weiner, K., 169
Weisberg, D. K., 7, 169–70
Weiss, C. L., 12, 35
Weissman, M. M., 146
Westerlund, E., 35
White, E. C., 200, 207–9
Williams, A. M., 165
Williams, J. E., 206, 210
Willoughby, A., 81, 170
Wilson, J. P., 29
Wingett, C., 76
Woititz, J. G., 158, 170
Wolberg, L. R., 130
Wolfe, J. L., 137–38
Wolpe, J., 137, 153
Women Organized Against Rape, 115
Wooden, W. S., 35
Wooley, O. W., 163
Wooley, S. C., 163

Yalom, I. D., 133, 152
Yllo, K., 5, 24
Yunker, C. E., 107

Zane, N., 207

Subject Index

Abortion, 86, 93–94

Acquired Immune Deficiency Syndrome (AIDS), 91–92, 170

Adlerian therapy, 139

Advocate: for legal intervention, 118–19; for medical intervention, 95–96; during resolution, 129. *See also* Helper

Agencies, choice of, 70–71

Agoraphobia, 153–54, 171–72 n.3

Alcohol, 25, 127, 170

Alcoholics Anonymous, 170

Anger, 148–50; as motivation, 22–23; political, 48; usefulness of, 77–78

Asian-Pacific population, 210–11

Authority, abuse of, 24–25

Awareness, 222–23

Behavior, disruption of, 73–74

Behavioral skills, 184–85

Behavioral therapies, 137; for depression, 145–46

Beth Israel Hospital (Boston), 56

Black population, 208–9

Blame, 32; projections of, 47–48. *See also* Self-blame

Blitz attack, 22

Body image, 162–63

Borderline Personality Disorder, 160–61

Brother to Brother (Providence, RI), 172 n.3

Catharsis, 178–79, 189

Children, 5–7; disabled, 212; evidence collection from, 88–89; information to, 52; legal intervention for, 107, 114–15; medical intervention for, 94–95; myths, 36–37; as property, 102; raising of, 226; stigmatization of, 37; welfare of, 71

Civil Action, 109–10

Clearinghouse on Child Abuse and Neglect Information, 17

Coercion, and seduction, 35–36

Cognitive restructuring, for intimacy problems, 165

Cognitive therapies, 137–38; for depression, 146; for guilt, 147–48

Confidence assault, 22

Control: abusive, 161–62; increase in, 78; issues of, 157–62; loss of, 27–28; of others, 159–60; return of, 50; strategies of, 23–26

Coping, by elderly, 215
Counseling: approaches to, 129–33; choice of, 70; goals of, 44; steps for crisis, 175–79; steps for individual resolution, 182–85. *See also* Intervention; Therapy; Treatment
Counselors, types of, 229–30
Courage to Heal, The, 140, 188
Crisis intervention, 42–43; acute, 64–65; counseling steps for, 176–79. *See also* Intervention

Decision making, 178
Denial, 66, 78, 158–59
Depression, 145–46; among elderly, 215
Deviance, feelings of, 152
Dignity, violation of, 30
Disabled people, 25, 211–13; legal intervention for, 115–16
Drug abuse, 127–70
Drug use, 25

Eating disorders, 127, 163
Eclectic integrated psychotherapies, 138–39
Elderly, 25; as clients, 213–26; coping by, 215; fear among, 214–15; independence of, 215–16; information to, 52; legal intervention for, 115; medical intervention, 214; stigmatization of, 37
Emerge (Cambridge, MA), 172
Empathy, 51
Employer, role of, 70
Empowerment, 137, 207; defined, 221; external, 224–27; steps toward, 222–24. *See also* Power
Equal Employment Opportunity Commission, 109
Evidence: collection of, 87–90; of sexual assault, 106; of sexual harassment, 105
Existential therapy, 139

Family: guidelines for, 173–74; loss of, 172–73
Family therapy, 131–32
Farmer, Frances, 25
Fear, among elderly, 214–15
Fear into Anger, 223

Femininity, 226; cultural values for, 34
Feminist therapy approach, 135, 141
Fight Back, 226
Flashbacks, 74–75
Force, defined, 26
Frenzel, G., 196 n.4
Freud, S., 35, 37, 136, 140 n.1
Friends, guidelines for, 173–74
Fundamentalists Anonymous, 168

Gender, and power, 34
Gender roles, 226; and abuse, 12; analysis, 202–3; exaggerated ideals of, 23; stereotyping of, 11
Getting Free, 158
Goals, development of, 179, 185, 203
Group therapy, 132–33; eighteen-week model, 192–93; five-week model, 191–92; steps in, 190–91
Guilt, 76–77, 146–48

Harm, fear of, 24, 27
Hearing officers, responsibility of, 118
Helper: burnout, 57–58; defining, 41; fears of, 199; functions of, 42–44; referrals by, 59; responsibilities of, 44–50; techniques useful to, 50–54. *See also* Advocate; Intervention
Helper-client relationship: and differences, 56–57, 199–200; negotiation of, 64, 128, 177, 183
Helplessness, learned, 157–58
Herpes Resource Center, 92
Hill-Burton Act (1946), 85
Hispanic population, 209–10
Holistic approach, 134–35
Homosexuality: fear of, 201, 203, 219 n.9; morality of, 102–3; stereotype of, 202–3
Homosexuals, 8; attitudes toward, 34–35
Hospitals, policies of, 84–85
Humanistic therapies, 138
Humanity, goodness of, 28
Humiliation, 75–76, 214–15
Hysteria, 37, 140 n.1

Identity, violation of, 30
Incest: and eating disorders, 163; effects

of, 29; family therapy for, 131; and
further victimization, 189–90; group
topics in, 197; individual counseling
model for, 131; legal intervention for,
107; male attitudes toward, 30; and
maternal support, 156; and risk category, 212
Incest Survivors Anonymous, 141
Independence, of elderly, 215–16
Information, accuracy of, 48–49
Informed consent, 45–46
Institute for Rational-Emotive Therapy,
140
Institutional grievances, 108–9
Institutions: advocate's role in, 43–44;
choice of, 70–71; and power dynamics
of abuse, 34–35; pressure on, 225
Intervention: avoidance phase, 65–67;
brief psychotherapies format, 129–30;
choice points for, 67–71; client choice
of, 51; clinical framework, 13–15; dual
format, 130; family therapy structure,
131–32; followup on, 78–79; goal of,
15, 66; group therapy structure, 132–
33; individual therapy structures, 131;
inpatient treatment structure, 133; long-
term psychotherapy format, 130; philosophical approaches to, 133–35; reasonable level of, 49–50; social
framework for, 10–13; with suicidal
clients, 79–80; support group structure,
133; termination of, 54–55, 78. See
also Counseling; Crisis intervention;
Helper; Legal intervention; Medical intervention; Therapy
Intimacy, 163–67
Intimate self, violation of, 29–30
Investigators, responsibility of, 116–17
Invulnerability, Illusion of 29
Isolation, 31

Judges, responsibility of, 117–18
Just world hypothesis, 28–29
Justice, process of, 68–69. See also Le-
gal intervention
Justice Assistance, 56
Justice system, improvements in, 103

Killing Us Softly, 224–25
Kinsey Institute, 203

Lawrence, T. E. (Lawrence of Arabia),
30
Legal intervention: assumptions harmful
to, 102–3; civil action, 109–10; criminal prosecution, 111–14; goals of, 101;
institutional grievances, 108–9; personnel involved in, 116–19; special pro-
tections, 114–16; types of, 103–7. See
also Intervention
Legislation, 56; for marital rape, 5
Lesbians, 203–5
Listening, reflective, 52–53
Loss: emotional, 145; of family, 172–73;
of self-esteem, 155–56; tangible, 144–
45; of trust, 21, 150–51
Love, violation of, 71

Males: as clients, 200–3; counseling of,
218–19; disclosure by, 14; helplessness
of, 33; as offenders, 11; power base
of, 33; rape of, 5
Manipulation, 159–61; psychological, 25
Martin, Robert A., 5
Masculinity, 23, 226; cultural values for,
34
Masochism, 37
Medical intervention: for elderly, 214;
evidence collection, 87–90; goals of,
83; negotiation of, 84–85; personnel
for, 94–96; preventive, 90–94; protocol
for, 99–100; selection of, 84; team approach to, 96; treatment, 85–86. See
also Intervention
Medical services, choice of, 67–68
Minority population, 8, 205–11; attitudes
toward, 34–35; help for, 46
Modus operandi, types of, 21–22
Multiple Personality Disorder, 161
Myths: effects of, 38–39; about men,
200–201; rape, 23; about sexual abuse,
35–38

Narcotics Anonymous, 170
National Alliance for the Mentally Ill,
141

National Committee for the Prevention of Child Abuse, 17
National Court Appointed Special Advocate (CASA) Association, 120 n.8
National Organization for Changing Men, 202
National Organization for Women (NOW), 225
National Self-Help Clearinghouse, 141
Nightmares, 74–75; dealing with, 80–81
Normalcy, of abuser, 20–21
Nurses, 95

Panic attack, 153–54, 171–72 n.3
Parents, 205, 225
Personal belief systems, disruption of, 28–29
Personal growth, as goal, 15
Phenomenological approach, for recovery, 14–15
Phobia Society of America, 172
Phobias, 153
Physician, 83, 87, 94–95
Plea bargaining, 113
Police: attitudes of, 201; policies of, 103; reports to, 4; responsibility of, 116–17
Post-Traumatic Stress Disorder, 71, 80
Power: and aggression, 11; and culture, 33–35; defined, 221; as motivation, 22–23. See also Empowerment
Pregnancy, 86, 93–94
Prejudice, 46–47
Process therapy, for anger, 149–50
Professional misconduct, 9–10
Professors, as abusers, 8–9, 20
Prosecution, criminal, 111–14
Prosecutors, responsibility of, 117
Prostitution, teenage, 170
Psychic numbness, 73
Psychoanalysis, 136
Psychodynamic therapies, 136–37
Psychogenic problems, 86, 94, 97–98
Psychopathia Sexualis, 20–21

Racism, 207–9
Rape: acquaintance, 4; case study of, 181–82, 185–87; of children, 5–7; date, 4, 186–87; effects of, 29; as fe-

male fantasy, 36–37; frequency of, 3; law reform, 103; marital, 4–5, 102; myths, 23
Rape kit, 88, 98–99
Recovery, 125; phases of, 14; as process, 53–54; reemergence phase of, 126–27; resolution phase of, 127–29
Referrals, 68; after intervention, 78; timing of, 54–55, 59
Rejection, 66
Relationships: changes in, 32–33; growing in, 226–27; problems with, 165–66
Religion, role of, 168–69
Repression, 31
Resolution, 178–79, 184, 189; assumptions about, 13–14; helping roles for, 128–29; as process of growth, 15
Rhode Island Rape Crisis Center, 226, 231
Rights of Women, The, 121
Running away, teenage, 169–70

Santa Monica Hospital, 56
Seduction, and coercion, 35–36
Self, reconstruction of, 184–89
Self-blame, 21, 38–39, 76–77, 147–48. See also Blame
Self-defense, 223–24
Self-destructive behaviors, 169–71
Self-esteem, loss of, 155–56
Self-help movement, 140–41
Self-image, sexual, 166–67
Sex, as weapon, 11
Sexual abuse: as aggression, 11; of children, 5–7, 107; cultural dynamics of, 33–39; emotional aftereffects of, 143–44; emotional reactions to, 71–78; experience aftermath, 28–29; legal perspectives of, 101–3; life affected by, 197; repetition of, 21–22; for social control, 34; social dynamics of, 30–33; sterotyping of, 12–13; trauma of, 26–28; and victimization, 29–30; from victim to survivor, 13–15
Sexual abuser: characteristics of, 20–23; control strategies of, 23–26; cultural power base of, 33–35; research on, 19

Sexual assault, legal intervention for, 105–7
Sexual Assault Treatment Center (Wisconsin), 56
Sexual dysfunction, 167
Sexual exploitation, continuum of, 10–13
Sexual harassment: case study of, 179–81; defined, 7; disbelief in, 37–38; federal statutes on, 120–21; legal intervention for, 104–5; letter to offender, 120; pervasiveness of, 8; for social control, 35
Sexual Harassment and Assault: Myths and Realities, 231
Sexuality: American view of, 211; lesbian issues of, 204; male issues of, 203; problems with, 163–67
Sexually transmitted diseases (STDs), 84, 91–93
Shame, 75–76
Silence, 75–76
Social support, absence of, 31
Stereotypes, 20, 47
Still Killing Us Softly, 224–25
Stone Center (Wellesley, MA), 137
Stress: control of, 14; effects of, 50–51; reactions, 127
Substance abuse. See Alcohol; Drug abuse
Suicide, 79–80, 161, 170–71
Support group, 54, 133; consciousness-raising, 194–96; for depression, 146; for lesbians, 205; for men, 202; for survivors, 193–94
Support systems, choice of, 69–70
Survivor, defined, 13

Tarassoff v. Regents of the University of California, 162
Terror, 72–73; patterns, 154–55; types of, 152–55
Therapists, as abusers, 9–10, 216–17
Therapy: major approaches, 136–40; structures for, 131–33. See also Counseling; Intervention; specific therapies
Thoughts, disruption of, 73

Transactional analysis, 139
Trauma: defined, 63; features of, 26–28; response to, 30–33, 65
Trust: abuse of, 22; establishment of, 177, 183; loss of, 21, 150–51; need for, 45; violation of, 30, 71

United States Supreme Court, 115, 162
Universities, and sexual harassment, 8–9, 37–38

Validation, 126, 177; need for, 51
Victimization, experience of, 29–30
Victims: blaming of, 12–13, 32; of blitz attack, 22; booklet for, 231–32; choices left to, 50–51; of confidence assault, 22; defined, 13; emotional reactions of, 13; empowerment of, 134; gender of, 12; helplessness of, 25, 27–28; medical treatment of, 84–85; among minority population, 205–11; morality of, 102–3; of prior therapist, 216–17; reports by, 4, 21, 68–69; rights of, 121–22; statement of, 88–89, 99; stereotyping, 12–13; suspicions about, 37–38; virtue of, 38. See also Children; Disabled; Elderly; Lesbians; Males; Minority population
Victim-to-survivor model, 50, 53
Violence, 3, 27; bias, 200; in media, 224–25; solutions to, 227; use of, 24

We Can Help, 231
When Bad Things Happen to Good People, 169
Witnesses, expert, 118
Women: as property, 102; and relationships, 54; as untrustworthy, 103
Women and Self-Esteem, 156, 187
Women in Science (University of Rhode Island), 196, 196 n.4
Women of Brewster Place, The, 204
Women Organized Against Rape (Philadelphia), 115, 231
Women's Lives: Themes and Variations in Gender Learning, 224

ABOUT THE AUTHORS

KATHRYN QUINA is an Associate Professor of Psychology and Women's Studies and Coordinator of the Psychology Program at the College of Continuing Education at the University of Rhode Island. She earned her doctorate in experimental psychology from the University of Georgia in 1973, working with developmental issues in visual perception. Her concern with sexual victimization became her major academic specialization in 1975. She has interviewed survivors and carried out research on long-term effects of sexual assault and harassment and on attitudes toward rape and other crimes. She has been a volunteer for the Rhode Island Rape Crisis Center, has taught undergraduate- and graduate-level courses on victimization, and is a frequent speaker and workshop leader on the issues of sexual harassment, rape, and incest. Her other areas of interest include gender role stereotyping, AIDS and other health issues, and effective teaching. She is coeditor of *Teaching a Psychology of People: Gender and Sociocultural Awareness* (1988), which won the 1988 Association for Women in Psychology Distinguished Publication Award.

NANCY L. CARLSON is a licensed Counseling Psychologist with a Diplomate in Counseling Psychology from the American Board of Professional Psychology. She holds a doctorate from the University of Kansas. She has been the director of university mental health centers for over ten years, directing the Counseling and Career Services at the University of Rhode Island from 1978 to 1987. She is now in private practice in Portland, Maine. Her work with rape, assault, incest, and harassment victims spans fifteen years and includes the development of three university campus women's crisis centers starting in 1971. She is a therapist, educator, administrator, consultant, and trainer in crisis intervention.

Together with colleague Hazel Temple, the authors wrote *Sexual Assault and Harassment: Myths and Reality*, a guide for the University of Rhode Island community, published and distributed to all students, faculty, and staff in 1981 and 1983.